OUR CHILDREN TOO:
A HISTORY OF THE FIRST 25 YEARS OF THE BLACK CAUCUS OF THE SOCIETY FOR RESEARCH IN CHILD DEVELOPMENT, 1973–1997

In celebration of the first 25 years

EDITORS
Diana T. Slaughter-Defoe
Aline M. Garrett
Algea O. Harrison-Hale

WITH COMMENTARY BY
Harriette P. McAdoo
Melvin N. Wilson
John P. Jackson, Jr.
John W. Hagen

Sandra L. Graham
Series Guest Editor

CABRINI COLLEGE LIBRARY
610 KING OF PRUSSIA ROAD
RADNOR, PA 19087

MONOGRAPHS OF THE SOCIETY FOR RESEARCH IN CHILD DEVELOPMENT

Serial No. 283, Vol. 71, No. 1, 2006

※ 64393788

LB
1103
.S6
no.283

Boston, Massachusetts   Oxford, United Kingdom

This issue of the *Monographs of the Society for Research in Child Development* (SCRD) departs from the usual presentation of new research and theory by tracing an important part of the history of the Society and of the field. It has a Guest Editor and a different cover than the other issues in this series to denote its different format and purpose. The Black Caucus, founded in 1973, broke new ground by establishing itself as an independent organization within the larger SRCD structure. Its dual goals of promoting high-quality research on children of color and providing professional support for African American scholars have been pursued actively since its inception, with positive consequences for our organization and for the field of child development. The history described in this issue of the *Monographs* goes well beyond being a record of a particular group within a particular society. It serves as a case study of how African American scholars assumed leadership in their field, both as researchers and as influential members of their profession. It is a marvelous story of a group organizing to provide professional socialization and support to individuals who often felt marginalized in the worlds of graduate school and careers. The insights expressed in these chapters should be useful for other fields and professional organizations facing similar challenges. The Black Caucus has provided important benefits to SRCD by assuring more research of high quality on important groups of children, by providing the profession with wisdom and perspectives that might otherwise be lacking, and by continually monitoring our progress, with its inevitable ups and downs, toward inclusiveness and respect for diversity. One indicator of success is imitation—within SRCD, a Latino caucus was recently organized, and an Asian caucus is being established. As President and Executive Officer, respectively, we are grateful to the editors and authors of this *Monograph* for their excellent efforts.

—*Aletha C. Huston, President*
John W. Hagen, Executive Officer

OUR CHILDREN TOO:
A HISTORY OF THE FIRST 25 YEARS OF THE BLACK CAUCUS OF THE SOCIETY FOR RESEARCH IN CHILD DEVELOPMENT, 1973–1997

In celebration of the first 25 years

CONTENTS

COMMENTARIES

WHEN YOU HEAR THE CHILDREN CRY

Suzanne M. Randolph, 1990
(all rights reserved)

When you hear the children cry
Stop and ask them why
Stop and heed their call
They're crying out to us all
"Please don't let us die."

When you hear the children laugh
Stop along their path
Stop to love and share
To show them that you care
Because we are all they have.

When you hear the children speak
Stop to hear them teach
Stop to hear the story they tell
And let them know all is well
And the world's within their reach.

When you hear the children playing
Stop to listen to what they're saying
They speak nothing but the truth
And their spirits are the proof
So for them we must keep praying.

So, when you hear the children crying
Know that you can stop the dying
Just turn and do your part
Grab hold of each little heart
And promise you'll keep on trying.

"Behold, children are a gift of the Lord." Psalm 127:3

Inspiration: Dedicated to people who labor on behalf of children and their families

I am honored to have been asked by Society for Research in Child Development (SRCD) President Aletha Huston and Executive Director John Hagen to be guest editor for this issue of the *Monographs* that chronicles the first 25 years of the Black Caucus of SRCD. The Black Caucus was founded in 1973 by a group of dedicated African-American developmental psychologists, including the three co-editors of this volume: Diana T. Slaughter-Defoe, Aline M. Garrett, and Algea O. Harrison-Hale. The Caucus was created at a time when there were few African American child development scholars represented in mainstream developmental research and few who held positions of leadership in SRCD. The goals of the Caucus were to provide an infrastructure to enable social and professional support for these Black scholars who often worked in isolation from one another and to promote a research agenda for Black children that was grounded in good developmental science. The three editors of this volume, in their collective and individual chapters, and the 10 other contributing chapter authors who also played pivotal roles in the Caucus's early years, describe the conception, birth and growth of the Black Caucus as it worked to achieve those goals during its first 25 years. Signs of progress that we in SRCD take as "givens" today—for example, that there will be scholars of color on Governing Council, that scholars of color will be on the invited program at the biennial meeting, and that scholars of color will serve on editorial boards of the Society's journals and *publish* in those journals—were virtually non-existent at the time of the founding of the Black Caucus in 1973. Paralleling the growth of the Black Caucus from 1973 to 1997 were SRCD's own initiatives to become a more inclusive entity.

There is precedent in the *Monographs* for chronicling the history of a professional society. Twenty years ago the *Monographs* devoted an issue to the 50th anniversary of SRCD (Smuts & Hagen, 1985). In that issue, Harriet Rheingold reviewed the first 25 years of SRCD (1934–1959) using archival data such as annual reports, minutes of business meetings, letters from members of Governing Council, and publications of the Society. From that review, we learned not only about the growth of SRCD during periods of great social and political upheaval, but also about the evolution of developmental psychology as a science and the particular challenge that it faced at the middle of the 20th century. The history of the Black Caucus in the current *Monograph* spans a similar 25-year time period and draws on similar archival material. Futhermore, its evolution accompanied (and prodded) our discipline's growing concern by the end of the 20th century with the need to address pressing social problems that impact children of color; to have a voice in the policy arena, while achieving the delicate balance between science and advocacy; and to embrace models of development for children of color that highlight strengths and resilience rather than deficits and risk. These are complex but necessary concerns for child development research in an era of increasing racial and ethnic diversity. Thus tracing the history of a professional society of an academic discipline can inform us about both the evolution of the society and the discipline with which it identitifes.

The *Monograph* is organized into four sections, which together highlight the multiple contributions of the Black Caucus. The first section, comprised of four chapters, is the most archival as it draws on historical documents (e.g., letters from Governing Council members) to describe the events that led to the founding of the Black Caucus and to trace its activities during its first 25 years. The chapters in the second section provide three examples of the ways in which the Black Caucus attempted to implement its commitment to teaching and mentoring of young scholars and of educating the parent organization about significant science policy and advocacy issues. Caucus founding members were at the forefront of early research and publications on African American children and the five chapters of Section III provide illustrations of how their collective activities helped to reconceptualize the ways in which Black youth were studied in empirical research. The two chapters of Section IV pay tribute to the contexts of institutional support provided by the University of Michigan and Howard University. Although Caucus members have been trained at a variety of institutions across the country, these two universities stand out for their unique contribution to nurturing the intellectual mission of the Black Caucus. The *Monograph* concludes with commentaries by Harriett McAdoo and Melvin Wilson, two Black Caucus members who have personally witnessed its evolution; by John Hagen, who can speak from the perspective of the SRCD parent organization; and by John Jackson, who can appraise the contributions of the Black Caucus through the intellectual lens of a historian of psychology.

As guest editor of this *Monograph*, I came into the process relatively late. The vision for a 25th anniversary celebration had been conceived many years ago by Diana, Aline, and Algea and the main writing of the chapters had been completed under their careful editorial guidance. Once the decision was made to publish this volume in the *Mongraphs* series, my main task was to shepherd it through the final stages of revision and polishing. For me, that was an uplifting experience that required little intervention. This is their history of the Caucus, in their own words, weaving personal experiences with historical events to produce a rich mosaic of a professional society that continues to have a unique place in SRCD.

—*Sandra L. Graham*

INTRODUCTION

Since its founding in 1973, the Black Caucus of the Society for Research in Child Development (SRCD) has been a significant source of academic and personal support to African Americans as they entered the developmental sciences to consume, produce, and critique research on children and youth that could benefit the lives of their people. Like us, most of the members of the Caucus are African American. We were educated through the doctoral degree at diverse top tier research universities around the nation. Early in our careers as developmental psychologists, we formed this network within the primary professional organization in our field for at least two purposes: first, to improve our professional positions and career options within our chosen field; second, to contribute to the improvement of the lives of children, particularly Black children, who, to that point, had been neglected in developmental research and theory. This *Monograph* tells the personal, but factual, story of what we believe to be an ultimately successful struggle to integrate SRCD in the broadest and deepest sense of the concept of "integration."

Throughout the Caucus's history, SRCD has been the central benefactor to its support network. The special people in leadership roles in SRCD between 1973 and 1997—Governing Council members and Executive Directors (e.g., Mary Ainsworth, Bettye Caldwell, Dorothy Eichorn, Willard Hartup, Frances Horowitz, John Hagen, Glen Elder, Aimee Dorr, Urie Bronfenbrenner, William Damon, Richard Lerner, to name a few)—improved the lives of Caucus members, frequently helping in important and strategic ways that pertained to members' professional development.

This *Monograph*, the collective product of the founding members of the Black Caucus, recognizes the bond between the Caucus and its parent organization, but also explores the sources of support apart from SRCD. Caucus members built relationships with program officers in government service, foundation staff, scholars in colleges and universities other than their own, Caucus colleagues, present and former students who became cherished friends, even causes. Embedded in the authors' acknowledgments of this support are portrayals of the relationships and processes associated with becoming a relevant developmental scientist. The authors share their motivations, fears, and concerns as well as their aims, objectives, and perceived record of accomplishments. They seek to leave a record for future generations of scientists that they themselves would have appreciated having when they were starting their careers in the early 1970s.

ON BECOMING A SCIENTIST

In 1991, a Pre-Conference session of the Black Caucus of SRCD focused on "Training Needs and Research Trends for the Next Generation of Ethnic Minority Scholars." The authors of the papers made some interesting observations that we as editors believe hold true today[1]:

1. In the 1980s, while the numbers of other ethnic minority students receiving doctorates increased, there was a decline in the number of doctorates received by African American and Native American students.

2. The demand for good, high-quality science has never been greater, particularly with reference to ethnic minority populations, including children, adolescents, and their families. A disproportionately high representation of ethnic minority populations is expected in the child and adolescent populations in community institutions serving those who are considered "at risk" for the psychological consequences of social disadvantage (e.g., poorer urban schools, child welfare system, juvenile justice system, and preschool programs such as Project Head Start).

3. We have ideas about the essential elements of this "good science": (a) rejection of "deficit models," which give little or no recognition to the strengths and resiliencies of ethnic minority groups, focusing solely on social and behavioral problems; (b) adoption of a cultural–ecological perspective, which emphasizes the varied contexts impacting childhood growth and development within ethnic minority communities; and (c) creation of interventions that address societal problems disproportionately affecting ethnic minority children, families, and communities—among them inadequate housing, restricted work and business opportunities, substance abuse, and the related mental health issues inevitably associated with inability to meet survival needs.

4. We emphasize the importance of well-designed research, with appropriately selected comparison groups. As one example, developmental researchers who observe "good science" no longer

compare middle- and upper middle-class White children with lower socioeconomic status African American children. Even more important, good scientists describe their research samples carefully, specifying sample source(s) as well as the racial, ethnic, and socioeconomic backgrounds of the study participants.

Good science requires good theory, sensitively related methods, and judicious powers of analysis and interpretation of obtained data. Mentoring the next generation of ethnic minority scholars to produce good science is especially important, as ethnic minority peoples have consistently led the critiques of the adverse effects of bad science upon their cultures and communities. Before the arrival of substantial numbers of ethnic minority scholars in the 1970s, these critiques were advanced by laypersons and special interest groups, including civil rights groups who, for example, bitterly challenged the assumptions of the Moynihan Report (Rainwater & Yancy, 1967). Although many of these sources continue to provide important and sophisticated commentary on social and scientific research,[2] in the generations since the early 1970s, a new cadre of ethnic minority scholars has acquired a legitimate voice in scientific matters.

The cadre is important because (a) it speaks the languages of research academies around the nation; (b) it typically has slightly more credibility with the ethnic minority populations of interest than majority researchers have; (c) the initial cadre of ethnic minority scholars was almost totally dedicated to critiquing and exposing false assumptions about the growth and development of the children and families of the communities they knew best; and (d) a number of members of this cadre recognized the importance of generating and patiently developing, through a program of research, fresh concepts and minitheories applicable to the populations.

Despite the presence of more progressive concepts and methods, there remains today concern about the resurgence of "deficit-oriented," "blame-the-victim" theories of African American behavior, in particular. As one example, in 1991, at the time of the second Black Caucus Pre-Conference, Caucus members observed that the National Institutes of Mental Health had funded more than $12 million for research into the social and biological aspects of human aggression. The research populations targeted appeared to be primarily inner-city residents. The design of the various studies permitted a narrow focus on the biological, social, and psychological antecedents of this phenomenon, neglecting the cultural, political, and economic factors also inextricably associated with the higher reported incidence of overt violence and aggression in such urban neighborhoods. Thus we surmised that there continued, and would continue, to be a need to train ethnic minority scholars in the ability to discern between good and bad science; concepts, methods, and data analysis; and the communication skills required to publicize their observations.

Historians (Holloway, 2002; Richards, 1997) have indicated that the first generation of ethnic minority scholars did not have an easy time assuming their scientific responsibilities with regard to the issues listed above. New publication outlets had to be developed and sustained, just to get their concepts and methods published and made available to the scientific community; examples include the *Journal of Black Psychology* and the *Hispanic Journal of Behavioral Science*. New modes of networking for public presentation of these ideas to interested scientists and practitioners had to be created (e.g., Division 45 of the American Psychological Association, the Society for the Study of Ethnic Minority Issues, Association of Black Psychologists, Association of Black Sociologists, Empirical Research in Black Psychology, and Black Caucus of SRCD). Challenges to academies in the form of expanded criteria for promotion and tenure had to be proposed; new courses and programs, inevitably interdisciplinary and policy oriented, were designed and advanced to enable institutions to respond to the training preferences and needs of culturally diverse students as well as students who wanted to learn about cultural diversity. Frequently, the first-generation ethnic minority scholars were expected to, and did, assume a leadership role in outlining the character and organizational structure of new institutional programs and policies. Finally, this first generation of scholars helped the willing institutions to rethink their criteria for selecting and admitting students from ethnic minority backgrounds.

Today, there is every reason to believe that ethnic minority scholars in research academies around the nation must continue to perform these same functions. If a recent favorable appraisal (Bowen & Bok, 1998) is any indication, such efforts are worthwhile from the perspective of subsequent salaried income as well as contributions to American society:

> American society needs the high-achieving Black graduates who will provide leadership in every walk of life. . . . We remain persuaded that present racial disparities in outcomes are dismayingly disproportionate. At the minimum, this country needs to maintain the progress now being made in educating larger numbers of Black professionals and Black leaders. . . . This goal of greater inclusiveness is important for reasons, both moral and practical, that offer all Americans the prospect of living in a society marked by more equality and racial harmony than one might otherwise anticipate. (pp. 283–285)

SCIENCE AND SOCIAL POLICY

Caucus members take the position that our history depicts a sustained struggle over paradigmatic approaches to science and social policy. For

4

example, the Black Caucus effectively broadened the discussion of the Atlanta child murders in the early 1980s: What was first perceived as purely a homicide investigation came to be understood as widespread child abuse. During the development of this *Monograph's* discussion of this subject (Chapter VI), members reflected on this trying period and how they attempted to galvanize the research community to respond to the abuses confronted by the children and their families. The Caucus's work offers insight on how organizations help determine what issues get on the national agenda and how crises can offer a window of opportunity through which a policy proposal may effect change.

In 1973, most majority status American researchers in child development did not think the psychological development of African American children and youth needed to be studied apart from reference to their socioeconomic status. Gradually, over the next 20 years, a rationale for considering the relevance of the racial, ethnic, cultural, and ecological/neighborhood backgrounds of African Americans emerged. Yet by the early 1990s, it seemed to Caucus members that newer generations of students and professionals (i.e., scientists, practitioners, policy advocates), whether in psychology, sociology, education, or other related disciplines, were still not being routinely exposed to the ideas and literature on cultural context and its influence on human development.

Traditional core and elective courses did not typically integrate such content. Mentoring in ethnic and racial diversity had virtually ceased unless there was an opportunity to teach courses in racial and/or ethnic minority development at Caucus members' colleges or universities. The story of the struggle to introduce this material into the mainstream scientific community has remained obscured. Therefore, the authors of this *Monograph* made special effort to insure that the voices of several pioneers who participated in the original struggle to introduce and propagate these concepts would be represented.

INITIATION OF THE SRCD BLACK CAUCUS HISTORY MONOGRAPH PROJECT

In 1993, Caucus members observed that 20 years, the equivalent of a generation, had been devoted to assisting developmental scientists in the reconceptualization of how children of color, in particular African American children (and their families), were portrayed in scientific and often, therefore, popular literature. Members also observed that "deficit-oriented perspectives" were reemerging in stronger voice. Furthermore, our own "adaptational perspectives" had to be tempered with newer understandings, given the impact of chronic poverty and associated continuing multiple problems confronting many African American communities. Thus members thought it was time for the group to reflect upon what it had taught, and what it had correspondingly learned, about the relationship between science and social policy. The early 1990s also seemed to be the time to reflect upon what had been revealed by the professional and institutional struggles of the generation immediately past. Even the SRCD parent organization had begun to revitalize its History Committee. In short, it was time to "sum it up" for the benefit of future generations of scientists and social policy analysts. We, the original leaders and members of the Black Caucus, concluded that if we did not claim intellectual and pedagogical ownership of our collective history, others, without our first-hand understanding, would do so for us. This monograph is an outgrowth of many hours of discussion and, in the end, individual members taking responsibility for summarizing various aspects of our quarter-century experience. We present the facts, but also share our beliefs and feelings about our history.

This monograph was first conceived as a mentoring tool for future generations of scholars and scientists—graduate students and junior professionals in child development and related fields. It is much more than a simple chronological history of the Caucus's first 25 years, 1973–1997. As the chapter authors tell their stories, they convey much about what the human spirit can accomplish, given a good education, a proclivity to networking as a strong family and community value, and a modicum of support from outsiders.

A number of organizations, including SRCD, have written reflections upon their own histories.[3] Sometimes ethnic minorities are featured. For example, Holliday and Holmes (2003) published a chapter on the history of ethnic minorities in psychology in the United States. To our knowledge, however, no contemporary scientific organization has been described from the perspective of its racial and ethnic minority constituent members. Therefore, as editors and authors we intend both to support our views carefully, and to allow interpretations and analyses to be flexible, individual, and, on occasion, even idiosyncratic.

Organization of the database for this history was daunting—a "labor of love" for editors and authors, each of whom had other major professional responsibilities. For example, in summer 1993 coeditor Diana T. Slaughter-Defoe (and an assistant) compiled a 22.5-page single-spaced inventory of available materials, including letters and other forms of correspondence referencing the Caucus's activities from 1973 to 1993.[4] Critical supplementary material to this inventory was provided by the other coeditors, Aline M. Garrett and Algea O. Harrison-Hale, given their strategic roles in the early years of the Caucus. Aline Garrett was the first executive officer of the Black Caucus of SRCD, and Algea Harrison-Hale was the first chairperson of the SRCD Standing Committee on Minority Participation.[5]

We hope that this volume will supplement and support the efforts of contemporary scholars in our own and related fields and contribute to the mission of giving inclusive voice to all of America's children. Finally, of course, telling the story in our own voices is a public way of thanking genuine friends and supporters, regardless of race and ethnicity.

REFERENCES

Bowen, W., & Bok, D. (1998). *The shape of the river: Long-term consequences of considering race in college and university admissions.* Princeton, NJ: Princeton University Press.

Holliday, B. G., & Holmes, A. (2003). A tale of challenge and change: A history and chronology of ethnic minorities in psychology in the United States. In G. Bernal, J. E. Trimble, A. K. Burlew & F. T. L. Leong (Eds.), *Handbook of racial and ethnic minority psychology* (pp. 15–64). Thousand Oaks, CA: Sage Publications.

Holloway, J. S. (2002). *Confronting the veil: Abram Harris Jr., E. Franklin Frazier and Ralph Bunche, 1919–1941.* Chapel Hill: University of North Carolina Press.

Rainwater, L., & Yancey, W. (1967). *The Moynihan report and the politics of controversy.* Cambridge: MIT Press.

Richards, G. (1997). *"Race," racism and psychology: Towards a reflexive history.* London: Routledge.

Senn, M. (1975). Insights on the child development movement in the United States. *Monographs of the Society for Research in Child Development,* (Series No. 161), Vol. 40, 3–4.

Smuts, A. B., & Hagen, J. W. (Eds.) (1985). History and research in child development: In celebration of the fiftieth anniversary of the Society. *Monographs of the Society for Research in Child Development,* (Serial No. 211), Vol. 50, 4–5.

NOTES

1. On April 16–17, 1991, the second SRCD Black Caucus Pre-Conference was held in the Grand Crescent Room of the Westin Hotel in Seattle. The conference theme was "Ethnicity and Diversity: Implications for Research and Policies." The symposium on "Training Needs and Research Trends," chaired by Elsie Moore of Arizona State University, was held from 2:00 to 3:15 p.m. It included the following panelists and papers: (a) Sherry Turner, Mount Holyoke College, "The need for models addressing Black child development"; (b) Brenda Allen, Smith College, "The mentoring process at predominantly Black universities"; (c) Sheree Marshall, Pennsylvania State University, "Facing the challenges: Pressing concerns for the present generation of minority students"; and (d) Dena Swanson and Michael Cunningham, Emory University, "Supportive Needs of African American graduate students: Issues of professional development." Subsequently, Diana Slaughter-Defoe was asked to draft a response to the papers; the draft became a template for this discussion.

2. Some of the best-written analyses of education research and policy, for example, were published regularly in *Crisis*, the quarterly journal of the National Association for the Advancement of Colored People (NAACP).

3. In 1985 Alice Smuts and John Hagen published a *Monograph* on the history of SRCD in honor of the Society's 50th anniversary. This *Monograph* focused upon the history of this scientific organization devoted to interdisciplinary study of children, but was more than a simple booklet of facts about SRCD's chronology, also presenting analytic and synthetic accounts of the founding of SRCD. Editors and authors of the present volume have generally

followed a similar approach in writing chapters for the history of the Caucus. Authors were also influenced by Senn's (1975) *Monograph*, which portrayed the child development movement in the United States from the perspective of early majority White developmental scholars.

4. Throughout this *Monograph*, each first author is responsible for the original documentation cited in her chapter. The Inventory referenced is available from Dr. Diana T. Slaughter-Defoe, University of Pennsylvania, Graduate School of Education, 3700 Walnut Street, Philadelphia, PA 19104-6216 at cost, as is a two-page single-spaced listing of cassette audiotapes from Slaughter-Defoe's private collection of memorabilia. The availability of this material, updated through 1997, ensures the accuracy and reliability of assertions made in the authors'/editors' discussions of members' experiences in reference to the Black Caucus of SRCD.

5. This committee is presently known as the SRCD Standing Committee on Ethnic and Racial Issues.

ABSTRACT

The Black Caucus of the Society for Research in Child Development (SRCD) was founded in 1973 to address concerns about the portrayal of Black children in scientific research, the lack of participation of ethnic minority members in the governance structure of SRCD, and the perceived need for a mutual support system for minority scholars aspiring to productive careers in the child development field. In this monograph, early members of the Caucus describe its history through the first 25 years, in 15 chapters distributed among sections on Caucus history, teaching and mentoring, publications and research-related issues, and supportive academic institutions. Among the topics explored are the formation and goals of the Caucus, its structure and membership, Caucus members' achieving stature and influence within SRCD, mentoring through the Toddler and Infant Experiences Study (TIES), response to the Atlanta child murders, the successful Pre-Conferences, SRCD *Monographs* and milestone developmental publications by Caucus members, the role of African American scholars in research on African American children (including the use of an ecological approach to study family processes), linkages between theory, research, and practice in Project Head Start, the contributions of the University of Michigan and Howard University, and looking to the future for students. Appendices trace Caucus chronological history and identify early sustaining members.

This volume celebrates the accomplishments of the Caucus while also revisiting challenges that have arisen both internally and through membership in the SRCD parent organization. Key thematic issues include:

- cultural deficit versus cultural difference;

- linkages between poverty, race, and empowerment;

- advocacy versus objectivity in scientific research; and

- how the cultural or racial identity of the researcher informs scientific knowledge.

The collaborations of Caucus members and others in SRCD modified the lens through which children of racially and ethnically diverse backgrounds are portrayed in the scientific literature.

SECTION I. FOCUS ON CAUCUS HISTORY

This section traces the beginnings of the Black Caucus of the Society for Research in Child Development (SRCD). It answers the questions: Why was such a group necessary? How did the Black Caucus grow and develop over the years, from its beginning in 1973? What strategies were used by the Caucus and by the majority parent organization, SRCD, to accomplish the goals of the Caucus regarding full stature in the Society? What were the consequences of attaining a presence on the Governing Council of SRCD?

Chapter I, by Diana Slaughter-Defoe, brings an historical perspective to the underlying need for an organization like the Black Caucus. Like other professional organizations, the Black Caucus could serve to provide support, mentoring, and networking for its members, especially for African American women in higher education, who dominated the area of developmental research with children.

Chapter II, by Aline M. Garrett, provides the intimate details regarding the structure and functioning of the Black Caucus. Garrett discusses the establishment of various membership directories, which served as important resources; the newsletter, which facilitated communication; and the dues structure, which has managed to support the development of the organization and to assist with activities such as the biennial Pre-Conferences. This chapter presents an overview of several issues discussed in detail in other chapters.

In Chapter III, Algea O. Harrison-Hale details her personal correspondence with Mary Ainsworth (then President of SRCD) as they strategized on their goal of getting a minority member elected to the Governing Council and minorities serving on SRCD committees. Their letters illustrate the commitment and dedication of the two individuals and their respective organizations to the goal of full representation. Chapter IV, by Diana Slaughter-Defoe, provides yet another perspective on the relationship of the Caucus to the SRCD Governing Council, by detailing her pathway to election and service on the Council, while simultaneously remaining faithful to the goals and aims of the Black Caucus.

I. A PERSONAL PERSPECTIVE ON THE BEGINNINGS OF THE BLACK CAUCUS OF SRCD[1]

Just before writing the first draft of this chapter, I read *Black Women in the Academy: Promises and Perils* (Benjamin, 1997). There I was reminded of the small numbers of African American women who occupy faculty and administrative positions in colleges and universities throughout the nation: less than 1% of these positions are held by Black women, and 50% of those appointments are in historically Black institutions. One of the concluding chapters, "Striking the Delicate Balances: The Future of African American Women in the Academy," by Mamie Locke, emphasizes the significance of mentoring and collective action for addressing and changing this situation. Locke states:

> Although the number of women in academic [positions] is increasing, racism and sexism remain a serious problem. . . . Mentoring is key to breaking the glass ceiling among African American women. . . . Career counseling and nurturing need to occur at all levels of education, from kindergarten through graduate school. The future of African American women administrators and faculty in the academy lies in their learning to empower each other and to foster cooperation, thereby diminishing competition among their own ranks. Through mentoring and the formation of women's networks, the number . . . will continue to increase. African American women faculty and administrators must learn to negotiate the maze, striking the delicate balances necessary to wipe away the glass ceiling and become effective, successful, contributing members of the academy. (Locke, 1997, pp. 340, 345)

Support groups within African American communities have a long tradition[2]—since at least the post-reconstruction period, when the Women's Club Movement began as an effort to assist Black rural migrants in their transition and adjustment to urban, frequently Northern regions of the country (Hine, 1994; Hine, King, & Reed, 1995; Hine & Thompson, 1998). By 1896, several national Negro Women's Clubs had been organized, each featuring "Negro uplift" as central to its purposes (Guy-Sheftall, 1990; Terrell, 1990).

When the Black Caucus of Society for Research in Child Development (SRCD) was founded in 1973, it was fundamentally a higher education support group, most of whose members were women. From the beginning, however, the Caucus has also had dedicated, influential male members, who were unusual in their commitment to developmental research with children.[3] Thus, the Black Caucus was founded by African Americans of both genders for the purposes of advancing their professional careers in SRCD and for contributing to the improvement of the lives of Black children.

As a member of the Black Caucus of SRCD, I am the beneficiary of a mentoring group and network that I helped to create at the beginning of my career in the human development field. In the remainder of this chapter, I share information about—and also personal recollections of—events in those early years, noting when possible the racial and gender-based historical context in which the reported events occurred.

BACKGROUND TO EARLY AFRICAN AMERICAN PARTICIPATION IN SRCD

What was the historical context in which future Black Caucus members, mostly women, had been educated? Historical studies of women in higher education are sparse (Brenzel, 1983; Collier-Thomas, 1982; Gordon, 1990; Graham, 1975, 1978), and such studies of African American women are virtually nonexistent (Brenzel; Collier-Thomas, 1982; Gordon, 1989; Perkins, 1983). In 1982, the *Journal of Negro Education*, following the appointment of Faustine Jones-Wilson as the first female editor in its 51-year-history, devoted its Summer Yearbook to the subject of Black women. In an article in that volume, Collier-Thomas stated.

> There is no book that documents the history of Black women in American education. ... Are there documentable differences in the historical experiences of Black women as students and educators as compared to Black men and White women? ... Is there any evidence that Black female educators developed a philosophy distinctive from that of Black males, White females and White males? (pp. 173–174)

For Collier-Thomas, the questions were merely rhetorical. She believed there were differences, and that they could be understood through considerations of prevailing societal images of Black womanhood.

Several authors (e.g., Bell-Scott, 1984; Carby, 1985; Davis, 1971; Noble, 1956, 1957; Perkins, 1983) have argued that prior to and immediately following the Civil War economic considerations fostered a pattern of gender-based educational equity among Blacks—that is, males and females were equally poorly educated; both men and women were slaves, and therefore generally legally forbidden to read (Perkins, 1983). Both Perkins and Carby (1985) concluded that within African-American communities, gender-based discrimination in higher education emerged during Reconstruction. Perkins reported that during the 19th century, the "cult of true womanhood" promoted by American society

> emphasized innocence, modesty, piety, purity, submissiveness and domesticity. Female education was necessary for the molding of the "ideal woman." ... The emphasis on these pieties was the antithesis of the reality of most Black women's lives during slavery and for many years thereafter. (p. 18)

Perkins (1983) and Guy-Sheftall (1990) argued that these stereotypes about the ideal woman increasingly came to be shared by educated Blacks, with African American women absorbing the greater responsibility for racial uplift in educational careers (primarily through elementary school teaching) and social service careers. Perkins further stated that " 'Race uplift' was the expected objective of all educated Blacks" (p. 22). To this day, "race uplift" is an enduring African American cultural value.

After Reconstruction, women's colleges or seminaries for African American women appeared but not in numbers comparable with those for White women (Slowe, 1933). Coeducational training was the dominant form of higher education experienced by African American women, in either the newly emergent historically Black colleges attended by the Black freedman or the predominantly White colleges and universities of the North. Many of the latter schools were populated by significant numbers of inhospitable students and faculty (Hill & King, 1990).

This brief description of the academic climate confronting African American women in higher education, which still existed when the founding SRCD Black Caucus members came together in 1973, illustrates why many of these women, myself included, believed they needed a support group to advance their careers and gain stature such that children would benefit from their skills as researchers and their status as academicians. Gender- and race-based discrimination remained pervasive in higher education, and thus presented many challenges to individual initiative, productivity, and creativity.

The founding members of the Black Caucus, to a person, had experienced these challenges themselves, as talented young African American women attending college and graduate school, whether in predominantly Black or mainly White educational institutions. As new young faculty members, they wanted a context for better mentoring of their own students. They also were aware of a long tradition of responsible service to the larger

14

African American community by those who were more educated and affluent—a core African American cultural value. And finally, they had attended high school and college at a time when advocacy for the moral, legal, and human rights of African Americans was perceptibly stronger than it had ever been, because of the influence of the civil rights movement.

Like most developmental scientists, they wanted the results of their research ultimately to become part of public practices and policies designed to benefit children. Though youthful, they instinctively knew they could not contribute to improving the lives of African American children unless their perceptions of these children's lives were to become valued by others in their chosen scientific field. Therefore, from the beginning, three strategies were considered likely to improve children's lives: (a) generating new, more conceptually defensible research on African American children; (b) linking research and contemporary social and public policy issues; and (c) serving wherever possible as an advocate for the children and their families.

AFRICAN AMERICAN PARTICIPATION IN SRCD IN THE 1970s[4]

In 1971, several founding members of the Black Caucus attended the Minneapolis SRCD biennial meeting: John Dill, Aline Garrett, Algea Harrison, Harriette McAdoo, and I met one another for the first time, obviously glad to see that other African Americans were attending the meeting, and hopeful that we could become new professional colleagues. Out of these contacts, the core of the Black Caucus was set in motion, becoming a perceptible group needing meeting space during the biennial conference in 1973. The first meeting of "Blacks Interested in Child Development Research" (BICD) was convened during the SRCD biennial meeting in Philadelphia, on Friday, March 30, 1973, at 5 p.m. in the Atlanta Room of the Marriott Hotel. A flyer distributed by myself and Ura Jean Oyemade to all Blacks who could be identified as attendees of the 1973 SRCD meeting described the objectives of the initial meeting of the BICD:

1. to provide an opportunity for Black people who are interested in research in child development to meet and to interact;
2. to establish intercommunication networks between Blacks in this area;
3. to become acquainted with other groups who have similar interests in Black Children, e.g., BCDI and NCBCD;
4. to adopt a position on future relationship of Blacks to SRCD and these other groups; and
5. to discuss issues of significance for Black researchers and Black children, such as training of Black graduate students.

15

The first meeting was convened by Joseph Hodges, Ura Jean Oyemade, Graham Matthews, Ido Rice, and me; I was the designated recorder. From the beginning, graduate students were involved, among them Matthews from the University of Michigan, Rice from Brown University, Margaret Beale Spencer from the University of Chicago, and Sherryl Browne Graves from Harvard University.

We pursued discussion of the five objectives listed above, including issues of significance to Black researchers and Black children, such as training of Black graduate students; the heredity versus environment controversy, a reexamination of issues of community control; the practical significance of research; and the role of the Black researcher. Founding Caucus members, in engaging these conceptual priorities, were influenced by prevailing ideas advanced by members of the newly created Association of Black Psychologists (Cross, 1991; Richards, 1997). As we talked, however, our lack of knowledge about the mission, structure, and function of SRCD became increasingly obvious. Several of us thought we needed stronger ties to the SRCD Governing Council to become better informed and more influential in the organization. Attendees were persuaded of the need to reach out to the Council.

Subsequent to the Philadelphia meeting, persons who had attended the BICD meeting approached members of Governing Council, who invited them to submit a list of potential participants. By December 1, 1973, I had prepared a "Directory of Some Black Americans Interested in Child Development Research"; compiled and typed by hand, this first directory listed 68 names of active professionals, university professors, and graduate students throughout the nation. By June 1, 1975, an updated directory, identified as "Prepared by Diana T. Slaughter for the Informal Black Caucus of the Society for Research in Child Development," listed 91 names. Both directories listed each person's professional location, membership status in SRCD, memberships in other national groups concerned with children, and research interests, where available.

The 1975 directory was especially useful because of a request made at the 1975 SRCD meeting in Denver. By that time, the "Group of Black Americans Interested in SRCD" had been meeting and communicating regularly among themselves, and sometime during the Denver meeting came to be called the "Black Caucus of the Society for Research in Child Development."[5] Representing members of the Caucus, Algea Harrison and Arthur Mathis met on a Sunday morning (April 13) with SRCD Governing Council members: Francis Graham, President; Leon Yarrow, Past President; Richard Bell, Chairperson, Committee on Interdisciplinary Affairs; Norman Livson, Committee Member and Psychology Representative on the Committee on Interdisciplinary Affairs; and Dorothy Eichorn, Executive Director of SRCD. At that meeting Governing Council members requested a list of the Black members of SRCD, thereby signaling official, but informal, recognition of the Caucus, and Harrison and Mathis were able to indicate the future availability of the directory. The Council also indicated it had a responsibility only to those members of the Caucus who were also members of the parent organization.

THE RELATIONSHIP BETWEEN THE BLACK CAUCUS AND SRCD, THE PARENT ORGANIZATION

The late 1960s and early 1970s could be generally characterized as a time when predominantly White organizations and institutions became open to including Black Americans among their ranks. In 1972, for example, President Richard Nixon proposed the famous "goals and timetables" that placed proactive force behind previous legislation emphasizing non-discrimination on the basis of race, gender, religion, or national origin in hiring or promotional contexts. The SRCD was no exception to this trend, reporting itself in conversations with Algea Harrison, first chair of the SRCD Committee on Minority Participation, to be especially receptive to the concerns initiated by Blacks then participating as members in the organization. In the earliest years, 1973–1977, before Jean V. Carew was designated the first official Chairperson of the Black Caucus (1977–1979) but was already its unofficial spokesperson, the informal organization struggled with learning how the parent organization could benefit "Blacks Interested in Child Development Research," experimenting with a variety of strategies, and in the process learning about the functional structures, values, and norms of SRCD.

In the same year that the Black Caucus of SRCD was created by African American members of the Society, the Governing Council created the Committee on Minority Participation (COMP). In doing so, the parent organization stressed that it was interested in accommodating the expressed concerns of individual Black Americans because it wished to diversify its membership and to include more minorities throughout its ranks. The Black Caucus, on the other hand, was founded by Black members for the purpose of extracting resources from the parent organization that would enable the productive advancement of professional careers in the area of Black child research, and thus provide "trickle-down" benefits to Black children and their families, historically ignored or devalued in the research literature in this field. COMP and the Black Caucus shared key members such as Algea Harrison, who worked hard to establish cooperative relationships. They likewise shared an interest in ethnic minority participation in SRCD; clearly, however, the Black Caucus had goals beyond simple inclusion and participation.

COMP has since become the "Committee on Ethnic and Racial Issues" and is perhaps no longer concerned only with creating a more diverse membership. Over time, the SRCD Governing Council has appointed minority members as Committee Chairs. The Black Caucus members elect their own Chairperson, who in turn generally appoints the Chairs of its committees. Continuing to pursue its original goals, the Caucus typically meets in the 1.5 days preceding the SRCD biennial meeting. Members include professionals, graduate students, and other interested persons (see Chapter II).

Space prohibits discussion of the many and varied ramifications of the enduring presence of the Caucus in this field. Suffice it to say that there is no African American who is a serious scholar in the broad developmental field who has not either participated in these meetings or been mentored through contacts made through these meetings. For example, the first Caucus Chairperson, the late Jean Carew, served as research mentor to me, and recommended my promotion and tenure at Northwestern University. I was elected the second Caucus Chair, and over the years I too have recommended a number of Caucus members for tenure and/or promotion. Throughout this 25-year-period of the group's history, Aline Garrett of the University of Louisiana, Lafayette served as Executive Director. Through her efforts, many members have come to know and appreciate the research of one another. Almost from the beginning, the networks of Caucus members broadened to include members of other ethnic minority groups (e.g., Luis Laosa, Cynthia Garcia Coll, Lillian Phernice, Ruby Takanishi). Some of these ties are discussed in the Chapter XII, by Ura Jean Oyemade Bailey and colleagues, in relation to Caucus members' participation in Head Start initiatives.

By 1979, the initiatives of Jean Carew, Algea Harrison, and other members of the Caucus as well as some SRCD majority members (e.g., Mary Ainsworth, Dorothy Eichorn, Bettye Caldwell) had provided for the presence of minority members on the majority of the SRCD standing committees. Their initiatives also increased the presentation of minorities in the various programs and publication boards of the Society, thus paving the way for the future appearance of articles, monographs, and other written documents by and about African-American and other minority children and families.

SOME PERSONAL RECOLLECTIONS OF THE SRCD AND THE BLACK CAUCUS, 1977–1981

The years 1977–1981 were important for me in terms of my professional ties with SRCD and with the larger scientific research community in child development. Beginning in 1977, I served as a member of the new

Social Policy Committee of SRCD, and by 1981 I had become the first ethnic minority to be elected to a term on the Governing Council. I also continued my service to the Black Caucus of SRCD, becoming its second Chairperson in 1979.

From my time on the Social Policy Committee, I recall that SRCD members varied in the extent of their support for the Society's new engagement in social policy activity on behalf of children and families. The greatest consensus among SRCD members concerned the need to demonstrate that scientific research in child development resulted in knowledge of substantial use to policy-makers, practitioners, and laypersons concerned with children's well-being and development. It was thought that research funding would be sustained by congressional sources and governmental agencies if the research were perceived to be useful; if not, further deep cutbacks in funding were anticipated for the 1980s.

Members of the new Social Policy Committee devoted many productive hours, and some not so productive, to considering how an organization like SRCD could be effective in the policy arena. The Committee decided to recommend to the Governing Council that SRCD act in consort with other scientific societies to sustain a Washington, DC, liaison office, with selected members representing SRCD as Fellows on the "Hill." Following Social Policy Committee recommendations, SRCD also supported the engagement of senior members of the Society in their postdoctoral training of Social Policy Fellows. Edward Zigler at Yale, Harold Stevenson at the University of Michigan, Norma Feshbach at UCLA, and James Gallagher at the University of North Carolina, Chapel Hill, directed these first Social Policy Centers, founded with primary funding from the Bush Foundation.

A social policy newsletter, *Social Policy Report*, was eventually established for the membership, and presentations at the biennial conferences in the broad area of child development and social policy were systematically encouraged. Caucus members have continued to serve on the Social Policy Committee, lending support to its initiative and contributing to its newsletter. I think my own visibility on the first Social Policy Committee, including work with the early Congressional Science Fellows' Selection Committee (1980–1981) and the Washington Liaison Office, probably contributed substantially to my successful election to Council. I engaged fully in these professional activities without missing a beat between 1977 and 1981, even though in December 1976 I had been denied tenure by my alma mater, the University of Chicago, and at the time of my appointment to the Social Policy Committee of SRCD, I was actively searching for a job. Fortunately, I was invited to join the faculty at Northwestern University, beginning *again* as Assistant Professor in fall 1977. By reputation, Northwestern was more receptive to both practice/intervention and social policy considerations, having established the Center for Urban Affairs and Policy Research in 1968 (now Institute for Policy Research).

Upon reflection, I think that the tensions between science and policy, in reference to child development and education, have been enduring elements in my professional life. I would never abandon scientific research in favor of a completely advocatory position, but I am also not attracted by any activity that appears to me to resemble "research for research's sake." I have always wanted to be an intelligent consumer *and* producer of research. I feel strongly that doing research is a special way to learn about human lives and that research can, indeed should be, especially useful to people who want to help others live better lives.

I believe two observations are appropriate here. First, the University of Chicago did not value my "rising star" in the leading professional organization in my field. Second, status within an academic institution, the primary factor motivating most academics in their external professional service activities, did not motivate me. What did motivate me to such great involvement in external professional service activities? Perhaps it was my commitment to the explicit aim of the Black Caucus: to set new standards for the beneficial aspects of research for African American children and families. Instinctively, I knew that I could not reach this lofty goal alone. Over the years, I would need committed colleagues—peers and graduate students—who would help to develop and sustain the effort. Thus, during my early tenure and adjustment to academic life at Northwestern, I had the support of the Black Caucus of SRCD.

Because of the importance of the Caucus to me at a critical time in my professional life, I conclude by briefly reminiscing about some of my observations as the second elected chairperson of the Black Caucus.

CHAIRING THE BLACK CAUCUS OF SRCD, 1979–1981

As Chairperson, I conducted the first empirical survey of the action preferences and needs of Black Caucus members. Survey statements were solicited from members, and then restated as potential priorities for the Caucus to pursue. Each statement was to be ranked on a continuum from $5 = $ *Very desirable* to $1 = $ *Not at all desirable*. Of 26 ranked statements, the top seven were to

1. identify key resource persons within such governmental and private foundation groups who might be of counsel, etc. as regarding obtaining research funds;

2. maintain close connections with the Committee on Minority Participation in SRCD in particular, so as to be a resource for

nominations for various committees, appointments, and sharing grievances within the hierarchy of SRCD;

3. maintain close contact with Black members of the various committees of SRCD so that we can promote the professional socialization of Black members of SRCD;

4. actively discover what research is ongoing that might positively or adversely affect Black children and families;

5. contact SRCD, ASA, AERA, and APA about the availability of training funds in various universities for support of Black scholars who would pursue careers in developmental and/or family research;

6. attempt to monitor the research priorities established by Congressional workers as these would affect Black families and children; and

7. encourage one to two off-year conferences whose major focus would be on research as it emphasizes development of Black children and families.

A steering committee was created to begin to address these priorities.[6] Black Caucus minutes written by me, dated April 3, 1981, reveal that the following observations were made to the approximately 75 persons attending that Black Caucus business meeting:

> Dr. Slaughter reported that her two goals as Caucus chairperson had been met ... (1) create an organizational structure which would have some permanency because it met the expressed objectives of the membership, and (2) facilitate increased participation in SRCD program activities.

The first goal was met through committees established by a Caucus referendum—seven committees were established by the referendum, and they are described in the first two, of three published, Caucus newsletters.

The second goal was also met largely because the SRCD Program Chair, Dr. William Hall, worked cooperatively and encouraged many Caucus members, including the Black Caucus Program Committee,[7] to be more involved. Attached is a flyer depicting the daily events involving many Black Caucus members. Particularly noteworthy was the Thursday evening Discussion Session entitled: "Some SRCD Black Caucus Perspectives on Directions in Developmental Research with Black Children and Families, Past, Present, and Future." It is the first time the Black

Caucus, as such, became part of SRCD's program. Drs. Slaughter, Peters, Dill, Garrett, Harrison, H. McAdoo, and Spencer, as early Caucus members, participated.

> Dr. Slaughter also noted that a Black Caucus Newsletter, edited by Dr. Aline Garrett, had been started at the suggestion of some D.C. Caucus members. Three newsletters were circulated to the membership between 1979–81 from Dr. Garrett's offices at the University of Southwestern Louisiana. Costs were borne by the Steering Committee Members and the Chairperson.

Thus, from all organizational indications, by that 1981 meeting everything was in place that has endured to the present day, including details as small as the Caucus newsletter logo that I created with Aline Garrett and processes as large as the minority members' report from the SRCD Governing Council to the Caucus, by then Governing Council member Harriette McAdoo.

There was, however, one important exception. To that point in the Caucus, we had avoided dues in hopes of maximizing continued member participation. Thus, at the conclusion of the minutes, I reported on a benchmark fiscal activity:

> After some discussion, it was decided and voted that Caucus membership is conditional upon membership in SRCD. Caucus dues will be $10 per year. Nonmembers of the Caucus can pay a $5 fee and receive the Newsletter. Student members will pay $5. A dues structure will (1) support the networking implicit in the need for a Newsletter, and (2) facilitate the activities of the Chairperson in this same regard.

I recall saying to myself at this point that the Caucus had finally arrived!

In retrospect, I think I took my University of Chicago education more seriously than the institution took me—a working-class Black girl from Chicago's Southside. In college, we were educated to believe that we could change social situations, and thus social facts, by changing how people think about them. In graduate school and my professional life, I applied that principle to working for children and families in African American communities. It was probably good for me that I did not know until later in my career how deeply many scientists, policy-makers, and practitioners feared those changes. It was probably even better for me that the Black Caucus of SRCD emerged and endured, as the Caucus openly embraced the possibility of realizing those changes. The remainder of this monograph provides specific examples and evidence of the challenges faced by early Black Caucus members.

REFERENCES

Bell-Scott, P. (1984). Black women's higher education: Our legacy. *Sage: A Scholarly Journal on Black Women*, **1** (1), 8–11.

Benjamin, L. (Ed.) (1997). *Black women in the academy: Promises and perils.* Gainesville: University Press of Florida.

Brenzel, B. (1983). *History of 19th century women's education: A plea for inclusion of class, race, and ethnicity.* Wellesley College, MA: Center for Research on Women. (ERIC Document Reproduction Service No. ED243796).

Carby, H. (1985). On the threshold of women's era: Lynching, empire, and sexuality in Black feminist theory. In H. L. Gates (Ed.), *Race, writing and difference* (pp. 301–316). Chicago: University of Chicago Press.

Collier-Thomas, B. (1982). The impact of Black women in education: An historical overview. *Journal of Negro Education*, **51**, 173–180.

Cross, W. E. (1991). *Shades of Black: Diversity in African American identity.* Philadelphia: Temple University Press.

Davis, A. (1971). Reflections on the Black woman's role in the community of slaves. *Black Scholar*, **3** (4), 2–15.

Gordon, L. (1989). Race, class, and the bonds of womanhood at Spelman Seminary, 1881–1923. *History of Higher Education Annual*, **9**, 7–32.

Gordon, L. (1990). *Gender and higher education in the progressive era.* New Haven, CT: Yale University Press.

Graham, P. (1975). So much to do: Guides for historical research on women in higher education. *Teachers College Record*, **76**, 421–442.

Graham, P. (1978). Expansion and exclusion: A history of women in American higher education. *Signs: Journal of Women in Culture and Society*, **3**, 759–773.

Guthrie, R. V. (1976). *Even the rat was white: A historical view of psychology.* New York: Harper & Row.

Guy-Sheftall, B. (1990). *Daughters of sorrow: Attitudes toward Black women, 1880–1920, Vol. 11. Black women in United States History.* In D. C. Hine (Series Ed.). Brooklyn, NY: Carlson.

Hill, R. & King, P. (Eds.). (1990). *The black women oral history project* (Vol. 3, pp. 111–83): Interview with Alfreda Duster (March 8–9, 1978). Westport, CT: Meckler.

Hine, D. (1994). *Culture, Consciousness and Community: The Making of an African American Women's History.* Greenville, NC: East Carolina University.

Hine, D., King, W., & Reed, L. (1995). *"We specialize in the wholly impossible": A reader in Black women's history, Vol. 17: Black women in United States History.* In D. C. Hine (Series Ed.). Brooklyn, NY: Carlson.

Hine, D., & Thompson, K. (1998). *The shining ray of hope: A history of Black women in America.* New York: Broadway Books.

Locke, M. (1997). Striking the delicate balances: The future of African American women in the academy. In L. Benjamin (Ed.), *Black women in the academy: Promises and perils* (pp. 340–46). Gainesville: University Press of Florida.

Noble, J. (1956). *The Negro woman's college education.* New York: Columbia University Press.

Noble, J. (1957). Negro women today and their education. *Journal of Negro Education*, **26**, 15–21.

O'Connell, A. & Russo, N. (Eds.). (1983). *Models of achievement: Reflections of eminent women in psychology* (Vols. 1–3). New York: Columbia University Press.

Perkins, L. (1983). The impact of the "cult of true womanhood" on the education of Black women. *Journal of Social Issues*, **39** (3), 17–28.

Richards, G. (1997). *'Race', racism and psychology: Towards a reflexive history.* London: Routledge.

Slowe, L. (1933). Higher education of Negro women. *Journal of Negro Education*, **2**, 352–358.

Terrell, M. (1990). What role is the educated Negro woman to plan in the uplifting of her race? In D. C. Hine (Series Ed.), B. W. Jones (Volume Ed.), *Black women in United States History: Vol. 13. Quest for equality: The life and writings of Mary Eliza Church Terrell, 1863–1954* (pp. 151–158). Brooklyn, NY: Carlson. (Originally published, 1902).

NOTES

1. An earlier version of this chapter was presented at the annual meeting of the American Psychological Association, Chicago, August 15–19, 1997.

2. June Patton, historian, reviewing a draft of sections of this chapter, observed that there is a tradition within Black communities of forming informal self-help groups to address the adverse impact of both racial discrimination and poverty (Personal Communication, June 2, 2002).

3. For example, Black Caucus records indicate that John Dill of the City College of New York and Board member of the National Institute of Black Child Development (NBCDI), Al Goins of the National Institute of Mental Health, Joseph Hodges of the University of Florida, Gainesville, and Graham Matthews, student member, were active contributing members to the founding meeting. In subsequent years, the late John McAdoo, William Cross, Dalton Miller-Jones, and the late Joseph Stevens contributed greatly to focusing our deliberations and directions, and to supporting individual members. One of our former chairpersons during that era, Melvin Wilson, contributed a commentary to this monograph.

4. Since SRCD was founded in 1933; African Americans have participated in child development research for much of that time. Ruth Howard (Beckham), for example, was educated at the Institute for Child Development at the University of Minnesota, and received her doctorate in 1934 after having conducted a study of the development of infant triplets in the state of Minnesota. She probably attended at least one biennial SRCD meeting, as she lived and worked in Chicago as a clinical child psychologist for virtually all of her life after receiving her Ph.D. (Guthrie, 1976; O'Connell & Russo, 1983). Another SRCD biennial meeting attendee overlapped with the earliest Caucus years: Dr. Sadie Grimmett. Grimmett, since retired from Indiana University, Bloomington, was active in the field of early childhood education/program evaluation, and regularly attended SRCD meetings between 1973 and 1997. In 1995, she was recognized by the Black Caucus of SRCD for her contributions throughout its early history. We do not know the names of many other African Americans who may have attended SRCD meetings regularly prior to 1971.

5. Geraldine Brookins (personal communication, September 13, 1996) reports that Evelyn Moore, Executive Director of the Black Child Development Institute, suggested that the group of "Blacks Interested in Child Development Research" be called the "Black Caucus of SRCD." Brookins, the 11th Caucus Chairperson, coauthored Chapter VII of this monograph, which discusses her initiation of the highly successful Black Caucus Pre-Conference programs.

6. I have copies of the original 1979 empirical survey, including the tabulated results. In my opinion, priorities 2–4 were addressed well during the early years of the Caucus. The achievement of priority 1 was initially undermined by the loss of Jean V. Carew in 1981, for at the time she had the most consistent track record of external research support. Priority seven was ultimately addressed by the initiation of the Caucus Pre-Conference (see Chapter VI).

7. This group became somewhat obsolete, especially when the Caucus initiated Pre-Conferences. The group initially was encouraged, however, by then SRCD Program Chair, William Hall, to give feedback on planned panels and other initiatives for the upcoming SRCD program.

II. THE BLACK CAUCUS OF SRCD: MEMBERSHIP GROWTH AND CRITICAL INITIATIVES

Although the Black Caucus was founded as an organization in 1973, it was very loosely structured. In the initial 5 years, what held us together was our belief and commitment to the five objectives outlined and agreed to in our first meeting in Philadelphia. Chapter I discusses the founding meeting and very early initiatives. However, as this *Monograph* presents the story of our first 25 years, I will provide a brief overview of how we, as a group, moved from the first Philadelphia meeting and earliest initiatives to become a recognized affiliate of Society for Research in Child Development (SRCD). Much of what is discussed here is elaborated in other chapters. For example, Chapters IV and V detail aspects of our relationship to Governing Council and Council members. Similarly, Chapter VIII details Caucus Pre-Conferences. Also appendices chronicle major Caucus events and core membership composition during the first 25 years. This chapter serves as point of reference for those readers who wish an overview prior to the more detailed accounts found elsewhere. Further, in describing approaches to membership recruitment, support, and expectations, as revealed from my content analysis of our 40 newsletters over 22 years, I reveal much about how the Caucus was sustained over a quarter century.

MEMBERSHIP RECRUITMENT

A major focus of the founding members of the Black Caucus was to increase the membership by trying to answer the following questions: (1) Who are the Black child development researchers? (2) What are their research interests? (3) What type of research are they doing? Thus, a concerted effort was made to identify individuals who fit these criteria. Therefore, in the 6 years following 1973, Black Caucus directories were compiled at each biennial SRCD meeting. At the meetings approximately 50 names were compiled. The directories then facilitated members of the Governing Council of SRCD in selecting appropriate and interested minority members for appointment to and participation in the various functions and committees of the Society.

The initial directory listed both members of SRCD and their self-identified ethnic group, as well as a section on minority persons who were interested in the field of child development, but were not members of SRCD. This directory became an important resource for contacting potential members for the Black Caucus.

As the biennial meetings of SRCD rotated to the different cities— Boston, Detroit, Toronto, etc., new members, especially students, were added to the list of Black Caucus members. Suzanne Randolph, Chairperson of the Black Caucus (1985–1987), prepared a membership directory of the Black Caucus containing 100 names. Additionally, in 1985 the Committee on Minority Participation (COMP) compiled a directory under the direction of John McAdoo. Over the years the number of Black Caucus members has continued to steadily increase. Caucus members have encouraged their colleagues and their undergraduate and graduate students to become members of the Black Caucus.

I believe that one very important factor which has led to the increase in membership has been the overwhelming success of the five Black Caucus Pre-Conferences held in the years, 1989, 1991, 1993, 1995, and 1997. Each Pre-Conference program focused entirely on topics/issues that were of primary importance to African Americans. In addition, the Pre-Conferences featured eminent researchers as presenters. Typically, there has always been a "full house" at the Black Caucus business meeting held on the Friday following the Pre-Conference because the pre-conference participants were eager to become part of an organization that featured a Pre-Conference that dealt entirely with issues of relevance to them.

Following the 1991 Pre-Conference there were many requests from non-African American professionals and students to extend membership in the Black Caucus to them. A vote of the membership was taken. The result of the vote was to allow non-Blacks to become members of the Black Caucus so long as their interests are consistent with the focus and established goals of the organization. As a result there was an increase in the Caucus membership; by 1997, the membership in the Black Caucus was approximately 140. The leadership and the members of the Black Caucus realized early on that in order to meet its goals, it would be necessary to communicate more frequently than every 2 years at the biennial meetings. As meeting together physically was generally prohibitive financially, another form of communication was needed. Thus the newsletter was established.

NEWSLETTERS

The first newsletter of the Black Caucus was organized under the direction of the Caucus Chairperson, Diana Slaughter for the expressed purpose of communication among the membership. Diana and I pieced together the mockup for that first newsletter on the floor of my sister's apartment in New Orleans in November, 1979. As stated in newsletter Number One, Spring, 1980, it was hoped that the newsletter would be used by the membership as a vehicle for:

(1) conveying its ideas, perspectives, and advice about the on-going structure and function of the Black Caucus;

(2) providing feedback on issues and items facing the Black Caucus, and the larger black community;

(3) sharing information (from a variety of sources) that might be helpful to the membership and to other groups with similar interests;

(4) and finally, just as a means of keeping in touch.[1]

The newsletter has been a consistent communication tool for members of the Black Caucus and other individuals interested in research about African American children and families. Through 1997, the newsletter was circulated three times per year. It was published twice in 1980, once a year from 1981 to 1984, twice in 1985, and not at all in 1986. From 1987 to 1997 it was published three times a year (with the exception of 1989, when two editions were published). As newsletter editor in those initial years, I worked closely with respective Black Caucus Chairpersons to ensure that the membership is informed about important issues related to African American children and families. As editor, I contributed a section entitled, "Editor's Notes" to each edition. This section conveyed an overview of each newsletter. Information regarding important dates and deadlines could also be found in this section.

As a communication device, the newsletter has been an important tool concerning African American children and families on multiple levels. Announcements of job opportunities were included in 35 of the 40 issues. The total number of jobs listed in the 35 editions of the newsletters is 331. Of the 331 job opportunities, 236 were tenure-track of senior tenured positions (the majority were junior faculty positions), 36 were non-tenure-track or visiting scholar position, and 59 were for postdoctoral fellowship positions. Although job listings are an important component of the newsletter, communication about and between the membership remained a key focus of the newsletter.

"A Message From Your Caucus Chairperson" was included in 19 of the 40 issues. This column normally highlighted the agenda of the current Black Caucus Chairperson. Issues related to research and social policy on African American children and families were frequently discussed in this column and other sections of the newsletter. Diana Slaughter stated in the inaugural edition of the newsletter, "This first newsletter is a beginning; whether it continues will depend upon whether you, as a member, or potential member, of the Black Caucus of the SRCD, will find it to be a useful organ of communication."[2] Diana and other Chairpersons emphasized reporting on contributions from Caucus members. These contributions about professional research activities are discussed in the newsletter section, "Issues Related to Research with Black Children and Families." This section appeared in the newsletter 13 times.

Another section titled "News From the Membership" highlighted information about the Black Caucus constituents themselves. Personal and professional recognition is given by acknowledging members' honors and awards including promotions, completion of doctoral degrees, successful awarding of grants, new job appointments, etc. A total of 100 listings of such honors and awards appeared in the newsletters. Additionally, recent publications by Caucus members were included in the newsletters. A total of 89 references to articles, chapters, monographs, technical reports, and books were listed in the newsletters. In addition, a listing of editors of journals who are Caucus members were included in the newsletter. The newsletter has also been a communication tool to announce upcoming events and conferences.

Along with promoting good news and professional opportunities for Caucus membership, the newsletter also has been a tool for announcements concerning the death of individual members including a special section entitled, "Remembrances." There were "remembrances" of Dr. Jean V. Carew in 1982; Dr. Marie Ferguson Peters in 1984; Dr. Joseph Henderson Stevens, Jr. in 1991; Dr. A. Wade Smith in 1994; Dr. John L. McAdoo in 1995; Dr. Maxine L. Clark in 1995. Caucus members offered reflections of personal interactions about the recently deceased member and their research. As the Black Caucus grew, the content of the newsletter also expanded. Therefore, the newsletter continued to be the focal mechanism for communication for the membership.

In response to the requests by the members, a Pre-Conference was held in Kansas City in 1989 prior to the start of the SRCD biennial meeting. The Black Caucus continues to sponsor a biennial Pre-Conference prior to the SRCD biennial meeting. Early on, the newsletter served as a vital tool for disseminating information about the Pre-Conference. Pre-registration forms, the programs for respective Pre-Conferences, and information regarding Caucus business meetings were also included in the newsletter along with Business Meeting Minutes, the Financial Report, and information regarding Caucus elections. Special topics appeared in nine issues of the newsletter, including a questionnaire on how to help/recruit student members to the field of Human Development; an announcement of a Teach-In during the SRCD general meeting to call attention to the Missing and Murdered Children Crisis in Atlanta; a list of SRCD convention events of interest to the membership; information about Caucus members' works in progress; and even a call to action by African American Women in Defense of Ourselves (in response to the treatment of Anita Hill during the Clarence Thomas confirmation hearings).

Students have always been central to the Black Caucus. The senior members of the Caucus have always recognized their roles as teachers and mentors to the future generation of Black researchers. In August 1987, when the call for papers for the special issue of *Child Development* on minority children was announced, the co-editors of the special issue, Margaret Beale Spencer and Vonnie McLoyd, envisioned this as a mentoring opportunity for the younger members of the Black Caucus. The mentoring system was conceived as a pre-review process in which established scholars would provide written or oral feedback to authors about manuscripts they planned to submit for publication in the special issue. The system was set up through the newsletter. The names and addresses of pre-reviewers, research areas of expertise, and the minority group with which they work were all published in the newsletter. Junior researchers simply needed to communicate with the appropriate mentor. The quality of that special issue of *Child Development* spoke to the success of the mentoring system.

Mentoring was a hallmark accomplishment of the tenure of Deborah Johnson as Black Caucus Chairperson. In her message to the membership, Deborah stated, "The organization has set a priority of mentoring. The graduate students have made their desire for this type of support known and we must respond quickly and with force." As a result, the "Graduate Network of the Black Caucus" (GNBC), a special feature in the newsletter, was established by Deborah. Like the Black Caucus newsletter, the network was set up to serve as a vehicle for graduate students to communicate with each other and with the membership. Graduate students were encouraged to submit their accomplishments, concerns, and other informational articles for publication. Deborah Johnson contributed to the GNBC by providing a list of articles that might prove helpful to graduate students in achieving successful careers. The list was published in issue twenty-four, Spring, 1992.

In addition, Deborah organized a forum for the graduate students to present their research at the Pre-Conference in New Orleans in 1993. Graduate students were able to receive constructive feedback from senior

Caucus members in a non-threatening environment. These "roundtable discussions" were continued at the Indianapolis Pre-Conference in 1995 under the direction of the Black Caucus Chairperson, Melvin N. Wilson.

The newsletter of the Black Caucus of SRCD began in 1980 with a rather crude format which was published on 11 × 14 sheets folded in half with a hand-drawn logo of a torch superimposed on a drawing of the United States and Africa. By 1997 and beyond, it had become a product of desktop publishing! I understand recent plans post my tenure, include converting to online contacts, and building a website, serve the same purposes addressed above.

MEMBERSHIP DUES

The issue of dues was first approached cautiously. Dues were first assessed in 1980 to cover the cost for the publication of the newsletter. For the next 6 years dues continued at $10.00 (students $5.00). However, the voluntary nature of paying dues, increased printing cost, increased frequency of the newsletter, and increased postage precipitated the decision in 1989 to increase the membership dues to their current level.

As the leadership of the Caucus added new goals and objectives to be accomplished, and the expectations of the growing membership increased, it became very evident that membership dues would need to be assessed. Further, dues mean commitment. The outgoing Chairperson, Valora Washington, who presided at the business meeting in Spring 1989 summated the rise and growth of the Caucus this way:

> All of us have reason to celebrate the momentum that the Caucus is experiencing right now: Our membership is growing, the Newsletter is being published regularly, and our influence throughout the Society is being felt more keenly. Imagine my surprise when my motion to increase the dues 100% was rejected in favor of a 300% increase![3]

Membership dues provide the seed money to support the Pre-Conferences. Operational costs and other incidental costs such as letterhead stationery and envelopes, and special mailings are also covered by membership dues. After the 1993 Pre-Conference, the new Chairperson of the Black Caucus, Melvin Wilson, appointed a committee to investigate the feasibility of establishing lifetime memberships as a means of stabilizing the organization's financial base. This issue is still under study. Additional funds have been added to the treasury through donations, sale of souvenir buttons and videotapes of Pre-Conference proceedings, and proceeds from the sale of copies of the poem "When You Hear The Children Cry" by Suzanne

M. Randolph. The Caucus now manages to operate without a deficit, given dues and the in-kind services of various members. Personally, I think this is an important achievement for an organization that began in 1973 with just a handful of interested people.

NOTES

1. Garrett, A. M. (1980, Spring). Editor's Note. *Black Caucus of SRCD*, **1**, 1.

2. Johnson, D. J. (1991, Summer). Message from the Caucus Chairperson. *Black Caucus of SRCD*, **22**, 3–4.

3. Newsletter, Black Caucus of SRCD, Number Seventeen, Summer, 1989, p. 3. The current dues of the organization are $60.00 for Professionals and $10.00 for students and postdoctoral fellows for a 2-year period. The income from the dues has remained sufficient to cover the cost of the three issues of the newsletter that are published per year. Over the years the cost for publishing and disseminating the newsletter has fluctuated, ranging from a low of $162.84 to a high of $261.32. However, beginning with issue thirty-four (Summer, 1995), the newsletter has been printed by the University of Southwestern Louisiana Print Shop averaging $115.00 per newsletter.

III. LETTERS FROM MARY: ACHIEVING STATURE WITHIN SRCD

Currently the biennial meetings, committees, and governing structures of the Society for Research in Child Development (SRCD) display the ideals of diversity and illustrate the model of multiculturalism described in the objectives and goals of numerous organizations. The SRCD that existed when I first attended in 1971 has changed tremendously in its governing structure, its integration of ethnic groups, and its membership demographics. The transformation is rewarding for those of us who were an integral part of the struggles for change. There are still challenges for the organization, yet the accomplishment of long sought-after goals that seemed impossible years ago must be acknowledged and celebrated. This discussion concerns the efforts of an international scholar who was a leader in promoting diversity and multiculturalism in the Society, Mary Ainsworth.

Mary Ainsworth's scholarly work speaks for itself in her prolific publication record. Little is known, however, about her role as a social force for change within SRCD. In her correspondence—especially the letters reproduced below, she describes in detail her perceptions and the strategies and actions she took to fully integrate ethnic minorities into all levels of SRCD. Of particular interest is the record of how, over time, she changed—and thus followed paths she had avoided when she first embarked on this endeavor. She was pragmatic in her actions when confronted with obstacles to full integration in the Society; she responded with determination and sensitivity in her various leadership roles. I hope that sharing these letters will enable readers to appreciate Mary Ainsworth not only as a great scholar, but also as an activist for diversity and multiculturalism.

There were many issues that influenced the decision of Black members of SRCD to coalesce and challenge its Governing Council. First was a major concern about articles on Black children and families published in SRCD journals and in the literature of developmental psychology. Black scholars thought these writings distorted the Black experience and lacked validity. Relying on both their professional observations and their personal experience of life in their communities, Black researchers perceived a gap between their own perspective of events in the Black community and that expounded by White researchers. Black members of the Society interpreted some of the major assumptions and inferences about Black children by White researchers as misrepresentative and racist in effect, if not intent. During this period Jensen (1969) was stressing a genetic component to differences in Black and White IQ scores, with attending assumptions of the genetic inferiority of Blacks. Although Jensen was not a member of SRCD, his position generated controversy among its members. The controversy was viewed by Blacks as a continuation of a long history, starting in the 1800s, of using racial research in American psychology to dehumanize and justify the oppression of Black Americans (Richards, 1997; Winston, 2004). Black members were concerned that perceptions of Black children in the larger culture would be affected by the pejorative impact of professional writings of Jensen. They did not perceive SRCD and its biennial meetings as a sensitive venue for expressing their concerns, although some members of the Society were speaking out as individuals against the trend of racial research.

A second concern was the issue of emphasizing the deficit model when describing the Black experience in the literature. If the family and community contexts for the development of Black children were different from those of the "traditional" White middle class, they were interpreted as deficient or culturally deprived. Black researchers thought this devalued their communities and slighted and overlooked the strengths and richness of their culture. Moreover, it was thought that one of the major reasons for this state of affairs was the lack of empowerment of Black members in the Society and the consequent disregard of their views and criticisms.

Blacks were not represented in the governance structure of the Society, and had limited or no representation at the various layers of the publication process. When manuscripts were submitted comparing within groups of Black children, comments by reviewers frequently referred to the lack of an appropriate comparison group, White middle class children. Black scholars, many of whom were interested only in within-group comparisons, considered this criticism an affront. They often interpreted these actions by editors and reviewers to mean that a White comparison group was required for their research on their community to be considered legitimate and worthy of publication. In addition, the publication process lacked reviewers who were sensitive to the Black experience. Resentment against other professionals in their chosen field of study and in the major organization representing both scholarship and collegiality in their scientific area began to smolder, creating tensions at the biennial meetings. It was thought that SRCD should not only be made aware that lack of representation of Blacks and the Black perspective was creating discomfort among its members, but also initiate processes to address the problems.

During this period, Mary Ainsworth was in leadership positions in SRCD and I was Chair of the Minority Participation Committee (COMP) and liaison person to the Governing Council from the Black Caucus. It was from our leadership positions that we began corresponding.

I had been introduced to Mary Ainsworth during the 1960s under the same conditions as other graduate students in developmental psychology: her publications on the concept of attachment were required reading. I was impressed with her innovative approaches, especially her studies from a community in Africa where multiple mothering was the cultural norm. Whenever she presented her research at SRCD meetings, I would attend her sessions, which augmented my interest in extended families as a context for development. Her presentations were as impressive as her writings. From my perspective in the early 1970s, she was a distant professional figure, an international scholar, and an active member in the affairs of the Society.

After my correspondence with Mary Ainsworth began, however, I was exposed to a closer view of this eminent scholar. She wrote a series of letters to me describing her concerns and explaining her efforts and strategies, for increasing minority participation in SRCD. The letters revealed how she responded to the challenges of proposals to change how SRCD conducted its affairs in regards to minorities.

This paper presents below Mary Ainsworth's letters and my comments on the contexts of her ideas and statements. (Because of the limitations of space in this publication, only extracts of the letters are printed here. To review all of her correspondence, please consult the archives of SRCD.) The letters are preceded by background information on what had occurred in the organization before the beginning of our correspondence in 1977.

In 1973, at the biennial meeting of SRCD in Philadelphia, Black members of the Society held an organizational meeting. A major objective of the group was to foster dialogue between members of the new Black Caucus and officers of SRCD. In 1977, the Committee on Minority Participation (COMP) was established to increase the participation of ethnic minorities in SRCD. It was suggested that the committee follow the HEW affirmative-action guidelines regarding the definition of minorities, Blacks, Native Americans, Asian Americans, and "Spanish" Americans. I was the first Chair of COMP, from 1977 to 1981. The other members of the committee were Bettye Caldwell, Ivonne Heras, and Lee C. Lee. Mary Ainsworth was president of SRCD for the years 1977–1979, and she served on the Governing Council from 1975 to 1981, as President elect, President, and Past

President, respectively. Her final leadership role was as Chair of the Nominations Committee.

31 May 1977
Dear Algea,

Anne Pick called me just before the long weekend to say that you had accepted the appointment as Chairman of the SRCD Committee on Minority Affairs. I am delighted to hear this news.

I am enclosing copies of all the correspondence that should concern the Committee on Minority Affairs, for your information. As you can see, much of it is concerned with the Black Caucus. Without wishing to frustrate the Black Caucus, the Governing Council nevertheless believes that the Committee on Minority Affairs should advise the Council on behalf of all minorities, and that the Black Caucus should in future submit its suggestions with the recommendations that the committee may wish to make on behalf of all minorities.

As you will note from the correspondence, the Governing Council has already made committee appointments for 1977–78, and indeed attempted to provide for "minority" representation on most of the committees. Except for filling vacancies that come about through resignation or refusal to accept appointment, there is no appropriate way in which minority representation can be augmented in committee appointments until the meeting of the Governing Council next spring. At that time, however, we should be pleased to take into consideration suggestions of the Committee on Minority Affairs.

As for the matter of a Council-appointed member-at-large of the Council itself, this too will be brought up for consideration at the Council meeting next spring—together with the whole issue of how to help our black members and members of other minority groups to feel more comfortable, participant and fulfilled in the Society. I do not wish to suggest to you that the Council will decide to act in the direction of reserving a Council slot for a minority member, for there are a substantial number of Council members who at this time hold that special action would be unwise and that we should count on the normal election procedures to accomplish this end in due course. But what I do wish to convey at this point is that next spring the Council will be looking forward to a report from your Committee as a basis for discussion. I have no doubt that this report will have an important influence on whatever decisions will be made. Nevertheless the major roster of committee appointments will be made at the 1979 Council meeting, which takes place just before the biennial meeting, and at that time suggestions from your Committee will have the best chance of affecting Council appointments.

Bettye Caldwell will also be in touch with you. She is the Council member appointed to your committee. She is eager to do what she can to help you in your endeavors, and indeed, before the establishment of your Committee she was responsible for advising the Council on minority matters.

May I wish you all success in the work of your Committee. Do not hesitate to call me, or SRCD's secretary, Anne Pick, if there is anything we can do to clarify your charge, or to help you in your work.

Yours sincerely,
Mary

8 September 1977
Dear Algea,

Thank you so much for your letter of August 26. Before I got round to replying (having been preoccupied both with a deadline for a chapter I was writing and the beginning of classes) Anne Pick called me today to tell me of her conversation with you.

I believe that your inquiry about the present "minority" membership on SRCD committees will have been answered in your conversation with Anne. She will have told you about the Archives, Distinguished Awards, and Nominations Committee. You are quite right that at present these have no minority representation: Anne will have explained to you how that came to pass.

The definition of "minority" that you proposed in your letter sits well with me. When I was at Johns Hopkins I was chairman of the Affirmative Action Committee, and had occasion thus to see how HEW defined minorities. It was obviously in terms of hyphenated Americans, and included "Spanish"-Americans, Oriental-American, as well as native Americans & blacks (What a muddle!). Nevertheless, I think we would be safe in following the HEW affirmative-action guidelines in this respect . . .

I am not quite sure how the Committee on Minority Affairs became the Committee on Minority Participation. I suspect that this may have been Anne Pick's bright idea. In any event I think the latter title more accurately represents our proper concern than the former. Second, should your committee become aware of non-psychologists who are also members of minorities, these would be of particular interest to the Governing Council and perhaps especially as a potential pool of candidates for the Committee on Interdisciplinary Affairs.

You have indicated that you plan to have a report ready for the Council meeting. It would be appropriate if you include in it suggestions about another Social Policy Committeemember, and the SPC would especially appreciate nominations from among the "Chicano" minority.

Thank you for your expression of interest. I am sure that the participation of minorities in SRCD affairs will be greatly forwarded as a result of the work of your Committee.

With all best wishes,
Mary

At the meeting of the Governing Council in 1978, I presented the first report and recommendation from the Committee on Minority Participation. Mary Ainsworth presided, in her position as President. As official meetings usually go, there were discussions and attempts by the group to reach a consensus on issues. In brief, COMP recommended that the Governing Council take action in three areas to increase minority participation: (a) governance, (b) professional socialization, and (c) professional integration. The following letter from Mary discussed the official position of the Governing Council on COMP's report.

May 12, 1978
Dear Algea,

It was indeed good to meet you at last, and to hear the report that you and Lee C. Lee presented to the Governing Council on behalf of the Committee on Minority Participation. We certainly thank you for a careful, thoughtful job.

Since the Council meeting was somewhat rushed, I though that it might have been difficult for you to know precisely what had been decided in regard to the recommendations made by your committee. Therefore, I am writing in the hope of clarifying the matter.

COMP had recommended, under the governance segment, some assurance of minority representation on the Governing Council, and minority representations on committees whose tasks have relevance to or direct effects on the minority community. COMP had also recommended that candidates for official positions in SRCD provide information about themselves, including, if they wished, information about their minority status. It was thought that very few members of SRCD had the opportunity to know ethnic minority members and their accomplishments, and if they did, this would influence their inclination toward voting for them.

A. *Minority Representation on the Governing Council*

    1. Council agreed that the election ballot be accompanied by information about each candidate. (I think that the Society has become so large that such information would be desirable quite apart from the minority participation issue.)

37

In addition, it was agreed that the Minority Participation Committee would provide the Nominating Committee with a list of individuals who identify themselves as minority members, for its use in preparing a slate of nominees.

2. The Governing Council did not wish to resort to appointment to the Council if the minority member is not elected through the normal procedure in the 1979 election. It was the consensus that the appointed slots were intended to ensure interdisciplinary representation on the Council, in accordance with the interdisciplinary aims of the Society from the time of its foundation.

3. Similarly, the Governing Council did not wish to initiate a change in the Bylaws to create additional appointed slots on the Council for minority representatives. It was clearly the hope of the Council, however, that normal election procedures would result in minority representation on the Council.

(Let's see what results from the implementation of your recommendation. The matter can always be raised again if the normal election procedures do not have the desired result in, say, the next two elections.)

COMP's second set of recommendations, under the segment of professional socialization, was for the Council to invite minority members to participate in the program planning of the Society's biennial meetings, invite young minorities to review journal articles for the Society's publications, and invite minorities to serve on editorial boards of the Society's publications.

C. Minority Representation on Editorial Boards of SRCD Publications

The Council concurred with this recommendation. Indeed the matter was raised with the Publication Committee in advance of the submission of your report to Council. The most relevant journal is, of course, *Child Development*. An Editor chooses the Editorial Board from among those who not only are experts in one or other developmental area, but also have in his/her editorial experience submitted thoughtful, competent reviews. Therefore, your suggestion of making a major minority push at the level of ad hoc reviewing is a very good one.

May I suggest that the Committee on Minority Participation provide the Editor of Child Development with suggestions of possible ad hoc reviewers.

Under the segment of professional integration, COMP had recommended a study group in the summer of 1979 and a summer institute in 1980.

D. Study Group

The Governing Council encourages you to frame a proposal for a study group. .... This proposal, when formulated, should be sent to the Committee on Summer Institutes and Study Groups.

F. Resource List

The Council approves the plan to compile a resource list. I am informing the Editor of the Newsletter that you wish to include a statement such as you suggest. I shall inform the Editor that you will be submitting something to her along the lines you proposed.

I trust that this helps to clarify the Governing Council's response to your report and recommendations. Thank you again for your efforts. Your new Committee is doing exactly the sorts of things that the council had hoped it would. If there is anything that either Anne Pick, our Secretary, or I can do to help, please let us know.

With best wishes,
Mary D. Ainsworth

On June 19, 1978 I wrote Mary Ainsworth in reply to her response to the COMP recommendations. In the letter I expressed disappointment that the Council decided not to initiate a change in the bylaws to assure that a minority member be on the Council. I also mentioned that to rely solely on the election process as a means of obtaining minority representation on the Council was a dubious solution to the problem. Minority representation would depend on election results, and the possibility remained that in some future years there would not be a minority member on the Council. I was not optimistic. Nonetheless, I agreed that we had to wait until after the election to decide what to do next. Mary responded as follows:

July 12, 1978
Dear Algea,

I am sorry to have been so long in replying to your letter of June 19. In fact there seems to be only one point that requires special mention. Perhaps you would be more optimistic about the outcome of "normal election procedures" if I mentioned some things that might be done within the framework of such procedures.

> 1. The Committee on Minority Participation can make nominations. At this point I would advise focusing on nominations for Member at Large on the Governing Council. I doubt that at the present time any minority member is well enough known or has sufficient experience with SRCD governance to have a chance at either the

President Elect or Secretary slots. So don't "waste" your most visible candidates by nominating them for these positions in 1979.

2. The Committee on Minority Participation can urge individual minority members of SRCD to exercise their rights as members by replying to the request for nominations that will be sent out by the Nominating Committee. I believe that a large percentage of the membership neglects to make nominations, so that a small, determined, and conscientious group can make quite an impact on the nomination process.

3. There is no minority member on the Nominations Committee at present, and, as I think I explained before, that could not be rectified at the last Council meeting, for the Bylaws specify a committee of three and there are already three members. Nevertheless the Council has charged the Nominations Committee to give special attention to nominations of minority member [sic]. One way to assure a minority member will be elected to Council is to place only minority members on the ballot for one of the slots for Member at Large of the Council. This is quite legitimate. The Nominations Committee is to be guided by the nominations sent in by the membership but they are quite within their rights to design the ballot in the way I have just described.

Incidentally, it would be a good idea to try to line up minority members of disciplines other than psychology for nominations for Council slots, as well as suggesting them to Council for committee appointments. Who knows! Two minority members might be elected to Council simultaneously by this means!

All of this was implicit in the Council decision to rely on the normal election process. I think it is entirely likely that the 1979 election will result in the election of one minority member. And the same thing can happen again and again as long as need be, provided that the Minority Participation Committee and others keep suggesting names of good candidates. Hopefully, in time, enough minority members will have become visible and experienced in SRCD affairs that there will be no further need to give special emphasis to pushing them for participation in Council and committees.

Congratulations on the fine progress you are making with the other issues that you mentioned in you letter.

With best wishes,
Mary D. Ainsworth

COMP recommended Lee C. Lee and Jean Carew as candidates for Governing Council. Their names did not get past the Nominations

Committee and were not on the ballot. Other minority members were recommended for SRCD committees. The Nominations Committee placed my name on the ballot for a position on Governing Council. I was the only minority candidate for the position, and I was not elected. I wrote Mary on November 21, 1978, commenting on how disappointed COMP was in the design of the ballot for the 1979 election. We had hoped that the Nominations Committee would follow her suggestions outlined in her letter of July 12. As noted above, one suggestion was to place only names of minority members as choices for one of the slots. In other words, minority members would compete only with each other for a position on Governing Council. Furthermore, it was through our trust in the sincerity of the Governing Council that we had accepted the election approach as a workable solution to the issue of minority representation thereon. From my experiences as a community activist, I knew it was highly unlikely that the membership would elect a minority member without strategic actions. Lack of credit-ability of the process emerged as a result of the wording of the ballot. There were two issues: (a) Whether the Governing Council was sincerely coop-erating with COMP to resolve the issue of minority representation on Gov-erning Council within a reasonable time period; and (b) whether the Committee's approach to Governing Council was perceived by ethnic members of SRCD as an effective and appropriate effort. A copy of my letter to Mary Ainsworth of November 21, 1978, was mailed to all members of the Black Caucus and self-identified ethnic members of the Society, using COMP's published directory of minority members of SRCD. I received a reply from Mary.

December 11, 1978
Dear Algea,

Further about the slate put together by the Nominations Committee. Not only were you and I unhappy about this, but also I have received feedback from Anne Pick, Bettye Caldwell, and Dot Eichorn, who have similar views.

I am enclosing a copy of a memo I have prepared for the Governing Council, asking them to vote on a proposal to change the By-Laws of the Society relevant to the composition of the Nominations Committee. I do not know, of course, how this will work out, but I hope that this will perhaps result in one step toward a better solution for minority representation.

Perhaps in earlier correspondence with you I was too optimistic about the slate that I felt sure would be presented by the Nominations Commit-tee—but which was not! I can understand that you and your Committee interpret the slate as a "breach of faith." Now I feel hesitant to share with you what I hope we may salvage from this situation, lest there may seem to be more promises unfulfilled. Nevertheless, please be assured that I shall do my best to forward the cause of Minority Participation before the end of my Presidency.

I shall keep you informed about further developments.

With Best wishes,
Mary D. Ainsworth

Memorandum

To: Governing Council
From: Mary Ainsworth
Re: Proposed Amendment to By-laws Relevant to Nominations Committee

It has long been the policy of the Governing Council to ensure that it has an interdisciplinary composition. More recently, we adopted a policy of encouraging minority representation in Council, we hoped, through "normal election procedures." The most recent ballot prepared by the Nominations Committee seems likely to me—and to others who have contacted me about it—to forward neither of these policies.

According to our present by-laws, the Nominations Committee is allowed considerable discretion in the preparation of the slate. Thus Article 11, section 3 specifics: "The Nominations Committee shall select the final slate of candidates. This selection shall be guided by the suggestions of the electorate and shall maintain representation of the various disciplines of the membership of the Society." My reading of "guided by" is not "determined by." Unfortunately, perhaps because of the increasing size of the Society, nominations from the membership in response to the mail invitation of the Nominations Committee tend to be sparse. In particular, they seem unlikely to give any clear mandate to the Committee in regard to either non-psychologist or minority candidates.

Therefore, it follows that the Nominations Committee is well within the specifications of the present by-laws if it disregards the quantitative aspect of the response from the membership—and even generates nominations of its own—in order to bring the slate into harmony with present policies of the Society. This must have been difficult for the present Nominations Committee, which was comprised of three members, all psychologists and none members of minority groups.

In our next Council meeting we shall have an opportunity to discuss strategies for implementing our policies, and I do not wish to discuss the possibilities here—except to propose that our present Nominations Committee is too small to be able to do the job that we expect of them.

I propose that we should recommend to the membership of the Society a change in the By-laws, specifically that Article V, Section 1 should read:

"The Nominations Committee shall consist of the Past President and four members appointed by the Council. The Past President shall chair the Committee." The only alteration is from "two" to "four."

My notion here is that at least one of the committee members to be appointed by Council would be a non-psychologist (perhaps preferably a member of the Committee on Interdisciplinary Affairs) and that at least one should be a "minority" member (perhaps preferably a member of the Committee on Minority Participation). If I am right in believing that you agree with my interpretation of our policy, there seem to be two ways in which this could be forwarded. Either we could leave it up to Council to be sure to make the appropriate appointment to the Nominations Committee, or we could specify a further amendment to the By-Laws, specifically: "The Nomination Committee shall consist of the Past President and four members appointed by the Council, to include representatives of at least two of the disciplines comprehended by the Society and at least one representative of the minority groups in the membership."

Personally, I would prefer to merely extend the size of the committee and leave it up to the Council at our next and at future meetings to act appropriately when considering appointments to the Nominations Committee. Nevertheless, it might by expedient to specify committee composition, in order to defuse agitation by members of minority groups who might otherwise create an unhappy disturbance at our Business Meeting. Obviously it would be desirable to prevent such disturbance, since I believe that we are all in favor of greater minority participation in the Society.

According to Article VI of our By-Laws, Section 1, 2 and 3, Council can, upon majority vote, propose an amendment to the By-Laws to the membership. Such proposed amendments should be transmitted to the electorate (by mail) at least 45 days prior to the vote on the amendment. A majority affirmative vote of those voting in a mail referendum is required for approval of the proposed amendment. I propose that Council consider proposing an amendment or amendments to the By-Laws, to be proposed to the membership early in 1979, the results of which can be announced at the Business Meeting in San Francisco.

Please vote, as a member of Council, in regard to the following alternatives enclosed herewith, and return your vote to Anne Pick by January 15.

Mary

After members of the Governing Council responded, Mary wrote to me again:

January 29, 1979
Dear Algea,

This is further to my letter of December 11. I should inform you that the outcome of the mail vote by Council was a lack of consensus about my proposal 1 for enlarging the Nominating Committee. Comments on the ballots indicated (a) that some were clearly in favor of minority representation on Council but thought that it was unnecessary to enlarge the committee to achieve it, and (b) that others wanted a discussion at the next Council meeting before taking the step of proposing an amendment to by-laws. So we shall have a thorough discussion of the issue at our next Council meeting. I hope that the focus will be upon ways and means and not on the validity of the issue of minority representation itself. (Ah me! Sometimes it is difficult to put up with democratic procedures in an organization! But since I believe in them I do put up with them.)

My chief purpose in writing, however, is to remind your Committee to supply us with suggestions for appointments to be made by Council—not only suggestions for the appointed slot of member-at-large of the Governing Council, but also suggestions for appointment to all of the other Committees (Alternates should be suggested for all "slots", [sic] so that we can be sure of a minority member on each committee, in case our first choice declines to accept. There is no reason why one person cannot be suggested for more than one position, for one as first choice and for others as an alternate.)

It would be a good idea to provide Bettye Caldwell with the list of suggestions, as well as appending it to your own report. (And I would like a list in advance also, just in case Bettye can't come to the meeting.)

Would Harriette McAdoo be an acceptable candidate for appointment to the Council slot? She is a sociologist—and Black, in case you hadn't heard of her. Most important, she has performed very well on other committee assignments and thus made an excellent impression on members of Council who have served with her. Another consideration is that she is a sociologist, and this would be a plus when one considers that this slot has been considered all along to be a slot for a non-psychologist. Personally, I don't really like the notion of killing two birds with one stone when it comes to affirmative action kinds of appointments, and will argue for a solution that smacks less of expediency. But if the only solution that Council can agree upon turns out to be to find a non-psychologist minority member for the appointed slot, it would certainly be better than appointing no minority member in 1979.

I may not have occasion to write again before I see you in San Francisco. In the meantime

All good wishes,
Mary D. Ainsworth

The next letter was written the following year, when Mary was Past President and Chairman of the Nominations Committee.

March 10, 1980
Dear Algea,

At the meeting of the Governing Council, May 6-7 [1979], the enclosed Call for Nominations and Nomination Ballot were approved. This is for your information now. Your official copy will arrive from the Chicago Office within a couple of weeks.

As you see from the Call for Nominations, we are asking that nominations for President Elect be restricted to members of disciplines other than psychology. Since this is the first time in many years that nominations have been restricted, Council did not see its way clear to restricting one of the two slots for Members-at-Large to members with minority status. However, as you will see, they have encouraged the membership to give consideration to minority members when making their nominations.

My chief purpose in writing at this point is to ask you and your committee to help in ensuring that somehow some good minority candidates come to the attention of the Nominations Committee. There are three possible ways of accomplishing this:

(a) The Committee on Minority Participation could confer and agree to submit a "short list" of names, together with commentary, for the Nominations Committee's consideration.

(b) COMP could draw up a short list of names, as above, but rather than submitting it to the Nominations Committee (or in addition to doing so) draw that list to the attention of others (friends and associates and/or other SRCD minority members) so that the returns from the membership do highlight a few minority candidates most likely to be elected rather than resulting in a scattering of minority candidates none of whom are nominated by more than a very few.

(c) COMP could decide that it wishes not to guide the nomination process beyond the suggestions already made in the Call for Nominations drawing attention to the desirability of considering minority candidates.

Please let me know the wishes of your committee.

In all honesty I must add that I do not think that there is a minority candidate who at present has much chance of being elected in open competition, even though I do think it desirable to especially urge the membership to nominate minority candidates, as well as candidates from disciplines other than psychology.

Speaking now as an individual (rather than as Past President or Chairman of the Nominations Committee) it is my hope that if no minority member is elected in the forthcoming elections, the Governing Council will give serious consideration to appointing another minority Member-at-Large to Council when they meet in 1981. If so, it might be very helpful for us to include one or more minority candidates on the election ballot, so that Council could use the election returns as some kind of guide as to the candidates they would consider for that appointment. Furthermore, it seems to me to be quite possible that when it comes to the next election (i.e., for Officers and Council in 1982–83) Council may decide to restrict one of the slots to minority candidates.

In conclusion, I do want to congratulate you and the rest of COMP, past and present, for the splendid work you have done. It has been statesmanlike and very constructive. I have no doubt whatsoever that it will in due course result in much greater minority participation in the Society, in its committee structure, and in its governance. However, remember that Council itself changes from biennium to biennium. I myself conceive of a continuing COMP that will serve as a conscience and as a reminder to Council to continue to emphasize minority participation.

With best wishes,
Mary

No minority member of SRCD was elected through the election process. Subsequently, Governing Council appointed Harriette McAdoo as its first minority member. Mary Ainsworth did accomplish her goals. Minority members were eventually appointed to the majority of the committees and were included in planning the biennial meetings. I was the Local Arrangements Chair for the 1983 meeting in Detroit, and also served on the Program Committee. I was instrumental in placing minority members on the Review Panels. After Harriette McAdoo's term ended, the election ballot was designed so that minority members competed only with one another for a slot on the Governing Council. Diana Slaughter was so elected.

I hope that this history has given readers insights into the complexities involved in the emerging composition of SRCD's governing structure, committees, and processes. We now have in place a procedure for the mentoring of young ethnic minority scientists, as established by LaRue Allen in her position as Chair of COMP. The 2003 program lists three African American scholars (Vonnie McLoyd, Sandra Graham, and Deborah Scott Jones) as Chairs of Review Panels. In 2004 the Society for Research in Adolescence (SRA), a sister organization to SRCD with a large overlap in members, elected Vonnie McLoyd as its president. The goals outlined in COMP's 1978 report to the Governing Council—increasing minority participation in the areas of professional governance, professional socialization, and professional integration—have been realized.

There are reasons these issues are important to the larger professional audience. Implicit in the accusations the Black Caucus made of the parent organization was how their failure to act in ways that empowered minority members was contributing to underlying tensions among members. SRCD and the governing structure had a professional responsibility to respond to the situation, as SRCD is a powerful society and a model for other professional organizations. Its decisions and activities impact policy decisions by other institutions and foundations that look to SRCD not only for published research findings but also for its actions on sensitive and controversial issues. Moreover, SRCD had addressed controversial issues in the past and successfully advocated for positive change (e.g., Head Start). Mary Ainsworth, from her leadership positions, responded to the challenges posed by the Black Caucus with pragmatic steps, planting the seeds for future inclusion and empowerment of minority members of the Society.

REFERENCES

Jensen, A. R. (1969). How much can we boast IQ and scholastic achievement? *Harvard Educational Review*, **39**, 1–123.

Richards, G. (1997). *"Race," racism and psychology: Towards a reflexive history*. London: Routledge.

Winston, A. S. (2004). *Defining differences: Race and racism in the history of psychology*. Washington, DC: American Psychological Association.

IV. ON BECOMING A GOVERNING COUNCIL MEMBER AND MAXIMIZING MEMBERSHIP

I think participating in the governance structure of the Society for Research in Child Development (SRCD) is important for ethnic minority members because usually we are the only ones who advance or nominate ourselves for important positions that sustain our professional, and therefore personal, lives. It should not be this way; but given American culture and issues of networking and social stratification, it all too often has been so. Sustaining our professional lives enables us to conduct research and perform advocacy and policy work on behalf of the communities we cherish. Members of our Black Caucus, and of the Committee on Minority Participation (COMP, presently Committee on Ethnic and Racial Issues), for that matter, have been relatively slow to recognize the crucial early support stemming from the first 25 years of the Caucus's history. This is the story of my own pathway to discovering how this system works, and of how I learned to use it to advance goals and aims supported by the Black Caucus of SRCD.

INTRODUCTION

On July 1, 1980, Rachel K. Clifton, then Secretary of SRCD, wrote to congratulate me on my nomination to stand in the upcoming election for Member-at-Large of the SRCD Governing Council.[1] She had been informed by Mary Ainsworth, Chair of SRCD's Nominations Committee, that I was willing to serve on Council if elected.

All three ethnic minorities nominated for the two Member-at-Large positions were developmental psychologists: Luis Laosa, Lee C. Lee, and I. Commensurate with the preferences of Council, and in response to the strong recommendations of the Nominations Committee, the three additional candidates were educated in disciplines other than psychology. They were Kathryn Barnard (nursing), Marilyn M. Smith (education), and Alfred Steinschneider (pediatrics). The President-Elect slate for the elections for terms beginning in 1981 included John H. Kennell, Arthur H. Parmelee, and Alex F. Roche.[2] Parmelee won. Kathryn Barnard won. And I won.[3] The efforts of Jean Carew and of Algea Harrison and colleagues toward achieving the appointment of an ethnic minority member to Council have been discussed earlier, in Chapters II and IV. This chapter describes, through brief discussion of my standing committee ties, my path toward Council membership. The information is drawn from a more comprehensive oral interview of me, completed and submitted to then SRCD History Committee Chair, Williard Hartup, on August 29, 1997. I believe my interview was actually deposited with the SRCD Oral History Archives at the National Library of Medicine in 1998.[4] I also describe my service while on Council, using documentation from letters and Council minutes. Of course, I alone am responsible for the interpretations given. In describing this service, I have the opportunity to offer what I have learned about the operations of each of SRCD's standing committees. Thus, the chapter briefly mentions how the Council used my services while I participated as a member from 1981 to 1987, and how I sought to benefit members of both the SRCD Black Caucus and the Committee on Minority Participation.

ON THE ROAD TO THE GOVERNING COUNCIL

As a tax-exempt, not-for-profit organization, SRCD has a public persona that today can be accessed through its excellent web site: www.srcd.org. When I was elected to the Governing Council, the standing committees were the Social Policy Committee (the newest Committee to be formed by Council), the Publications Committee, Program and Local Arrangements Committees, Committee on Minority Participation, Interdisciplinary Affairs Committee, Summer Institutes and Study Groups Committee, Preservation of Historical Materials Committee, Committee to Review Ethical Standards for Research, and Distinguished Scientific Contribution Awards Committee. The Executive Director of SRCD was Dorothy Eichorn, on the faculty at the University of California, Berkeley. Eichorn was later succeeded by today's Executive Director, John Hagen, on the faculty at the University of Michigan. Hagen is a former student of Eleanor Maccoby, who was President and Immediate Past-President of SRCD during some of my years of service to the Social Policy Committee (1979–1981) and Council (1981–1987). Today, several of these committees, as evidenced by the SRCD web site, have new names (e.g., COMP has become the Committee on Ethnic and Racial Issues), but their structure and function within SRCD endure, thanks to the strong spirit of volunteerism among the entire SRCD membership.

In 1981 I became the first ethnic minority member to be elected to the Governing Council of SRCD, a majority-White scientific organization. It was a great honor, and culminated the efforts of both the SRCD Black Caucus, initiated by the late Jean Carew, and COMP, initiated by Algea Harrison and Bettye Caldwell (Council ex-officio member of COMP) in the 1970s. Prior to this election, I had visibility in the Society through my membership, from 1977 to 1981, in the new SRCD Standing Committee on Social Policy. In my oral history interview, I commented as follows on the early meetings of the SRCD Standing Committee on Social Policy:

> There was a concern to get the organization (SRCD) more involved with the public face, I think in part to insure that support dollars would continue to come into the field relative to child and family research. There was a general sense at that time that research dollars were being cut back dramatically and that it was important to get out to the public the benefits of research. Information about how research had benefited human lives. The membership ideas about the relationship between the Society and the public at large ranged from preferring that the Society be an advocacy organization at one end to preferring that ideas get out so that people will have a kindly view of research. And [James] Gallagher, I think, correctly assessed the situation, the Committee did, that we could get unanimity in the Society by focusing on the contributions of research rather than the [purely] advocacy role per se . . . we did decide that we would, for example, open a Washington liaison office, which we did. That we would collaborate in a consortium with other organizations that were trying to lobby relative to public policy support for research. That we would thirdly, establish fellowships where persons could take a year off from their traditional academic endeavors and maybe work for a year in the public policy arena, presumably representing through their fellowship support, the Society . . . supported by the Bush foundation to do post-doctoral training in Public Policy. So during this period, roughly 1979–1981, the Society, in effect, developed a very strong face toward social and public policy that it had not previously had in its 50-year history and I was very pleased to be part of that process.[5]

Once a member of Council, I learned something I had not known while performing services for the Social Policy Committee. Positions on any of the standing committees are a strong path toward becoming elected to Governing Council membership. Although at least one other candidate for Council and I had strong backgrounds of service to the Social Policy Committee, I alone also had academic rank at a university and was conducting research on early intervention. Furthermore, I had served on two other important, non-standing SRCD committees that were by-products of my membership on the Social Policy Committee: (1) the Selection Committee for the Congressional Science Fellowship Program, cosponsored by SRCD and AAAS (American Association for the Advancement of Science), and (2) the Ad Hoc Committee on National Register and Licensing, for which I was

Chair. I was also Chairperson of the Black Caucus, but I chose not to include this information in the biographical sketch that I shared with what I believed to be the largely conservative SRCD membership. I deemed the membership "conservative" because both the Caucus and COMP had to work hard to secure a commitment to electing an ethnic minority member to Council. COMP had even urged that, to ensure such an election, only ethnic minorities should be slated. Council had rejected this approach (see Chapter IV).

PERCEPTIBLE STRUCTURE AND FUNCTION OF THE SRCD GOVERNING COUNCIL

It was my impression that, whether surprised by my election or not,[6] most continuing Council members[7] and Dorothy Eichorn, Executive Director, greeted me as if nothing unusual had happened. Nonetheless, all knew that my presence signified a victory in which many had been invested.[8] One exception to the "business as usual" approach was Harriette McAdoo, who had been earlier appointed to Council. Harriette sent the following letter[9] to me at my former address at the University of Chicago on February 2, 1981, just a few days after I received the official congratulatory letter from Rachel Clifton on January 26, 1981:[10]

Dear Diana:
Congratulations on being elected to the Governing Council!! I am really glad to have you come on board.... Will you present a 15-minute paper on some aspect of parenting in Black families from your Chicago infant study, at the National Council on Family Relations' meeting in Milwaukee in October 1981? ... If you are interested, send me a one-page abstract within the next two weeks.

Sincerely,
Harriette

Later, in a 1982 letter to me,[11] Harriette commented that she had missed the companionship of both Mary Ainsworth and Bettye Caldwell when they departed from Council. (Council appointments are staggered with two members leaving at the end of each biennial meeting, although appointments are for 6-year terms. Committee appointments are also staggered, but generally run 2 years, with reappointments to 4 years. Both Caldwell and Ainsworth were no longer active Council members when I began serving in 1981.) Harriette said she was, therefore, very pleased that I had joined the group.

In spring, 1981, Harriette's outreach to me was both helpful and informative. I learned that Council members typically liaise themselves with one of the standing committees.[12] For example, Harriette and Rachel Clifton continued their memberships on the Publication Committee, and were joined by Kathryn Barnard who became the Council's ex-officio member to this important SRCD committee. Willard Hartup was liaison to the Program Committee, serving with Algea Harrison, who had left her role as COMP chairperson to become a member of the Program Committee and chair of the Convention Arrangements (Local Arrangements) Committee. Herbert Pick was liaison to the Committee on Summer Institutes and Study Groups, which supported the efforts of the Study Group, chaired by Margaret Beale Spencer, Geraldine Kearse Brookins, and Walter Allen (see Chapter XI). Other Council members with whom I interacted included Sandra Scarr, Eleanor Gibson, and Arthur Parmelee, President-Elect.

Harriette strongly encouraged me to select the new Committee on Minority Participation as my liaison group, thus to work closely with the chair, Raymond Yang (who had replaced Algea Harrison). On April 27, 1981, I wrote to Dorothy Eichorn that I wished to commit to COMP as a liaison committee assignment, commenting:

> I think issues of professional recruitment, socialization, and development as these interface with current research and service funding crises in our field will be particularly critical over the next few years. Naturally, this dire situation will impact minorities most severely as many are just starting their research and service careers in human development. For this reason, I'm especially interested in working with the Committee on Minority Participation, for at least the next two years.[13]

I learned that because each committee, through its chair, annually files a written report of its activities to Council, Council liaisons become supplementary spokespersons, together with the Executive Officer, for the particular committee in the annual Council meetings, interpreting and generally supporting the anticipated written reports filed by committee chairs. I also learned that the SRCD President serves as chair of the Nominations Committee, and the three Presidents—Past, Present, and President-Elect—constitute the Distinguished Scientific Contribution Awards Committee. Before joining Council, I had no knowledge of these matters, and I do not think many other Black Caucus members did either. Therefore, we had struggled to achieve ethnic minority representation on Council so that we could learn how the primary professional organization in our chosen field conducted its business.

Apart from the Governing Council, several committees had racial and ethnic minority members: Publications (McAdoo, Nakamura), Program (Harrison, Hall), Social Policy (Laosa, Pizzigati[14]), and Summer Institutes and Study Groups (Spencer). I quickly learned that Council also has influence through its capacity to recommend fellow members for appointment to committees. Committee appointments are career perks that assist scientists in making the case for promotion and tenure in their institutions. The appointments, when strategically made, also influence the direction of the field by determining who will edit and review articles for the core SRCD journals and assist biennially in the development of the scientific programs presented.

I also learned that as of June 1981,[15] the committee to which I was liaison (COMP) had only ethnic minority members: Raymond Yang (Chair), Billy Burgess, Juarlyn Gaiter, and Felicisima Serafica. In my opinion, this composition contributed to its marginalization. I determined that I would first seek to appoint minority members to all standing committees, and second, seek to identify majority-White SRCD members who would serve on COMP. Until writing this chapter, I had not thought much about it, but the decision—following Harriette's advice to work with COMP—probably helped to salvage what is today known as the Standing Committee on Ethnic and Racial Issues. On June 24, 1981, Rachel Clifton informed me in writing that she would advise Raymond Yang, then Chair of COMP, of my willingness to serve, and that I should be hearing from him. I soon learned whereas I was focused on the organizational and structural aspects of COMP, Raymond Yang was concerned with how COMP could respond to important policy changes becoming evident in American society under the new Reagan Administration—changes such as the increasing decentralization from federal to local control of health and human services.

SERVING AS LIAISON TO THE COMMITTEE ON MINORITY PARTICIPATION

It is important to note that between 1981 and 1987, SRCD experienced many new developments, most of which did not directly relate to ethnic minority issues. For example, in 1983 members of the Society wrote to the Council objecting strenuously to so little time on the Program being given to scientific studies of adolescent development; these objections probably eventually led to the founding of the Society for Research in Adolescence.[16] As another example, the SRCD Governing Council decided to simplify the process of becoming an SRCD member, so that primary and secondary sponsorship would no longer be required.

One development, however, was of considerable significance to SRCD's ethnic minority members: discussions of the relationship of social and public policies to child development research and researchers. This new thematic focus in the parent organization affected concerns among members about the long-range future of this interest and the future of initiatives around it, in the Society.[17] When SRCD celebrated its 50th anniversary at the biennial meeting in Detroit in 1983, Council, under the leadership of Eleanor Maccoby, addressed this and other developments in the context of discussions about SRCD's future as a professional scientific organization. Thus, as part of its anniversary celebration, Council decided to create an Ad Hoc Long-Range Planning Committee, with the goal of paying closer attention to strategic planning. This committee, chaired by Frances Horowitz, issued a Report to the Governing Council in April 1985.[18] The report was based in part on survey results obtained from about 30% of the membership (about 1,000 respondents). Essentially, the report stated that members believed the Social Policy initiatives described earlier in this essay should become a permanent part of the organization's identity. Even though the Society could not support the effort as in previous years, strategic supports given by the Bush Foundation to four influential SRCD members (Edward Zigler at Yale, Harold Stevenson at Michigan, James Gallagher at NC, Chapel Hill, and Norma Feshbach at UCLA) were expected to support the area within the SRCD membership. In effect, SRCD could support these efforts, but senior members of the Society, rather than the Society itself, would be responsible for fiscally sustaining them at strategic academic institutions throughout the nation.

Integrating research in child development with social policy initiatives into the SRCD as a whole provided an important bridge between majority-White and ethnic minority members. Even those who could not appreciate the importance of cultural factors in human development could appreciate the significance of social and public policies in the lives of both majority and minority populations. Although some members (e.g., Robert McCall[19]) called for a more assertive approach to public information and advocacy, SRCD seemed most comfortable emphasizing applied developmental and intervention research, thus maintaining its scientific banner. Nonetheless, some SRCD members felt that the 1985 Report on Long-Term Strategic Planning was not assertive enough regarding the benefits of the ongoing Social Policy initiatives to the Society. For example, in a pointed letter to Frances Horowitz,[20] one member suggested that the recommendations of the Long-Range Planning Report were not nearly as strong as the survey results indicated. During this period, I observed how seriously SRCD Council members deliberated in reference to these complex membership issues, most of which, by definition of being related to longer-term strategic planning, would eventually confront the incoming Executive Director, John Hagen, and future Council members.

The Council's early and intense attention to the new Social Policy Committee initiatives and the strong interests of significant segments of the SRCD membership in this emerging area did not go unnoticed by COMP, and particularly its new chair, Raymond Yang. Notably, during this same period (1980–1982) of great transition from a smaller, informal, face-to-face organization in which many SRCD members shared similar social and professional backgrounds to a larger, more professionally diverse, and formal organization, perceptible direct focus on COMP waned. Council and Committee members, having expressed a desire to be more inclusive, primarily expected COMP members to produce an updated ethnic minority membership directory that they could use to identify helpful volunteers with ethnic minority backgrounds.

In 1982, Raymond Yang was asked to continue as chair of COMP. Subsequently, in a report to Council, COMP requested increased contact with Council and with other SRCD committees. COMP particularly wanted to connect with the Social Policy Committee to focus on social policy issues of importance to ethnic and racial minority children and families. Yang and his committee believed that closer contact between the two committees would facilitate interchanges that would ultimately support new initiatives in this area. COMP also requested funds for an off-year meeting intended to consider a potpourri of similar goals and objectives that COMP might pursue. Council subsequently requested a detailed budget describing the funds needed to support such a meeting.

Yang, as Chair of COMP, advised his members in writing on May 17, 1982, of his disappointment that Council's most recent communication about COMP's mission indicated it viewed COMP's primary responsibilities to be "in an area carefully circumscribed by SRCD's scholarly and scientific functions."[21] He had hoped for more, given the apparent devolution of human services from federal to state and local governments. He had hoped that SRCD, as parent organization with both COMP and a standing Social Policy Committee, would engage in more of a political and advocatory role because, as he stated, "These are tough times for poor people." Yang was aware that under these circumstances large numbers of ethnic and racial minority children and their families would be adversely affected. However, he had not been (as I had) part of the discussions and debates surrounding the creation of the Social Policy Committee, so it is not surprising that his expectations exceeded mine. I knew SRCD felt it could not keep its reputation for "scientific objectivity" and its tax-exempt status and engage, in open, direct, partisan political activity.

Yang resigned shortly after COMP's requests were rebuffed by Council.[22] In 1983, as Karabelle Pizzigati became incoming Chair following Yang's resignation, updating the directory was again emphasized. Pizzigati's ties with the Social Policy area made her a natural for the COMP Chairperson role. What was needed immediately, however, was a membership directory of the racial and ethnic minority members of SRCD, similar to what I had earlier produced on two occasions, and to what had been produced by COMP when Algea Harrison was its Chair. Minutes of the Meeting of the Governing Council in April 1983[23] indicate that Council wanted to have the directory distributed to all Council members, editors, and all committee chairs.

In 1984, as Council-COMP liaison, I tried a somewhat different strategy to redirect Council's attention to the broader issues associated with minority participation in SRCD, a strategy that would determine COMP's future within the Society's governance structure. I reasoned to myself that as chairs and members of all SRCD standing committees come and go, the important item was to secure COMP's future. I hoped to encourage Council to better define COMP's purpose, and pressured Council members to do so by outlining the "worst-case scenario." As noted in Governing Council minutes:

> Diana Slaughter raised the question of whether there should be such a committee.... Council worked to clarify the charge.... Slaughter wondered if the need for this committee has disappeared. Minority participation is good within the Society at present.... Slaughter recommended either disbanding the committee or having total turnover in membership. [24]

As an alternative to dissolving COMP as a committee, it was proposed by a key Council member that a completely new committee be appointed, with John McAdoo as Chair, and with at least two majority-White members (Minutes of the Meeting of the Governing Council, May 17–18, 1984, p. 17). I was pleased. However, by April, 1985, COMP still had not produced the updated directory under Pizzigati's leadership.[25] SRCD committee chairs relied upon the directory to diversify committee memberships, yet the parent organization also relied upon the voluntary commitment of members to execute this labor-intensive project. Pizzigati pledged[26] to assist John McAdoo, incoming COMP chair, in making the updated directory a reality, reporting also that Vonnie McLoyd, at the University of Michigan, had offered direct assistance in efforts to update the directory, and that COMP had thought of a number of strategies to pursue in updating the present membership listing.

By summer 1985, John McAdoo chaired COMP, and SRCD members Margaret Beale Spencer and Beverly Birns had been appointed to it. Faced with the possibility of eliminating COMP altogether, Council leaders and members of the governance structures had rallied support of the then fledgling and weak committee that, combined with the early and continued assistance of committed Black Caucus members, endures today as a standing committee in SRCD's governance structure.

The distinction between COMP and the Black Caucus of SRCD was clearly drawn at this point. COMP focuses on minority participation, whereas members of the Caucus have always been freer to affiliate with and to engage in social policy initiatives, using one another as intellectual supports in the process. In this *Monograph*, some chapters nicely illustrate the variety and vicissitudes of such efforts (e.g., Chapters VI and XII). As affiliates of the parent SRCD organization, neither group engages in direct advocacy.

MAXIMIZING GOVERNING COUNCIL MEMBERSHIP

Several of my Council initiatives were more directly effectual. For example, my letter of reply to Program Chair John Hagen, in January 1982,[27] together with Ray Yang's letter,[28] also written in January, probably insured that a program review panel entitled "Social and Public Policy" continued to be included as a panel for proposal submission. Appointed by Hagen, Ray Yang served as chair of the salvaged Social Policy Panel, actively recruiting minority and majority reviewers for the 1983 meeting. In March 1982, John Hagen wrote me of his active efforts to maintain minority representation on the various program panels.[29]

Similarly, in April 1982, I wrote to John Ogbu[30] of the University of California, Berkeley that I had nominated him to the Committee on Interdisciplinary Affairs. As I learned the routine, I nominated other minority members who were appointed. For example, Aline Garrett was appointed to the Committee on Ethical Research with Children, and Karabelle Pizzigati to first the Social Policy Committee and later COMP. Her path, from being a Congressional Science Fellow to becoming an active member of the Social Policy Committee, was one later taken by Valora Washington, a former President of the SRCD Black Caucus. Furthermore, the presence of Harriette and later myself on Council probably encouraged other majority-status members to nominate ethnic minorities to positions. For example, I think another majority Council member nominated John McAdoo to chair COMP.

Much time and effort went into demonstrating to the Executive Director and to Council that I could be a member who contributed to the Society. The same was true for other ethnic minority members appointed early to the SRCD governance structure (e.g., Algea Harrison, Harriette McAdoo). We were also determined, though, to serve the Black Caucus and ourselves too. Thus, throughout this period, my loyalty to the SRCD Black Caucus never wavered. It became a tradition, for example, for first Harriette McAdoo and later me to report to the SRCD Black Caucus at each of the Caucus's biennial business meetings about those thematic issues deliberated by Council that could conceivably affect the livelihood and posture of the Caucus. In those days, Council and standing committee members who were African American acknowledged the importance of the Black Caucus to their newly-found career advantages; we all gave back by sharing helpful information that would support Caucus members' career advancement. Notably—because the heart of SRCD is its publications—several Caucus members found themselves at last able to contribute to the publication process, first through memberships on the editorial boards (having been chosen by members of the Publications Committee) and second through publications in the journals themselves. Both processes are discussed elsewhere in this monograph (see Chapters X, XI, and XIII in particular).

The triple responsibilities of serving SRCD, advancing one's personal career, and serving the SRCD Black Caucus did not always neatly overlap. In fact, before initiation of Black Caucus Pre-Conferences, serving SRCD may even have occasioned some neglect of the primary purpose of the Caucus having been established: to develop an organizational infrastructure permitting special attention to the need for developmental research, interventions, and theory construction in reference to African American children. When I was the Caucus Chairperson (1979–1981), this challenge was anticipated and feared by one Caucus steering committee member, John Dill. Between February 1980 and January 1981, Dill wrote a series of brilliant and prophetic letters stressing the importance of the organizational development of the SRCD Black Caucus.[31] The letters, written to key Black Caucus leaders, may well have contributed to the continuity of our vision and the stability of the Caucus over its first 25 years, despite the deep involvement and participation of many key Caucus members in the ongoing life of the parent organization. Dill stressed that we must never forget that the purpose of the Black Caucus is to provide a home base for the greater participation of Blacks in child development research—to enable them to produce high-quality research that would fuel and support public policy and advocacy efforts. In short, the Caucus is neither obliged nor obligated to consider other ethnic minority researchers/research, or to pursue interdisciplinary or intercultural initiatives—and especially not to the point of neglecting the African diaspora.

On other occasions, however, there were wonderful points of overlap between the efforts of SRCD, the goals of the SRCD Black Caucus, and the advancement of individual careers. For example, Jean Carew, as a member of the Program Committee, convened a research symposium featuring the research efforts of Black Caucus members like myself at the April 1975 Denver meeting, entitled a "Symposium on New Directions in Research with Black Children." As another example, once we learned of the utility of Discussion Sessions (while I was SRCD Black Caucus chairperson, and still a member of the SRCD Social Policy Committee), I organized one entitled "Some SRCD Black Caucus Perspectives on Directions in Developmental Research with Black Children and Families: Past, Present, and Future," at the New Orleans SRCD meeting in 1979. The following caucus members participated: Jean Carew, John Dill, Aline Garrett, Algea Harrison, Harriette McAdoo, Ura Jean Oyemade, Margaret Beale Spencer, and myself. I continued this practice, convening a symposium on the "Contribution of Research on American Minority Children to the Field of Child Development" while still a member of Council at the biennial meeting of SRCD held in Baltimore in 1987. This symposium was eventually published under the title "Black Children and Poverty: A Developmental Perspective" in a volume (Slaughter, 1988) that was part of a series edited by William Damon for

Jossey-Bass on *New Directions For Child Development*. In such symposia, members of the parent organization were informed about the developmental pathways and socialization experiences of culturally different children in America, minority members of the Society were able to engage in scientific study of both majority and minority children in the United States, and careers were advanced by public presentations. In addition, as Council member I thought it fortunate that other Caucus members were also fueling and realizing original Caucus goals. Therefore, I enthusiastically supported the SRCD Study group that led to the publication of the volume *Beginnings: The Social and Affective Development of Black Children* (see Chapter X, by Margaret Beale Spencer, for an overview of this process).[32]

EXITING GOVERNING COUNCIL: MANY REWARDS

Of necessity, this chapter is a selective overview of my experiences with the SRCD governance structure, including Council membership (1981–1987). I have focused on those experiences likely to be of particular value to future generations of members of the SRCD Black Caucus, to ethnic minority and majority members of today's Committee on Ethnic and Racial Issues, and to other members of the Society who have a special affinity for research questions and issues associated with child development and social policy and cultural influences on human development.

There were many unexpected "perks" of Council membership, and I am confident this was true for Harriette McAdoo as well. In 1984, I traveled to China with members of SRCD; a discussion session about our observations and experiences was later shared with the SRCD membership. In 1987, I used my influence to arrange for a lecture by Lee C. Lee, at the biennial meeting of SRCD in Baltimore, about parenting research within mainland China, thus expanding my own horizons to include international interests in childhood growth and development. Finally, and perhaps most important, I used my influence to insure that an ethnic minority member would succeed me on Council. Having earlier nominated John Ogbu to the Interdisciplinary Affairs Committee, in my last year of Council membership I advanced his name to the Nominations Committee for Governing Council membership. John Ogbu served on Council from 1987 to 1993.

While on Council, I came to appreciate the devotion of the SRCD leadership to children and to child developmental studies that would ultimately benefit children and their families and even whole communities. I even came to see SRCD as a maverick in the larger American culture, a maverick that probably would not have minded, at least not as much as I had originally thought, my listing "Chairperson, Black Caucus of SRCD" on my preelection biographical sketch. Of course, this perspective does not generalize to beliefs of individual members, most of whom still function within closed, scientific support networks. I was simply fortunate enough to be pursuing a career at a time when the SRCD leadership had particular commitments to the quality of life experienced by all the nation's children, and in which SRCD itself felt either vulnerable or empathetic enough to attempt to embrace all members with respect. Thus, leaders of the Society graciously helped Caucus members who were also members of SRCD to create a network that was professionally workable for them.

What I valued most, however, upon completing my term as Governing Council member, was the recognition I received from the Black Caucus itself. At the April 1987 meeting in Baltimore, I received the Black Scholar Achievement Award, which described me as a "Scholar, teacher, mentor, advocate, and friend." To me this award, given during Valora Washington's term as Chairperson of the SRCD Black Caucus, meant that the Caucus perception was that I had made life better for members while serving SRCD through my Governing Council membership. Of my awards to date, this is the one I especially cherish.

REFERENCES[33]

Slaughter, D. (Vol. Ed.). (1988). *Black children and poverty: A developmental perspective*. W. Damon (Series Ed.), *New directions for child development: Vol. 42*. San Francisco: Jossey-Bass.
Spencer, M. B., Brookins, G. K. & Allen, W. R. (Eds.). (1985). *Beginnings: The social and affective development of Black children*. Hillsdale, NJ: Erlbaum.

NOTES

1. Letter from Rachel K. Clifton to Diana Slaughter, July 1, 1980. The footnotes in this chapter document the original sources used in constructing this overview of my service on Governing Council, 1981–1987. Copies of all letters, minutes, reports, and other Council documents are part of the author's private collection and available from her: Dr. Diana T. Slaughter-Defoe, University of Pennsylvania, Graduate School of Education, 3700 Walnut Street, Philadelphia, PA 19103.

2. Election of Officers Ballot, SRCD, January 2, 1981.

3. Subsequently, Marilyn Smith, then Executive Director of the National Association for the Education of Young Children (NAEYC), was appointed to Council. Her services were important to SRCD at a time when its Executive Director, Dorothy Eichorn, was anticipating retirement, and the membership of the organization was rapidly expanding. NAEYC was accustomed to managing a larger membership group, and was perceived as having done so successfully.

The full text of Rachel Clifton's letter, dated January 26, 1981, is printed below. Both of Clifton's letters, written in relation to her service as Secretary to SRCD's Governing Council, reveal how the organization conducted its business:

> *Dear Dr. Slaughter:*
>
> *It is with pleasure that I announce your winning the election to a seat on the Governing Council of SRCD, 1981–1987. Your term will officially begin at the end of the 1981 Boston meeting and extend through the 1987 meeting.*

> *The electorate was fortunate to have many excellent candidates to choose among, and Council was extremely grateful that you agreed to run. As you may know, it is customary that election results be held confidential until the Business meeting.*
>
> *I'm looking forward to meeting you in Boston, and to working with you on Council. Please accept my warm congratulations.*

Cordially,
Rachel K. Clifton

4. Initially, I believe I was contacted about an Oral History interview by Neil Salkind on November 18, 1992. Salkind chaired the SRCD History Committee when the interview draft, expected to be completed within 2 hours, was crafted. He graciously sent copies of materials, and referred me to the new Chair, Judy Rosenblith, on April 14, 1993, when I phoned him to follow up on an earlier contact about conducting an oral history interview because of my former Governing Council membership. I agreed to participate, and began in earnest following a letter from Judy, dated November 15, 1994. Her letter stated that the entire oral history collection based upon SRCD leadership would be deposited in the Archives of the National Library of Medicine. Her letter was supplemented by an open-ended two-page interview schedule to be used by the person I chose to conduct the audiotaped interview (a former Northwestern student and subsequent research colleague, Adrianne Andrews, had been selected as my academic biographer, and she conducted the interview). By the time the interview was completed and transcribed for feedback from me, Willard Hartup was Chair of the SRCD History Committee.

At his request on March 25, 1998, I provided a personal photograph to supplement the audiotaped and transcribed interview in SRCD's possession. Thus this process, begun in 1992, a couple of years after I became full Professor at Northwestern University, was completed 3 months after I left Northwestern to assume an endowed chair at the University of Pennsylvania—the Clayton Professor in Urban Education.

5. Slaughter-Defoe, Diana. SRCD Oral History Interview, National Library of Medicine, August 29, 1997, p. 3.

6. I believe that my election was a surprise, given how the electoral ballot was constructed, listing all six members, without regard to social background. When preliminary knowledge of the ballot's layout was made known to Bettye Caldwell, then Council ex-officio member of COMP, she drafted a "note of despair" (dated July 25, 1980) to the SRCD Executive Director, Dorothy Eichorn:

> The purpose of my letter is to respond with a note of despair to the memorandum of June 20th from the Nominations Committee. For reasons which are not specified, the Committee has recommended that all six candidates for Members-at-Large of the Governing Council should be listed on the same ballot. You will recall that the Committee on Minority Participation had strongly requested that these two positions be separated on the ballot, with only minority members being shown for one of the two positions. ... The slate as now published could again result in the selection of two people, neither of whom is a minority.... I feel that as a Council representative to the Committee on Minority Participation I have failed either the Council or the Committee as a liaison person.

On that same date, July 25, 1980, Bettye Caldwell drafted a similar letter to Algea Harrison. Because Council has the capacity to appoint Members-at-Large, Marilyn Smith, a financial wizard who had served as Executive Director of the considerably larger NAEYC, was appointed to Council in 1981 for a similar 6-year term, just as ethnic minority member Harriette McAdoo had been appointed in 1979. It is important to observe that some majority-White SRCD members like Caldwell demonstrated considerable temerity during these difficult times by openly supporting COMP and the integration of SRCD ethnic minority members into the governance structure, including standing committees of the Society. For their integrity, we should all be forever grateful.

7. In 1981, the members of the Governing Council I joined included Eleanor Maccoby, President, Arthur Parmelee, President-Elect, John Flavell, Past-President, Rachel Clifton, Secretary, and Members-at-Large: Eleanor Gibson, Willard Hartup, John Kennell, Harriette McAdoo, Herbert Pick, and Sandra Scarr. Kathryn Barnard and Marilyn Smith joined me in being new Council Members-at-Large.

8. COMP submitted a list of nominations to the Chair of the Nominations Committee, Mary Ainsworth on May 14, 1980. I was listed last on a list that included William Hall, Lee C. Lee, Luis Laosa, and Charles Nakamura. Individual members of the SRCD Black Caucus (e.g., Margaret Spencer) told me they had also nominated me.

9. Letter from Harriette McAdoo to Diana Slaughter, February 2, 1981.

10. Letter from Rachel K Clifton to Diana Slaughter, January 26, 1981.

11. Letter from Harriette McAdoo to Diana Slaughter, April 1, 1982.

12. 6/81 (Roster of) Governing Council and SRCD Committees, updated: June, 1981.

13. Letter from Diana Slaughter to Dorothy Eichorn, April 27, 1981.

14. Pizzigati, who was African American, had been recommended to Alberta Siegel as a member for the Social Policy Committee by me, when I resigned upon joining Council. She was a former Congressional Science Foundation Fellow in Child Development. (The program was funded by the Grant Foundation and the Foundation for Child Development, but implemented and managed by SRCD.)

15. Letter from Rachel K. Clifton to Diana Slaughter, June 24, 1981.

16. Letter from seven SRCD members to SRCD President Arthur Parmelee (copied to Council), April 27, 1983.

17. For example, a Summer Institute on Child Development and Social Policy was held at Cornell University, June 17–29, 1984. The Preliminary Program of this Institute indicates that it focused on "Historical Perspectives on the Evolution of Child Development Research and Public Policy Related to Children," thus addressing a theme commensurate with SRCD's 50th anniversary. SRCD Black Caucus member and former Congressional Science Fellow, Valora Washington, then on the faculty in the School of Education at the University of North Carolina, Chapel Hill was a participant. By December 1985, four issues of the *Washington Report of SRCD* (later renamed *Social Policy Reports*) had been distributed free of charge to SRCD members.

18. *Report to the Governing Council of the Society for Research in Child Development from the Ad Hoc Long Range Planning Committee*, Frances Degen Horowitz, Chair, April, 1985.

19. Letter from Diana Slaughter to Robert B. McCall, December 7, 1981.

20. Letter to Frances Degen Horowitz from SRCD member, January 29, 1985.

21. Within 12 months of my election to Council, and 9 months of my appointment as ex-officio Governing Council liaison to COMP, Raymond Yang, Chair of COMP, distributed an annual report to Council (February, 1982) which summated COMP's status as follows:

(COMP) has made two contributions to SRCD: (a) the compilation of a Directory of Minority Members; and (b) the placement of minority members in decision positions in SRCD. These positions include editorial/review as well as Committee assignments .... Relative to that original charge, the current responsibilities of the COMP are not as heavy as they once were. It was in this light that the Committee recommended that it be abolished . . . . Apparently, the recommendation was not accepted. If the recommendation was too abrupt, it at least suggested that the Committee could appropriately reassess its purpose and function. It was to this reassessment that the Committee turned after the Boston meeting . . . . The Committee decided to move in two directions . . . . Update the directory and index individuals by their area(s) of specialization [and] Political activities. The COMP feels that it is appropriate for SRCD to increase its activities to representing families and children who may be further disenfranchised by the shifts in political responsibilities from federal to state and local levels. SRCD can and should act as a lobby for families and children. The Society should provide expert professional assistance to local and state governments . . . . To start this process a local directory of the SRCD members could be mailed to state and local governmental representatives . . . . [to] provide information about SRCD members nearby, their areas of interest, and their availability to work with state or local governments . . . . There is no reason to confine these activities to ethnic minorities. Any SRCD member should be able to pursue these activities with the Society's support. It was in this light that the Committee on Minority Participation has considered its relation to SRCD's Social Policy Committee. The political activism that the COMP is suggesting may [be] related to issues being discussed by the Social Policy Committee . . . ."

I do not recall having any spirited disagreements with Council's ideas presented in reply to the reassessment of COMP as depicted by Yang, nor do I recall disagreeing with him about any of its initial contents. It is entirely possible, given all that I was doing at the time, that this enormously important discussion completely eluded me! Probably more to the point, I agreed with COMP, but I also agreed with the alternatives suggested by Council.

On June 22, 1982, in a letter to the members of COMP, Raymond Yang quoted Council's official reply through its Secretary, Rachel Clifton. To summarize briefly, Council approved the plans for an updated, indexed Directory, disapproved the steps proposed toward political activism as described in Yang's report, but provided a number of acceptable alternatives (none of which I recall being pursued by COMP), and disapproved of a proposed name change to the "Committee on Minority Issues," apparently feeling at the time that "the present name reflected the proper orientation and charge of the Committee." Raymond Yang offered his resignation as COMP Chair in a letter dated August 12, 1982, indicating that new work responsibilities prohibited his continuing as Chair. During this time, COMP was not a permanent, standing committee in SRCD.

22. Minutes of the Meeting of the Governing Council, March 25–26, 1982.

23. Minutes of the Meeting of the Governing Council, April 20–21, 1983.

24. Minutes of the Meeting of the Governing Council, May 17–18, 1984, p. 17.

25. Minutes of the Meeting of the Governing Council, April 24–25, 1985.

26. Pizzigati, K. Report of the COMP to the Governing Council of SRCD, April 3, 1985.

27. Letter of reply to John Hagen (Program Committee Chair) from Diana Slaughter, January 12, 1982.

28. Letter from Raymond Yang to John Hagen , January 29, 1982.

29. Letter from John Hagen to Diana Slaughter, March, 1982.

30. Letter from Diana Slaughter to John Ogbu, April 12, 1982.

31. On February 13, 1979, Dill wrote to all members of the Black Caucus Steering Committee, including me:

I have read the recent correspondence that Jean Carew and Algea Harrison have mailed to all of us. . . . As we approach the 1979 meeting, it is indeed important for us to consider what stance and action we should take. . . . I believe an initial perspective would be to recall the overall purposes and goals of the Black Caucus. For me, the caucus is directed toward fostering greater participation of blacks in child development research. A secondary goal is for the group to serve as strong advocates for black children and their families.... My recommendation... [is] to generate greater unity of purpose in the Black Caucus by using the SRCD convention as a forum to foster communication among black child development researchers.... The one serious problem with the Black Caucus is that there is so much variability in attendance at each meeting. Furthermore, the reality of American developmental research is broader in scope and extends beyond the organizational structure of SRCD. If we direct our energies mainly toward greater participation in SRCD, I wonder how beneficial such efforts would be in terms of the larger picture. I guess I have felt a sense of frustration as my first SRCD meeting in 1969 about not being able to develop our own mechanism for dealing with the needs of black children. We have had few opportunities at the biennial meetings to counsel students, hold seminars on our current research, scrutinize public policy—all from a black perspective.

On September 25, 1980, Dill wrote me:

My only real suggestion for our 1981 meeting is to focus on more substantive black child development issues at Caucus meetings.... I [also] think that the black conferees need to get together among themselves away from the conference.... I would also like to urge you to run again as chairperson. You have done an excellent job during your tenure and another two years under your leadership should create the level of stability that the Black Caucus needs. Please, please consider this recommendation.

And on January 26, 1981, Dill wrote to Aline Garrett, Black Caucus Executive Director, responsible for working with each Chairperson (in this instance me) in preparations for the biennial meeting:

I would think that there should be three objectives for the SRCD Black Caucus in Boston: (1) to maintain an extension of our network of black people at the meetings; (2) to strengthen the structure, organization, effectiveness of the Black Caucus relative to SRCD, developmental research, black children; (3) to share and learn current ideas, theories, strategies from each other. I cannot overemphasize the importance of the last objective, at least for me. I must reiterate my request to have Margaret and her study group formally present to the Caucus a brief version of the work being done by her group. Once again, you're doing a fine job with the newsletter. I really enjoy receiving it.

I believe that the Black Caucus through the medium of SRCD publications and the SRCD Black Caucus Pre-Conferences, as described in other chapters in this volume, realized many of John Dill's aspirations, with one important exception: majority-White and other ethnic minorities also participate and benefit from these activities and processes. Nonetheless, the status of Black children today indicates that considerable work still remains for future generations.

32. A list of the original 23 members of the Study group convened by Margaret Beale Spencer, Geraldine Kearse Brookins, and Walter Allen includes several majority-White members of SRCD who were invited and were willing to stand in support of the Study group, among them Urie Bronfenbrenner, Aimee Dorr, Glen Elder, and Morris Rosenberg.

33. The letters, minutes, reports, and other documents from Governing Council consulted in writing this chapter are listed in individual footnotes, rather than below. These are part of the author's private collection and are available from her: Dr. Diana T. Slaughter-Defoe, University of Pennsylvania, Graduate School of Education, 3700 Walnut Street, Philadelphia, PA 19103.

SECTION II. TEACHING AND MENTORING

Section II describes several different types of important contexts of teaching and mentoring developed and experienced by members of the Black Caucus of the Society for Research in Child Development (SRCD) between 1981 and 1993. The teaching and mentoring experiences probably helped to insure the visibility and endurance of the Caucus to this day.

Chapter V, by Grace Carroll, thoughtfully depicts how a traditional style of mentoring by two of the earliest SRCD Black Caucus members expanded her view of the developmental field. Carroll also conveys the tremendous loss to her, and to the field, when ties to the special role models provided by these extraordinary scientists, Jean Carew and Marie Peters, were abruptly terminated.

Chapter VI, by Diana Slaughter-Defoe, Margaret Beale Spencer, and Ura Jean Oyemade Bailey, recounts the Caucus members' interaction with majority members of the Society over engagement with science policy and advocacy issues while obtaining SRCD support of a resolution deploring the ongoing Atlanta child murders in the early 1980s. The encounter further crystallized differences, alluded to in Chapter IV by Slaughter-Defoe, between many Caucus members' views about the relationship between science and advocacy and those of many other members of the Society.

Direct interactions and confrontations with SRCD majority members about matters of pubic policy and advocacy were not the only contexts for teaching and mentoring. The establishment of biennial Black Caucus Pre-Conferences that permitted sharing of research ideas and studies has provided an ongoing source of intergenerational, interracial, and interethnic mentoring. Chapter VII, by Deborah Johnson and Geraldine Kearse Brookins, describes the initiation of these Pre-Conferences, including the consequent support for international and interdisciplinary research by Caucus members. The authors demonstrate how initiatives from Pre-Conference planning broadened the horizons of Caucus members and strengthened connections with SRCD. The humanistic values of the youthful Black Caucus members did not always resonate with the needs of the

SRCD parent organization for institutional preservation and self-sufficiency. Through the introduction of biennial Pre-Conferences; however, Caucus members discovered a meaningful way to collectively (and individually) interface with the SRCD parent body. Thus, the dual goals of (a) racial and ethnic diversity within SRCD and (b) change of scholarly paradigms that previously were highly disrespectful of and discrediting to African-American peoples could begin to be met. In the process, the research was eventually broadened to include study of variations within the African diaspora.

V. TIES: TODDLER AND INFANT EXPERIENCES STUDY— CARROLL AND COLLEAGUES

In 1978, Jean Carew, Principal Investigator, in collaboration with Marie Peters and myself, Grace Carroll, as Co-Principal Investigators, launched a small 3-year descriptive study of young Black toddlers and infants, named TIES, an acronym for Toddler and Infant Experiences Study. We were each excited about the prospect of doing a longitudinal observational study from a multidisciplinary approach. Jean, a psychologist, had invested a decade in her observation instrument and was both challenged and fascinated by the new technology that allowed us to capture and store the behavior of children on videotape. Marie, a Black family specialist, courageous and unswerving in her ongoing battle with cancer, was equally adamant in her desire to challenge the frequently perpetuated myth that Black children were like Topsey, "They just grew." My work in education and sociology, as well as my dive into parenthood, led me to see this as a great opportunity to open an office where Black children were thought to be bright and beautiful, where their parents could have a voice, and where I could learn more about parenting. We were all idealistic in thinking that this small study would make a positive difference in how Black children and their families were viewed—with an emphasis on their strengths rather than on their deficits and deficiencies. These ideals, however, motivated us and served to bond us together.

Over the next 2 years, this bonding occurred in the day-to-day operations of the nonprofit organization we had established for the purpose of conducting this research. The organization was appropriately named the Institute for Developmental Studies (IDS). We got all of the necessary papers and official approval for a 501(c) organization and set up offices in downtown Oakland, CA. We were each excited about the prospect of venturing out on our own, planting the seeds for a new organization. We wanted to serve children and families through culturally sensitive research. We hoped that such research would provide the foundation for developing better social services to support families and children from diverse cultures.

We wanted to shatter the conception that the White middle-class family model was appropriate for all families irrespective of cultural differences. More importantly, we wanted to contribute to the data that looked at strengths of our families rather than the myriad of reports and research findings that focused on our dysfunctions and deviance.

Jean was based in Menlo Park, CA, and operated from her home once her appointment with the Stanford Research Center was completed. She was engrossed in fine tuning her observation measure for coding the behavior of infants and toddlers. She had invested nearly a decade in this instrument. Jean was driven. Her attention to detail and her desire to add to the research literature and make a difference in how we view the development of children were evident in all she did. She focused on the methodological issues surrounding the gathering and reporting of observational data.

Marie initially was based at the University of Connecticut and made monthly transcontinental flights so that we could meet and make conceptual as well as operational decisions about the direction of IDS and the TIES research project. She loved and was fascinated by Black families. She constantly spoke of how amazing it was that so many Black families functioned well and performed the necessary duties of raising healthy children despite being in an environment that constantly gave them negative messages and little support.

Both Jean and Marie were seasoned researchers, whereas I was a neophyte. I was only 25 and had just completed my Ph.D. from Stanford in 1975, when I first met Jean. In 1977, she approached me with her vision for creating a research center. We had many late night discussions about Jean's vision and what this would mean for our careers. We discussed how nontraditional this path would be. I guess this is what fascinated me, as I clearly wanted a nontraditional avenue to pursue my personal and research interest in stress and coping mechanisms among our families. Jean convinced me to join the team, which was not a difficult task, especially after I met Marie, a wonderful mother figure and mentor—warm, generous, loving, and always positive.

When we actually began the project in 1978, I had recently moved to Oakland, the city with the largest concentration of African American families in the Bay Area. We subsequently based our research center there, and I had the responsibility of office operations. Jean's mentor, a Harvard psychiatrist, Chester Pierce, who later became a mentor to all of us, was our primary consultant. His input was invaluable in the first year of our study, when we were setting up and making hard choices about process and procedures and conducting our pilot work. We hired a wonderful staff of female researchers—former students and colleagues who wanted to engage in this new venture.

TIES was exciting and fresh for all of us who wanted to get into the community and use the academic skills we had developed to help improve family lives in important ways. Because videotaping in home settings was a new phenomenon at that time, we had a video expert who also became a researcher during her work with TIES. The technology had not yet progressed to the small lightweight camcorders available today. Quite the contrary, our researchers had to be strong enough to support an awkward and fairly large 10-pound recorder on their shoulder as they videotaped. The equipment was purchased, the literature reviews conducted, a beautiful logo developed, measures and instruments created, the pilot families selected, training on inconspicuous videotaping initiated, and recruitment for study families begun. TIES was coming to life!

The overarching purpose of the toddler and infant experiences study was to examine the socio-emotional, intellectual, creative, physical, and language development of Black toddlers and the corresponding childrearing practices, attitudes, beliefs, and values of working-class and middle-class Black parents, who, because they are Black, are outside of mainstream American society. Reflecting back, this was an enormous undertaking. At the time, I was too new to the research to really understand just how ambitious it was. I felt we could do anything! Based on our own family experiences, we truly believed that our families respond to the differences being Black makes to our economic, social, and political lives, and we needed to document this affirmatively. Thus, a primary goal for TIES was to examine, in depth, the intricacies and uniqueness of Black family life, child socialization, and child development.

The specific objectives of TIES were: (a) to document and trace longitudinally, from age 1 to 3, the daily experiences (behaviors, interactions, and activities) of Black children, including both the experiences that children generate for themselves in independent pursuits and those in which their caregiver and other family members play some part, (b) to document and trace the development of major socio-emotional, intellectual, language, creative, self-care, and physical competencies, (c) to examine the connections between the children's daily experiences (both self-generated and environmentally produced) and the development of the competencies referred to, using three types of assessments, based respectively on videotaped observations of children in their home, caregiver reports, and performance in a standardized test, (d) to document and trace longitudinally the childrearing practices and styles used by Black caregivers in socializing their infants and toddlers and to identify the underlying rationales, life experiences, life conditions, and personal characteristics that influence these practices and their associated attitudes and expectations, and (e) to document and describe the lives of Black families, focusing on both (1) factors that commonly cause stress for Black mothers and influence their ability to cope with the problems of parenthood and of living in a society in which racial and social discrimination are pervasive aspects of daily life and (2) sources of happiness, satisfaction, self-esteem, hope, and pride.

"Ambitious but do-able" was our unwritten but often spoken motto. Jean came to the office regularly and we went to her Menlo Park office, where she had set up a for-profit sister organization called Research for Children. Her observation measure and process was mapped out and tested in our pilot work. Jean spent hours training our observers so that reliability and validity issues could be resolved to her high standards, ultimately getting an intercoder agreement above 85% with the error variance for each code attributable to intercoder unreliability below 5%. Jean, Marie, and I agreed on protocols for interviews so that all of our interests could be met. I felt I had really arrived when they both agreed to my "debrief and race as a stress factor" final interview. Marie made a bold move as we engaged in the data collection phase of the research: she took an apartment in Oakland. We knew of her cancer and had shared her times of high and low energy, treatments, and hospital stays. Thus, we were truly surprised that in spite of her health, she wanted to be with us in this project on a day-to-day basis. Her mother-in-law and a few other extended family members lived in the Bay area, but her husband and children were still on the East Coast. Realizing her love for life and resolve in making TIES work, they too supported her decision. I was in awe of her commitment, passion, and strength. We forged onward.

TIES was in full swing. We had selected a sample of 25 Black families who, at the time of recruitment, were rearing their infant or toddler at home. These toddlers and infants were all age cohorts of my daughter, born shortly after my move to Oakland. Her timely birth gave us an excellent opportunity to try out our measures on her prior to piloting work on other infants and toddlers in the study. Although the sample was small, great efforts were made to insure that participating families represented a broad range of social classes, family structures, and other demographic characteristics.

Beginning in the fall of 1978 through the end of 1980, we conducted 3-hour visits to our TIES families' homes each month. Five types of data were gathered on each family: (1) videotaped and eyewitness observations of the child's behavior and interactions in his normal home environment, (2) child-focused interviews with the mother or primary caregiver, (3) child assessments (Bayley mental development scales at 24 and 30 months and the Stanford Binet at 36 months), (4) adult-focused interviews with the parents, and (5) assessments of the physical environment, such as materials and cultural resources in the home. The data gathering procedure was organized in four 6-month cycles, with appropriate modifications of procedures and measures for each cycle. Most of the observations and child-focused interviews occurred in the first three cycles, while most of the in-depth, adult-focused interviews were concentrated in the fourth and last cycle. Needless to say, we had no shortage of data!

During the course of developing the study, recruiting the families and staff, and opening an office in Oakland, Jean, Marie, and I developed an intimate friendship with one another. Professional and personal successes and problems were shared. We used one another as sounding boards for ideas. We rarely agreed about anything, and we each were known for pushing our own point of view. Because we listened to and respected each other, however, our perspectives evolved, producing a more healthy and informed research team. Thus TIES, originally only an acronym, became a symbol of our own personal ties to the project, our cases, our staff, our ideas, and one another.

Jean and Marie were intent on making me respect and participate in academe. Although I had received a doctorate emphasizing research, I was a reluctant academic. I had often viewed myself more as a practitioner because my passion was working with children and families, not presenting research findings to a bunch of strangers. My formal training, which involved constant doses of deviance data in reference to Black families, had made me wary of research and its effect on the greater Black community. Viewing the care that both Jean and Marie took in respecting our case study families and in truly trying to understand the nuances of the data made me rethink my perspective. Working intensely together gave me an appreciation for the breadth of the impact that research can have. Jean felt that African American researchers needed to get together in the larger professional organizations and share research, information, issues, and concerns that affect our lives in ways that White researchers may not understand. She worked diligently to get the Black Caucus of the Society for Research in Child Development (SRCD) together. I felt this to be a bit ironic, as Jean and I constantly argued about what Blackness meant in the day-to-day lives of families. She felt that I was too radical in thought and too tough on White folks. I felt that she was too compromising and had not really experienced being African American, having been brought up in a foreign country and sheltered at Harvard. Eventually, however, we came to a profound understanding about our internal diversity. We experienced first hand that Black folks were not monolithic, nor should they be categorized as such. Within social class or any given community, Black folks have a wide range of differences, too often not captured in research about our families. Jean made me keenly aware of this internal diversity. She also increased my ability to be tolerant of those who do not think like me.

Marie was equally insistent on making changes in professional academic organizations. She wanted them to be more understanding of Black family issues, to see African American families as culturally different, not culturally deprived, to better comprehend the legacy of racism and its impact on families. Her organization of choice was the National Council on Family Relationships (NCFR). She, like Jean, attended conferences, presented papers, and tried her best to advocate for Black families with the powers that be in these academic arenas. Marie even used her own family and the McAdoo family as live cases on a panel for NCFR. The Peters and McAdoo families, including children, presented their own lives, and responded to questions about being Black families in America. She was very proud of this presentation and often spoke of it fondly.

Both Jean and Marie rationalized that if the Black professionals got together within these predominately White professional organizations to which they belonged, and pushed an agenda for change, they could collectively make these organizations more relevant to the issues of Black researchers, families, and children. I went along, kicking and scratching, as I respected my mentors, but at the time I did not see clearly how these endeavors were the best use of my time, space, and energy. I would later learn.

Jean and Marie insisted that we begin sharing our findings as soon as we made sense of them. We had weekly meetings to discuss procedures, data, and analyses. We reached out to others who were engaged in similar work. We presented initial findings to various professional meetings and were able to generate a series of early papers: a *Monograph* for SRCD, a chapter in a book edited by Hamilton McCubbin on family socialization, and various journal articles. Jean and Marie supported me in ways that I have come to appreciate as being rare for a young scholar. I did not truly know how fortunate I was. They solicited and respected my views, encouraged me to think outside of the box, introduced me to key theories and researchers, opened doors to many of the hallowed halls of academe which I had frequently rejected, and, most importantly, helped me navigate a professional life consistent with my personal convictions.

My respect for my two colleagues grew. They nurtured my professional growth and served as the mentors and role models I sorely missed in my Stanford graduate experience; I had never had an African American female professor throughout my 8 years in college and graduate school. My colleagues supported my desire not to have to choose between academia and community service. They provided for me a safe and sturdy bridge between the two. Then this wonderful magical spell was broken. The hurricanes of illness came and my bridge was irreparably damaged. Jean died in her sleep after a serious case of manic depression in the summer of 1981. This was to be our writing year. Marie, who attacked her cancer as she lived her life, with vigor and optimism, succumbed to it in the winter of 1982.

The passing of my two friends and mentors overwhelmed me: I felt so alone, with such a responsibility to publish the work of TIES. I knew it was so very important to both Jean and Marie. But I could not. It was too painful. It took me over a decade to return to our work. Prodded by Reginald Jones, I completed a chapter about TIES in his measurement and testing compilation (Massey, Milbrath, Hayes, Buchanan, David, & Rosenberg, 1996).

I had lost track of much of the data, but I had kept the final interviews with our sample mothers conducted by Marie and me in her last year. I wrote about the data that focused on parenting, race, and stress. It became my favorite chapter in my book *Environmental Stress and African Americans: The Other Side of the Moon* (Carroll, 1998). The title of this chapter, "Parenting: Mothers, Magic, M.E.E.S. and Myths," captured my feelings for my too brief time with Jean and Marie. They were outstanding mothers who truly gave unconditional love to their children. They helped me become a better mother to my two children by their encouragement and through their personal examples. We broke many of the myths in our coming together and in our research. We proved that Black women of extremely different backgrounds and orientations could not only work together but bond in very special ways. We were able to put forth, with supporting data, the multiple ways that Black children and families are able to cope and thrive in the midst of a hostile environment. Myths of Black deviance did not enter our space. M.E.E.S. stood for "mundane, extreme, environmental stress," a term to describe the stress associated with being African American in an environment that did not value your assets and gifts. I felt that Jean had experienced this stress as she tried to negotiate her professional career, parenting role, and racial identity issues. Although stressful toward the end of our time together, my workspace with Jean and Marie was overall a safe space for me to grow and develop my professional identity. I will be eternally indebted to them for their mentorship, guidance, and friendship. As I reflect back, this was indeed a magical time for me. I feel truly blessed to have had this time with two very wonderful and remarkable women.

REFERENCES

Carroll, G. (1998). *Environmental stress and African Americans: The other side of the moon*. Westport, CT: Greenwood Press.

Massey, G. C., Milbrath, C., Hayes, W. A., Buchanan, A., David, J., & Rosenberg, J. (1996). Observation instruments of Toddler and Infant Experiences (TIES). In R. Jones (Ed.), *Handbook of tests and measurements for Black populations* (Vol. 1, pp. 19–30). Hampton, VA: Cobb and Henry.

VI. THE ATLANTA CHILD MURDERS
AND THE BLACK CAUCUS OF THE SRCD

The Atlanta Child Murders dramatize early tensions between the Black Caucus and its parent organization, the Society for Research in Child Development (SRCD). A brief description of the context surrounding the murders is essential to understanding these tensions.

In June 1981, Wayne Bertram Williams, aged 23 and African American, was arrested on suspicion of the murders of 28 African American children, all residents of Atlanta, GA, over the previous 22 months. Prior to the arrest, local and national media were regularly reporting the disappearance of predominately lower income African American youth from their homes, their corpses later being discovered on the streets of some of Atlanta's poorest and most marginalized neighborhoods. The murders, and the dramatic reports of each incident, were terrorizing, not only to the families involved, but also to members of their surrounding communities and to African American communities throughout the country, which beseeched the nation to address this horror.

The prize-winning African American author and expatriate James Baldwin focused on this story in one of his last books, *The Evidence of Things Not Seen* (1985), recording memories, emotions, and actions that were stimulated in him by living in a world that produces such atrocities. Of Williams's conviction and incarceration, he wrote:

> Wayne Williams was arrested for the murder of two grown men. Once he was placed on trial for these two murders (*if* they were murders) he was *accused* of twenty-eight murders (of children) and, once he was condemned to prison, for life, seven cases were closed, leaving him guilty, then, of twenty-one murders: murders for which he was not arrested. This is untidy. It also establishes a precedent, a precedent that may lead us, with our consent, to the barbed wire and the gas oven. . . . The man may be guilty, but I smell a rat; and it is impossible to claim that his guilt has been proven, any more than it can be proven that the murders have ceased. . . . It is perfectly

possible that Wayne Williams must be added to the list of Atlanta's slaugh-tered Black children. I do not think that the Black community, or for that matter, the White one, can afford to ignore the moral dilemma as well as the moral opportunity posed by his incarceration. The author of a crime is what he is—he knows it, can make no more demands, nor is anything more demanded of him. But he who collaborates is doomed, bound forever in that unimaginable and yet very common condition which we weakly suggest as *Hell*. In that condition, and every American walking should know it, one can never again summon breath to cry *let my people go!* (pp. 98, 125)

Baldwin seems to be saying that, whether or not Wayne Williams was guilty, we are all party to the condition that occasioned the attacks upon vulnerable, impoverished Black children in Atlanta. Either we are part of the solution to such horrific conditions or we are enablers, party to the problem. Even today, his message is highly relevant to developmental scientists, whose research on children presumably has the ultimate goal of improving the quality of the children's lives.[1]

PATH TO THE SRCD RESOLUTION ON BEHALF OF THE MISSING AND MURDERED AFRICAN AMERICAN ATLANTA CHILDREN

There was little division within the Black Caucus over its responsibilities in reference to the Atlanta Child Murders. A 1980 survey of Black Caucus members (see Chapter I) indicated that the welfare of children, particularly Black children, was a top priority. The priority was expressed as a desire to "establish closer working relationships with other, more advocacy-based groups which impact Black children and families (e.g., Black Child Development Institute, National Council on Black Child Development, etc.) at the local and national level." The statement was endorsed as "highly desirable" or "desirable" by 23 of 26 respondents. Caucus members expressed an even stronger preference for maintaining "close connections with the Committee on Minority Participation in SRCD ... to be a resource for nominations for various committee appointments, and as a resource for the sharing of grievances within the hierarchy of SRCD"; this priority was endorsed as "highly desirable" or "desirable" by 24 respondents.

Clearly Caucus members knew that SRCD, as a research organization, was not devoted to child advocacy, but the situation of the Atlanta child murders was so extraordinary that they thought all available institutional resources should be applied. It was precisely on this issue, however, that the Caucus and many other members of SRCD, including members of its Governing Council, differed. The opposing views mirrored those cited in reference to the Society's involvement in social policy initiatives—specifically, how much should/could a prestigious, primarily scientific organization like SRCD involve itself in social policy activities, however worthy? Many in SRCD took the position that individual members were free to respond as they saw fit, but the scientific organization should not become involved in social policy. Others, including Black Caucus members, strongly believed that the prestige of the Society should be applied to influence public opinion in the service of stopping what appeared to be targeted hostilities against defenseless, impoverished Black children. Black Caucus members, therefore, collectively engaged in a variety of notable activities in 1980–1981, demonstrating their unwavering commitment to the physical and psychological survival of Atlanta's Black children.

In April 1981 in Boston, at the meetings of the Governing Council preceding the biennial conference, Algea Harrison, Chair of the Committee on Minority Participation (COMP), urged the Council to issue a statement on the Atlanta murders at the SRCD business meeting on April 4. Minutes of the Governing Council's meeting, recorded by Secretary Rachel Clifton, stated that:

> While Council generally accepted that a statement should be made, the exact wording was difficult to agree on. ... McAdoo [Harriette McAdoo, then the only sitting minority Council member] asked that a discussion be put off until Harrison could write a statement that would be brought back to the floor. Council agreed.

The SRCD business meeting, however, was preceded by a Teach-in, organized by Caucus members. In correspondence regarding a planned SRCD Discussion Session, addressed to Diana Slaughter and dated February 26, 1981, John Dill, Black Caucus Steering Committee member, elaborated his vision of a Teach-in on the Atlanta Murders:

> I believe that a lot of us around the country are very much concerned about the murders of Black children in Atlanta. I also dread the announcements on the evening news about another child disappearing. The murders are tragically important but perhaps even more so are the attendant mental health problems that seem to be rampant among Black children in the Atlanta schools. I would suggest that the Caucus should make this an issue at the SRCD meeting. Any of the following, I believe are worth considering: 1) Present a resolution at the SRCD membership meeting that the society strongly supports more Federal law enforcement (investigatory) assistance and funds for dealing with the mental health concerns for the Black children; 2) Although I despise symbols, I would suggest that SRCD sell black satin ribbons to be attached to the SRCD badges as a symbol of remembrance, concern or protest. ... The proceeds should go to Atlanta investigatory efforts. Also get SRCD to match these funds. At the least, the Black

caucus members should wear black ribbons; 3) We should petition Bill Hall [William Hall, SRCD Program Chair and a minority member] to cancel or rearrange the scheduled time slot and have a special panel . . . on the Atlanta situation.

In a reply dated March 3, Slaughter, then Chair of the Black Caucus, urged Dill to organize a Teach-in, offering detailed suggestions about possible participants and organizational strategy. Slaughter also encouraged Dill to contact William Hall, as well as other members within the Caucus, reminding him that:

> There are important reasons for continuing the Discussion session as planned—it should not be a single issue forum. However, in my personal opinion you are so right, there should be an open forum on Atlanta and, I believe . . . you should organize it. . . . Every effort must be made not to appear to be capitalizing on other Black folks' misery for our own interests. The forum should be essentially a "teach-in" given that the *New York Times* this past Sunday has led the way toward a strategy of "blaming the victim."

By March 25 Dill had convened a panel; writing to William Hall and to SRCD Executive Director, Dorothy Eichorn, he stated that the panel would minimally address the following issues:

1. What strategies are Atlanta's social institutions using in dealing with the behavioral and emotional reactions of children to the murders?

2. What is the emotional climate in Atlanta's homes and schools really like?

3. Are there specific roles and activities that Atlanta child development researchers and behavioral scientists are playing?

4. What implications for child development research exist?

John Dill convened the Teach-in at a late afternoon session on April 3—a last-minute program addition, facilitated by William Hall.[2] Instructors at the Teach-in, all from Atlanta, were Asa Hilliard, Georgia State University; Sandra Sims, Spelman College; Margaret Beale Spencer, Emory University; Joseph Stevens, Georgia State University; and Walter Hodges, Georgia State University. Diana Slaughter's notes on the Teach-in suggest that the four previously listed issues were discussed, and that the informative event was highly successful—well attended by majority scientists (e.g., Urie Bronfenbrenner, Freda Rebelsky, the late Janet Blumenthal) and minority scientists alike.

Dill and panelist Beale Spencer had participated in a new, refereed SRCD program event the previous day (together with Jean Carew, Aline Garrett, Harriette McAdoo, Ura Jean Oyemade, and Diana Slaughter): a Discussion Session focusing on "Some SRCD Black Caucus Perspectives on Directions in Developmental Research with Black Children and Families—Past, Present, and Future." This session had introduced the majority membership to a group of SRCD Black Caucus members, persons who clearly shared a commitment to the more general research goals and mission of the Society. One might conclude that through the Discussion Session and the Teach-in together, Caucus members came to be perceived as members of the "SRCD family" with a special request for help. These two events, involving the public endorsement of several respected minority and majority SRCD researchers, undoubtedly facilitated the writing of a statement on the Atlanta murders and its eventual support by the SRCD membership at its business meeting.

It is noteworthy that the Teach-in emerged from a cooperative spirit within the Black Caucus, and between the Caucus and SRCD leadership. John Dill and Algea Harrison were duly elected members of the Black Caucus Steering Committee, and Slaughter had appointed Margaret Beale Spencer and Asa Hilliard to that Committee. Furthermore, on October 22, 1979, well before planning for the Teach-in, Margaret Beale Spencer's Black Caucus Steering Subcommittee (whose members were Jessica Daniel, Juarlyn Gaiter, and Velma LaPoint) had given written feedback to William Hall on proposed Panel Titles for the SRCD meeting in 1981. This followed Hall's expression of appreciation at the prospect of assistance earlier that month. In summary, prior to plans for a Teach-in at the SRCD program, a cordial working relationship existed between that year's Program Chair and Caucus members who would have a leadership role in the Teach-in.

On April 4, the day after the Teach-in, the text of the resolution printed below was presented at the SRCD Business Meeting by incoming Black Caucus chairperson, Teach-in participant, and Atlanta resident Margaret Beale Spencer.

Whereas the SRCD is the major professional organization of child developmental research, be it resolved that SRCD offer its organizational resources and expertise of its membership to the Atlanta community in connection with the "Missing and Murdered Children," if requested, and urge through appropriate communications that the Federal Government provide resources and support to the Atlanta community for conducting research, provide mental health programs, and develop educational services.

Whereas murders of children or infanticide can be viewed as an extreme form of child abuse, be it resolved that SRCD contribute its expertise to assist interested agencies to determine the causes, both individual and societal, of this example of child abuse with the aim of preventing future murders.

Whereas the incidence of murders of Black children in Atlanta continues to rise and has received much negative attention in all forms of communication media, be it resolved that SRCD set forth a variety of mechanisms (e.g., television, literature, symposia, etc.) to educate Black children and their families concerning strategies for prevention of further assaults on Black children and systematically monitor the quality of media coverage for the specific purpose of assuring that Black children and their families are depicted in a positive, authentic, and non-exploitative fashion.

Whereas the continuing murder of Black children in Atlanta highlights the normative socialization of racist attitudes and behaviors in America, and whereas such attitudes, like other objects in motion, will remain in motion until intentionally and systematically put to rest, be it resolved that SRCD should support the development and implementation of programs that attack this problem at the source, i.e., the socialization of racial attitudes of all American children.

Whereas the development of accurate information which describes the impact of the "Missing and Murdered Children" on the process of child development is essential to the development of effective responses to the crisis, and whereas many individuals have expressed their opinions about the impact, but do not have benefit of hard data, this creates a situation which is ripe for rumor and for the development of inappropriate and inefficient strategies. Children have been described as anxious, fearful, and as exhibiting a wide variety of stress-related symptoms, etc., and whereas, while we are convinced that there has been and will be major impact on the general development of children, we need to determine more precisely the evidence for that impact. Be it therefore resolved that SRCD request of the Federal Government that it provide resources for a survey of practicing professionals such as teachers, school administrators, school psychologists, ministers, mental health workers, physicians, crisis intervention workers, etc. to describe the actual incidence and nature of the impact on the behavior of children, both problem and coping behavior.

The resolution concerning the "Missing and Murdered Black Children Tragedy in Atlanta, Georgia" was passed by the Society's membership by a "near-unanimous" majority vote. Minutes of the meeting at which this retrievable Resolution was presented and voted upon indicated that:

> Margaret Spencer presented a resolution from the Black Caucus concerning the missing and murdered Black children in Atlanta. Some members from the floor felt the resolution was too long and complicated to respond after a brief verbal presentation, though they shared the sentiments behind the resolution. After some discussion, it was felt that the matter was too

pressing to wait until copies had been distributed to the membership. The motion was made that the membership endorse the resolution as presented, and the motion carried. (Minutes of the Business Meeting of the Society for Research in Child Development, April 4, 1981)

"BACKLASH" WITHIN THE SRCD PARENT ORGANIZATION AND RESPONSE BY BLACK CAUCUS MEMBERS OF SRCD

Despite apparent support for the resolution on the Tragedy in Atlanta and sentiment at the SRCD Business Meeting, within 6 months it became apparent that SRCD leadership had expressed reservations about the actions taken at that meeting. Therefore, on December 21, 1981, Caucus Chairperson Margaret Beale Spencer wrote a letter to SRCD President Eleanor Maccoby, stating:

> I was quite dismayed ... to hear that individuals with whom you have been in contact have communicated their discomfort with the mechanism employed for presenting the Caucus Resolution during the business meeting of the biennial meeting. In fact, the argument that scientists should remain apolitical is problematic for several reasons. ... Given the history of the women's movement which conveniently benefited ... from the Civil Rights movement, it would appear that issues become overtly political when informal and/or covert mechanisms or contexts for dialogues are deemed inadequate or nonexistent. ... I am surprised at the reactions to the Resolution when its treatment in the SRCD (1981) Newsletter neutralized potential effectiveness. ... The minutes of the Business Meeting did not report that the Resolution had been passed by the membership in a floor vote. ... It was disconcerting to hear that members felt that a vote had been "railroaded." Although the Resolution was not as effective as I would have desired, however, [sic] we do know that the Resolution's passage and its subsequent visibility at the Child Abuse Conference was correlated with a cessation of child killings in Atlanta. In essence, for whatever reasons, the murder ceased. ... Ideology has always influenced research and science. ... American scientists who initially used Binet's test were quite familiar with its purpose and assumptions inherent in its construction. However, this knowledge never inhibited its use as a screening device when a larger proportion of southern Europeans began immigrating to America. Given that it is expected that the current minorities of non-whites (e.g., Blacks and Hispanics) will represent the majority population in another 100 years, the question of specifying precisely how ideology impacts ... research seems imperative. Generating a research base solely on the "temporarily advantaged" does not respond to the serious questions which will plague society during the 21st century.

81

As is indicated in Beale Spencer's letter, Caucus members did not stop addressing the "Missing and Murdered Children" after the Boston SRCD meeting. A few days later (April 7) in Milwaukee, Wisconsin, the Atlanta situation became the focus of a Symposium panel, developed by Caucus members Diana Slaughter and Ura Jean Oyemade, for an annual conference of the National Center on Child Abuse and Neglect.

Slaughter, then a member of the National Advisory Board to the Center, was moderator/co-convener of the panel. Oyemade, serving as a panelist, reported findings from her study (conducted with colleagues) on the relationship of social factors to the incidence of child abuse and neglect in lower income African-American families in Washington, DC. She emphasized the societal abuse perpetuated upon the children and families through (a) the societal context in which they live—cultural differences and patterns that are ignored or disrespected by majority culture; (b) social pressures on families, which have a disorganizing, debilitating effect; (c) inadequate and ineffective social services, and (d) services expected to be compromised by projected budget cuts and reductions.[3]

Panelists also included a sister of one of the slain children and professionals who stressed that whatever the cause(s) of the murders, communities must organize to prevent their occurrence. It was also emphasized that Day Care, Head Start, and Child Protective Services must work together with families and law enforcement officials to accomplish this objective.

CONCLUSION

In the process of being helped by the Caucus to develop a response to the heinous Atlanta murders, SRCD as an organization was dramatically and simultaneously confronted with a multiplicity of different ideas about the relationships between science, social and public policies, and social responsibility. The Society was forced to recognize that many American children are socially vulnerable, through poverty, ethnic/racial status, prejudice, and discrimination. The confrontation within SRCD itself waned with the cessation of the Atlanta child murders. Nevertheless, the issues raised by the Caucus endure for a scientific organization whose membership aims to promote children's human development and welfare through scientific scholarly study and research.

DOCUMENTS

Letter from Margaret Beale Spencer to President Eleanor Maccoby, dated December 21, 1981, regarding SRCD membership reactions to the Caucus Resolution.

Minutes of the Business Meeting of the Society for Research in Child Development, April 4, 1981, Boston, MA, by Rachel K. Clifton.

Resolution Concerning the Murdered Black Children in Atlanta, dated April 4, 1981.

REFERENCES[4]

Baldwin, J. (1985). *The evidence of things not seen*. New York: Holt, Rinehard, & Winston.

Slaughter, D., Washington, V., Oyemade, U. J., & Lindsey, R. W. (1988). Head Start: A backward and forward look. *Social Policy Report*, **3** (2). [Available from the Society for Research in Child Development, University of Michigan, Ann Arbor, MI.].

NOTES

1. It is appropriate to set the tone of this article with a quotation from the book by the late and acclaimed James Baldwin. Black Caucus member Margaret Beale Spencer spent an evening with him discussing the events in Atlanta and her work with over 300 children in that community and the local police department when he began research on the Atlanta Child Murders.

2. The discussion of the background to the Teach-in and the subsequent resolution passed by the SRCD at its Business Meeting is based upon a series of letters exchanged in February–March, 1981, prior to the meeting in Boston:

(1) Letter from John Dill to Diana Slaughter, dated February 26, 1981, regarding the need for SRCD involvement in the effects of the Atlanta murders on Black children in Atlanta schools in particular.

(2) Letter of reply from Diana Slaughter to John Dill, dated March 3, 1981, suggesting the planning of a special SRCD session on the matter at the upcoming program, and suggesting solicitation of the involvement of Atlanta based Caucus members Asa Hilliard, Margaret Beale Spencer, Joseph Stevens, and James Young.

(3) Letter from John Dill to Dorothy Eichorn, SRCD Executive Officer, and William Hall, Program Chair, dated March 25, 1981, regarding planning a special SRCD session— a Panel on the Atlanta murders. (This subsequently became the "Teach-in"; a last-minute flyer was distributed announcing the Teach-in for Friday, April 3, 1981, 3–4 p.m.)

3. Oyemade, Ura Jean (1981, June). Unpublished presentation. In D. T. Slaughter-Defoe (Chair), The Atlanta Child Murders: Defending Black children from abusive societal violence. Symposium conducted at the meeting of the Fifth National Council on Child Abuse and Neglect, Milwaukee, WI. Some of the information presented was later reported in Slaughter, Washington, Oyemade and Lindsey (1988).

4. References are included as documentation of the original sources used in constructing this overview of how the instance of the Atlanta child murders dramatized the sources of tension between the Caucus and its parent organization. References are listed in order of initial referral to them in the text. Copies of letters and other Council documents are part of the author's private collection and available from her: Dr. Diana T. Slaughter-Defoe, University of Pennsylvania, Graduate School of Education, 3700 Walnut Street, Philadelphia, PA 19104. The December 21, 1981 letter may be requested from Dr. Margaret Beale Spencer at the same address.

VII. PRE-CONFERENCES' HISTORY AND REFLECTIONS: CONCEPTUALIZING A PROCESS

TWO REFLECTIONS

The Pre-Conferences[1] of the Black Caucus of the Society for Research in Child Development (SRCD) have drawn appropriately on new leadership and scholarship in a manner that energizes the Caucus's membership. They have highlighted significant work by Caucus members and other researchers in the field focused on African American child and family issues or policy issues needing new attention and the perspectives of scholars of color. They have helped to set a research and practice agenda that goes beyond the confines of the SRCD and developmental psychology. This chapter contains an account and personal reflections on the development of the Pre-Conference format (described by Brookins) and a detailed example, the 20th Anniversary Pre-Conference, "Reviewing Black Child Survival: Old Issues New Directions" (described by Johnson). Both accounts emphasize the organizational, conceptual, intellectual, and personal processes that led to institutionalization of the Pre-Conference for the Black Caucus and the development of particular Pre-Conferences for each SRCD meeting. Pre-Conferences emerge in response to the Black Caucus's organizational concerns about issues that affect communities of children, in relation to both the development of the field and the collective scholarship of its members. Pre-Conferences facilitate linkages between policy, research, and practice. Ultimately, the Caucus Pre-Conferences are intended to provide a shared perspective and voice for child development issues in underrepresented or unrepresented arenas.

HISTORY AND PERSPECTIVE

Pre-Conferences were developed to fill several voids in the program offerings of the larger organization and in the experiences of African American scholars both within SRCD and within the field. Soon after the Black Caucus of SRCD was formed in 1973, there was recognition that the

84

proceedings of the biennial convention did not address some of the issues considered to be salient to Caucus members. Important functions of a professional scholarly organization include the provisions of pertinent data, of outlets for the dissemination of new theories, and of a forum for face-to-face interaction among its scholars. These provisions facilitate the processes of mentoring and long-range development of the discipline. Despite their importance, these processes were not happening consistently or well for African American scholars or other scholars of color in SRCD. A scholarly supportive arena was needed. In addition, the perspective of African American researchers had a unique and worthwhile impact on developmental research. What follows is a personal recollection of the chronology of events ending in the Caucus sponsoring Pre-Conferences.

In spring 1975, at the biennial meetings of SRCD, a small but energetic and committed group of both budding and seasoned African American scholars gathered in a suite of the convention hotel to discuss its role in SRCD. As the discussion proceeded, someone recommended that we, as the Black Caucus, organize symposia or a Pre-Conference session that addressed issues germane to the growth and development of African American children. Thus the idea for a "Pre-Conference" was born. At the suggestion of Jean V. Carew, some members of the group worked separately on this concept in the interim prior to the next SRCD conference. Sherryl Browne Graves, Arthur Mathis, and I (Brookins) developed a questionnaire to query the membership of the Caucus about potential conference topics. Data from the survey were made available, yet for reasons that remain unclear, nearly 15 years—and several SRCD conferences—passed before Jean Carew's suggestion to develop the Pre-Conference formats came to fruition: the vision became a reality at the biennial meetings of SRCD in Kansas City, MO in 1989.

The chair of the Black Caucus in 1987–1989, Valora Washington, chose as a theme for the Pre-Conference "The Next Generation of Black Children: Our Roles and Our Goals." Having been drafted by Valora into chairing this event, I (Brookins) set about the task of working with the Program Committee to ensure that this first, very public, effort merited attendance by Caucus members and others. As I reflect on the first Pre-Conference, I remember being especially concerned that there be a dialogue not only among scholars but also with individual practitioners and policymakers in the Kansas City community, who were laboring in the "vineyards" every day on behalf of our children. We spent considerable energy locating those harvesters and were overwhelmed by the generous responses and genuine interest they expressed in hearing from scholars—African American scholars! There was clear recognition that our goals were the same, although our paths perhaps varied. Velma LaPoint, a Program Committee member, was especially resourceful at identifying potential presenters within the Kansas City community. The participants represented a broad spectrum of the community, including municipal government, health care organizations, and various levels of the educational arena—public school boards, higher education, and alternative ventures. There were also representatives from employment training establishments and the religious community, and we were graced with the prescient wisdom of Joy Schultebrandt, who talked with us about critical mental health issues for middle-school African American children. Research such as Schultebrandt's was presented at Caucus Pre-Conferences nearly a decade before early adolescence was widely addressed in the field of child development and developmental psychology.

The plan was that as SRCD crisscrossed the country every 2 years, the Caucus would build a constituency of comrades who participated in the knowledge transfer process toward enhancing life chances for our children. As is the case with many new efforts, lots of hard work with modest formal support was the order of the day. The Program Committee and I worked tirelessly with no budget. We recognized, however, that a successful Pre-Conference would inaugurate a new chapter for the Black Caucus and SRCD because it would accrue wider visibility, affirmation, and credibility to the Black Caucus and, by extension, the Society.

When Sherryl Browne Graves assumed leadership of the Black Caucus in 1991, she requested that I again take leadership in chairing the Pre-Conference. I agreed to do so only if there were a cochair and so Margaret Beale Spencer agreed to take this position. She and I had exciting telephone conversations as we developed the Pre-Conference theme, "Ethnicity and Diversity: Implications for Research and Policies." It was our goal to broaden the discussion of child development to include other peoples of color. One of the more gratifying aspects of this planning was the gracious, sometimes eager, acceptance by diverse minority scholars. We drew reasonable representation from the Asian American, African American, and Latino communities. Another aspect of being inclusive was inviting scholars from other disciplines and individuals from other arenas, whose perspectives could broaden and assist our understanding of the various contexts in which development takes place and the broader macrofactors that influence developmental outcomes. Thus economics, anthropology, sociology, and a range of fields within the discipline of psychology were also represented. In addition, individuals representing philanthropic foundations and federal agencies participated.

Another objective of the Pre-Conferences was to highlight our junior scholars and doctoral students, as their role in advancing future scholarship is critical. Several have presented their work and taken part in panel discussions on preparing the next generation of minority scholars.

In 1991, as Keynote Speaker of the Pre-Conference, Professor Edmund Gordon took us on an intellectual journey through the wilds of cultural psychology. His address set the tone for the vividly textured and rigorously arrayed scholarship that followed. As African American scholars have argued, there is considerable variation within the African American population, and more research needs to focus on this within-group diversity. Much of the audience learned that this phenomenon exists among other racial and cultural groups too. Thus, when within-group diversity is aggregated into one category, we lose opportunities to explore the complexity of human development among these groups, and therefore diminish our knowledge base.

Although the first Pre-Conference was successful, the second, because of obvious changes in demographics in the United States, was lauded as timely, informative, and provocative. Like the earlier Pre-Conference, it provided a platform for cutting edge research on children and communities of color. On this occasion, in a presentation entitled "Asian American Identity: Media Image and Research Issues," Lee C. Lee and Kathay Feng reported on the pressures of "model minority" long before subsequent research documented the stress on Asian American adolescents.

Another gauge of success for the Pre-Conference and the Black Caucus itself was the request from members of other ethnic groups to become members of the Black Caucus. Following the 1991 Pre-Conference in Seattle, Aline Garrett, newsletter editor, polled the membership about opening our doors to diverse groups. The motion to open the membership to persons of non-African American descent who were interested in supporting the goals of the Black Caucus was passed in June 1991.

I handed the torch to Deborah Johnson to chair the 1993 Pre-Conference in New Orleans. It was obvious that our biennial Pre-Conferences had become an institutionalized event, as the Black Caucus and SRCD expected them to occur, and SRCD willingly assisted with mailing labels and space allocation. In 1993, the theme of the Black Caucus 20th Anniversary Pre-Conference was "Reviewing Black Child Survival: Old Issues, New Directions."

TWENTIETH ANNIVERSARY PRE-CONFERENCE

Formulating Interests

In the late 1970s and early 1980s several African American child development researchers were making theoretical and empirical linkages between Black child development and African cultures and traditions. Janice Hale-Benson (1982) studied families and children of the Sea Islands off the coast of South Carolina, where African ways of being were said to have remained nearly unchanged. Hale compared childrearing themes and traditions among the Islander families and African American families on the mainland. Conceptual linkages to traditional Africa were made by Leachim Semaj (1980, 1981). Semaj posited that worldviews existing along a continuum from African to European were responsible for childrearing approaches of African American parents and self-concept outcomes of African American children. William (hereafter Bill) Cross (1981) also drew upon historical connections with Africa to develop his theory of Black identity. Some of these researchers had been members of the Black Caucus or had participated in early Caucus/SRCD-sponsored activities; for example, Semaj was a member of a Caucus-initiated SRCD study group that led to an edited volume (Spencer, Brookins, & Allen, 1985).

During this formative time in the expansion of research and theory on Black child development, both Semaj and Cross mentored me (Deborah Johnson) during graduate school at Cornell University. Partly because of their influences, I developed a keen interest in incorporating Africa into my graduate studies on Black children and families. My ambition was temporarily postponed while I completed doctoral work under Diana Slaughter at Northwestern University, but Diana later facilitated my professional dream by introducing me to the late Joyce Cain, from Michigan State University. In 1989 Cain was recruiting faculty for a Fulbright-Hayes project in Zimbabwe. There, along with colleagues such as Harriette McAdoo and John McAdoo, I worked on studies of racial identity development and early childhood education. In 1991, after returning from Zimbabwe, I became chair of the Black Caucus.

Amidst numerous changes in the field, members of the Black Caucus began to cull their ambitions to link Black child development with African culture and traditions. Algea Harrison had received a Fulbright to teach in Zimbabwe, and Harriette McAdoo had returned there to engage in family research with a different group of colleagues. Others were making academic tours to Africa and other lands. International interests were taking hold, and Caucus members were participating in international excursions sponsored by SRCD and other professional organizations (e.g., the Association of Black Psychologists).

Later, Caucus members expanded their international activities, particularly their international affiliations and research endeavors. For example, Algea Harrison, who had done much teaching abroad, began publishing some of her comparative work in adolescence while also adding other countries to her scholarly travels. Harriette McAdoo published her comparative research on family values and idioms (McAdoo & Rukuni, 1993), and began a myriad of projects that included a major exploration of HIV in African families. In 1984, Diana Slaughter, then a Governing Council member, joined other SRCD members on an SRCD-sponsored trip to China. This trip, hosted jointly with Beijing University, marked the reintroduction of psychological studies in China, and in spring 1985 Diana and other SRCD members reported on the emerging developmental work with "only children" and their extended families.

Thus my interests in the connections between African American children and African children existed in a context of a credible amount of intellectual focus on comparative international studies of children and families of color. Fortunately, as Caucus Chairperson, I had the responsibility to take the lead in shaping a vision for the Black Caucus Pre-Conference in 1993. The synthesis of my evolving interest and the previously described developments in the field and the state of research among Caucus members was encapsulated in the concept and title of the Pre-Conference, "Reviewing Black Child Survival: Old Issues, New Directions."

Black Caucus Pre-Conference 1993

It happened that the 20th anniversary of the Black Caucus coincided with my tenure as chair (1991–1993). The progress of the Black Caucus had been tremendous up to this point and it was critical, in my view, to culminate this experience. A steering committee was set up, whose members—Diana Slaughter-Defoe, Walter Allen, Oscar Barbarin, Ura Jean Oyemade-Bailey, and Aline Garrett (Executive Director and undisputed cornerstone of the organization)—were my supports through the process and were key in generating topics and ultimately making a simple vision a reality. Although in previous years we had relied exclusively on dues and conference fees to pay the costs of the Pre-Conference, this celebration year brought additional costs; fortunately, we received contributions from the University of Wisconsin and SRCD, and Caucus members spontaneously provided significant contributions when dues were collected. As always, Aline Garrett made good deals with the hotels.

Anniversaries are prime times for both reflection on the past and looking into the future. Conceptually, it was important that the 1993 Pre-Conference, "Reviewing Black Child Survival: Old Issues, New Directions," consider the Caucus's work and interests over the previous years, as well as our future role in shaping child development knowledge. I attempted to cover this vast ground by including an international session and emphasizing other key areas of concern for the Black Caucus: education, health, family, and individual development. Valora Washington, a policy person concerned with Project Head Start and early development of Black children, was chosen as the keynoter.

It was important to make the Pre-Conference both inclusive and reflective of Caucus members' many interests. We wanted young graduate students and both new and established Caucus members to participate. Caucus members were invited to organize some of the sessions. For example, Diana Slaughter-Defoe, a longstanding expert on Head Start and family-school linkages, chaired the session on education, which evolved into a collection of presentations reflecting on the past, present, and future status of Head Start. Capturing the Executive Director of the National Head Start Association, Sarah Greene, proved to be a huge coup, and attendance was quite high at that session, despite its having been schedule late in the day. It is clear that the Head Start Program has been a focal point in the research of numerous Caucus members (see Chapter XII).

To address health issues, Oscar Barbarin was enlisted to organize a panel on chronic illness, a close interest for him at the time. He and a student were invited to present their work on a joint project in that area. Discussions of disability had always raised concerns about how Black children have or have not been represented. Nevertheless there were those interested in language, disability, and other developmental or physical challenges. To supplement Barbarin's session, I invited Reginald Redding, an administrator of a school for deaf students and a member of the African American deaf community, to present on Black deaf children as an issue of disability that had not previously been addressed by Caucus or SRCD researchers. Dr. Redding consented to do the presentation, but its placement was difficult because it crossed the areas of education, health, and racial identity. The decision was made to place Redding's presentation with the chronic illness and disability panel, which had only two other presentations. Barbarin, however, was concerned that the placement of deaf issues under the topic of chronic illness projected a poor message about the status of deaf children and the relation between chronic illness and disability. Barbarin's view was validated, but we could not overcome the constraints of time and space. Adding a speaker who was deaf resulted in our engaging sign language interpreters for the first time in the history of SRCD.[2] Our invitation to Redding actually paved new territory for SRCD, which in subsequent years added interpreters to key events.

Three sessions remained to be organized—International, Identity, and Family—and I either organized them myself or enlisted help. To identify speakers for the international sessions, I called UNICEF and the World Bank, and invited Harriette McAdoo, with whom several of us had recently shared the Fulbright experience. Aline Garrett alerted me to a group of scholars associated with Tulane University's International Health Program/ Public Health and Tropical Medicine Department, where African scholars were working in the area of child survival. Those who participated in our session were Drs. Nkhoma, Maina, and Bona Lana, from Malawi, Kenya, and Nigeria, respectively. I contacted Dr. Penny Jessop at Tulane, and she consented to recruit another three scholars for the presentation. "Child Survival in the African Diaspora" set the tone for thinking about African American child development as an issue of child survival in the West. All other sessions were linked to this idea conceptually.

By organizing the Identity session on "Reviewing Race Preference," I was able to pull together scholars who worked in this area from disparate parts of my career and express the central part of my own work on racial identity and race-related socialization of children. Margaret Beale Spencer's work had been a central influence on this focus; I considered her to be a key expert—one who had achieved field-altering changes in the research direction of race identity studies. Bill Cross was a senior scholar who had recently published a book reviewing in historical and contemporary detail the area of racial identity while also presenting his model of racial identity development (Cross, 1991). Rounding out the panel were my young peers, Craig Brookins and Emilie Smith, who had already completed some important measurement work that pointed the way to the future. It was really exciting to see this "dream group" come together.

In the last session, Children and Families, the speakers were phenomenal. Linda Burton was becoming a well-known scholar, Melvin Wilson was being recognized for his work in intergenerational Black families, and Andrea Hunter was the new family scholar among the group, pushing forward on her studies of the nuances of Black family life. Finally, Vonnie McLoyd and Suzanne Randolph ended our session, Vonnie with a futuristic look at Black child development issues in brief, and Suzanne with a rousing and touching self-penned poem, entitled "When You Hear the Children Cry."

Feedback on the Pre-Conference was very favorable. Caucus members reported that it was a great celebration of the work of the Caucus and an excellent demonstration of what the next generation had to offer the field. Despite the varied and unique interests among Caucus members, the Pre-Conference was additional evidence that the Caucus still pulled together to focus on the larger issues of Black children here and abroad. Inserting the international perspective seemed to reflect the many directions and activities that Caucus members already had in motion. For some members, others it may have spawned international interests. The Caucus and its activities have often been a doorway to new professional opportunities. This was certainly true for me.

As a direct consequence of the exposure created by the Pre-Conference, I was asked to be on SRCD's International Committee for a 6-year term. In this same year I learned of the International Society for the Study of Behavioral Development (ISSBD), a close cousin to SRCD (with many members in common), and was able to present my work at its conference in Brazil. Subsequently, I have expanded my international focus to include racial identity work with indigenous (aboriginal) peoples in Australia. Like my research in Zimbabwe, my work in Australia centers on ways in which one's position as a minority group member in a society impact self-perceptions and skill development. International work such as this helps to place the experiences of African Americans more broadly in Western society.

There have been many important Pre-Conferences and many Pre-Conferences with excellent presentations both before and since the 1993 sessions. In 1995, in Indianapolis, the Pre-Conference had the theme "The Family and Ecological Challenge: Community and Social Issues." In 1997, as the SRCD Black Caucus celebrated its 25th Anniversary in Washington, DC, the theme of the Pre-Conference was "The Pursuit of Talent Development: An Approach to Optimizing Child Outcomes."

PRE-CONFERENCES, CAREERS, AND FUTURES

The shaping and management of the research and professional careers of Caucus members as well as the body of contributions to the field are evident through the lens of the Pre-Conference history and work presented in this chapter. The opportunities that were created through the vehicle of the Pre-Conferences by Caucus membership/leadership and Pre-Conference coordinators throughout the years facilitated experiences that were beyond the scope of the parent organization at the time. In other instances, Black researchers' imaginations were stimulated to operate outside of the ivory tower influences and traditions of the larger organization. The Caucus's activities provided those new insights in a safe, supportive environment. The 1993 Pre-Conference presentations coalesced many critical issues pertinent to African American scholarship and visibility over a 20-year period. The celebration culminated our efforts to expand the purview of child development and highlighted the successes of the organization in creating a stimulating and nurturing intellectual environment for ourselves. Moreover, these opportunities forged the way for the entire SRCD membership to access perspective and innovations in scholarship being presented in the Black Caucus Pre-Conferences.

Brookins's generation represents the foundation of the organization, where struggles were staged and necessary battles won to create a metaphorical time and space in which Pre-Conferences could occur and be accepted. Johnson's generation, immediately following, built upon this foundation, enjoying the freedom it made possible to expand and innovate. Together, our generations have made and sustained a way out of no way, in which a solid foundation has been cast for the future. Our collaborations with the parent organization have expanded, there is more visibility and integration of African American scholars into the scholarly activities and inner workings of the organization, the unique offerings of the Pre-Conference broadly attract SRCD membership, and finally, the pre-conference remains a context in which new and seasoned scholars of color presenting their research feel stimulated and valued. We hope that the next generation of scholars and Pre-Conference organizers can continue to build on these structures in ways that expand the possibilities for future scientists yet undiscovered.

REFERENCES

Cross, W. E. (1981). Black families and Black identity development. *Journal of Comparative Family Studies*, **7**, 19–50.

Cross, W. E. (1991). *Shades of Black: Diversity in African American identity*. Philadelphia: Temple University Press.

Hale-Benson, J. (1982). *Black children: Their roots, culture and learning styles* (revised edition). Baltimore, MD: Johns Hopkins University Press.

McAdoo, H., & Rukuni, M. (1993). A preliminary study of family values of the women of Zimbabwe. *Journal of Black Psychology*, **19**, 48–62.

Semaj, L. T. (1980). Reconceptualizing the development of racial preference in children: A socio-cognitive approach. *Journal of Black Psychology*, **6**, 59–79.

Semaj, L. T. (1981). The Black self, identity and model for a psychology of Black liberation. *The Western Journal of Black Studies*, **5**, 158–171.

Spencer, M. B., Brookins, G. K. & Allen, W. R. (Eds.). (1985). *Beginnings: The social and affective development of Black children*. Hillsdale NJ: Erlbaum.

NOTES

1. The list of SRCD Black Caucus Pre-Conference themes, dates, and locations between 1989 and 1997 is:

(1) Raising the Next Generation of Black Children: Our Roles and Our Goals, April 26–27, 1989; Westin Crown Hotel, Kansas City, MO.

(2) Ethnicity and Diversity: Implications for Research and Policies, April 16–17, 1991, Westin Hotel, Seattle, WA.

(3) Reviewing Black Child Survival: Old Issues, New Directions, March 24–25, 1993, New Orleans Sheraton, New Orleans, LA.

(4) The Family and Ecological Challenges: Community and Social Issues, March 29–30, 1995, Hyatt Regency Hotel, Indianapolis, IN.

(5) The Pursuit of Talent Development: An Approach to Optimizing Child Outcomes, April 1–3, 1997, Sheraton Washington Hotel, Washington, DC.

2. The naiveté associated with this new venture meant that I did not request African American interpreters. Redding had a couple of miscommunications by his Euro-American sign language interpreters during his discussion of Black deaf individuals. The problem was one of voice and perspective; they had the power of voice but not his perspective.

SECTION III. RESEARCH AND RELATED ISSUES

The heart of the Society for Research in Child Development (SRCD) is its publications. Presentations and related publications are the shared means for conveying what has been learned from scientific studies in this broad field. No history of the Black Caucus of SRCD would be complete without attention to the critical ideas and issues addressed through the primary vehicle of teaching and mentoring in this field: research studies and related writings. Section III, a core section of the *Monograph,* discusses Black scholarly research in child/adolescent development, including both the scholars' intentions and the historical and ideological contexts surrounding their studies and writings.

Section III extends this *Monograph* beyond simple description of the relationship between SRCD and the Black Caucus of SRCD to detailed discussion, from the authors' perspectives, of some of the key ideas and issues that Caucus members sought to address during the first 25 years. As editors, we identified these ideas/issues to be: (a) cultural deficit versus cultural difference; (b) the appropriate linkages between poverty, race, community, and individual empowerment; (c) advocacy versus objectivity in scientific research; and (d) whether and how the cultural or racial identity of the researcher informs scientific knowledge.

Of necessity, this section of Caucus history is selective, intended to illustrate with a few examples how Caucus members addressed these issues when they participated in research and policy presentations and publications on African American children and youth between 1973 and 1997. Chapters VIII and IX discuss early research. In Chapter VIII, Diana Slaughter-Defoe describes the first SRCD *Monographs* published by African American scientists, Jean Carew and herself (then Diana Slaughter). She discusses how Carew emphasized parental/environmental contexts in shaping the intellectual development of White working-class children. In other research addressing African American children, both Carew and Slaughter-Defoe shared strong beliefs in the cultural difference paradigm. Slaughter's SRCD

Monograph emphasized early intervention and applied development in relation to African American children.

In Chapter IX, Aline Garrett reflectively describes her research study in which linkages are drawn between the ecological-community context, poverty, and individual psychological outcomes within a small impoverished Southern town that is home to both Black and White families. Her study used an ecological approach to research with African American children and families several years before Bronfenbrenner's writings in this area appeared in scholarly journals and books.

Chapters by Margaret Beale Spencer (X), Vonnie McLoyd (XI), and Ura Jean Oyemade Bailey, Trellis Waxler, and Valora Washington (XII) discuss the path-breaking publications of the mid-1980s, publications focused on (a) attending to the normative development status of African American children, including racial identity development; (b) understanding the evolution of ideas and influences that shape one's identity as a scientist and scholar; and (c) comprehending the strengths and challenges posed by building linkages between theory, policy, and practice in the applied developmental field. In Chapter XII, Oyemade Bailey and colleagues use as one example ethnic minority scholars' response to the research, evaluation, and programmatic needs of Project Head Start, the national public policy program most supportive of the needs of children and families from poverty-stricken backgrounds.

If there is one Caucus voice, then that voice—clearly articulated in Chapters X and XI by Beale Spencer and McLoyd—pertains to liberation of African American communities from deficit-oriented scholarly writing and research paradigms. The delight of Section III, however, is that there are many voices—voices that vary in emphasis on theory, on the practice of empirical research, and on policy and service. Thus Section III demonstrates how all Caucus members were mutually influenced, not just by the larger SRCD parent organization, but also by diverse perspectives on research and scholarship brought to fruition by the support provided by the Caucus itself. The diversity is apparent in the authors' formulations about what they did during those early years and why they did it. Although at times a source of conflict and tension within the group, the diversity also reflects the Caucus's lively and vibrant structure.

This chapter describes the earliest contributions to the *Monographs of the Society for Research in Child Development* by two pioneering African American scientists, Jean V. Carew and myself (then Diana T. Slaughter). Published in 1980, the Carew *Monograph* was entitled *Experience and the Development of Intelligence in Young Children at Home and in Day Care*; published in 1983, the Slaughter *Monograph* was entitled *Early Intervention and Its Effects on Maternal and Child Development*. Both *Monographs* were published while future Society for Research in Child Development (SRCD) President Frances Horowitz was editor of *Monographs*, and no empirical research-based *Monograph* has since been published with an African American as lead author. At the time the Carew *Monograph* was published (1980), I was a member of the Board of Consulting Editors to *Monographs*.

Fortunately, Carew and I knew each other. Carew mentored me in my first major postdissertation study, which led to my *Monograph*. At that time, roughly 1973–1979, I was building on a scholarly research path initiated by my doctoral dissertation research (Slaughter, 1969), and the research of scientists like Carew, K. Alison Clarke-Stewart, and Bettye Caldwell. The relationship between Carew and myself was warm and cordial, but professional: Carew contributed a letter toward my tenure at Northwestern University, being familiar with the study that was published as my *Monograph* in 1983 and also knowing me through our founding member-ships in the Black Caucus of the SRCD. Carew was the first elected chairperson of the Caucus, I the second.

JEAN V. CAREW'S 1980 *MONOGRAPH*

Born in Trinidad and educated in the British cultural tradition, Jean V. Carew approached her subject with influences from both of those cultures. As an adult, she supported herself and her daughter, and conducted her research on grant funds obtained primarily from governmental research sources while she was a Research Associate at Harvard's Graduate School of Education. I visited her when she was a Fellow at the Palo Alto Center for Advanced Studies in the Behavioral Sciences, and found her actively planning to establish her own consulting firm in the Berkeley/Oakland area.

Far ahead of its time, Carew's research was conducted entirely without benefit of the security of an academic appointment at a university. Her pioneering 1980 *Monograph* demonstrated the importance of the maternal role in children's intellectual development, using Burton White's competence model (Carew, Chan, & Halfar, 1976; White, Carew-Watts, Barnett, Kahan, Marmor, & Shapiro, 1973) and Piagetian formulations (Piaget, 1952) to guide the conceptual framework. Like other scientists (e.g., McCall, Eichorn, & Hogarty, 1977), Carew believed that the "intelligence" assessed by traditional IQ performance tests could be affected by motivational (White, 1959) and environmental influences.

Carew reported longitudinal observational data on White middle-class and working-class children ($N = 23$ dyads), ages 12–36 months. Children were individually observed in their homes at four time periods: 12–15, 18–21, 24–27, and 30–33 months. Each child was observed for 1 hour on three to five separate occasions during these periods. Nine of the children were also observed in the day-care centers they attended, at 18–23, 24–29, and 30–34 months. Carew reported that the amount of early joint reciprocal interaction (before 30 months) between mother and child correlated .76 with the child's Binet performance score at 36 months. Moreover, the child's solitary play activities, again before 30 months, did not contribute to Binet scores at 36 months. The early maternal and child interaction that preceded high cognitive performance among children later in their development accounted for only a very small percentage of observed time. Furthermore, the defining maternal style was described by Carew as "participatory," not merely supportive or facilitative: the mothers of higher IQ children literally created the intellectual content of their children's play activities by guiding, expanding, and entertaining them.

Clarke-Stewart's commentary on the study, found in its concluding pages, prompted Carew to elaborate in some detail on her approach to coding and categorizing the observational data (Carew, 1980). Defending her concept of "intellectually valuable experiences," Carew defined "concrete reasoning/practical problem solving" in several examples (pp. 78–79):

> Piaget has described certain classes of experiences, which he regards as fundamental to the development of true intelligence (1952). This type of intellectual experience seems to provide the child with a clear opportunity to learn basic reasoning skills, such as differentiating means from ends and cause from effect, and to learn about the basic physical regularities underlying concepts such as volume, gravity, momentum, buoyancy,

trajectory, equilibrium, and reflection. Often it is the child himself who creates the opportunity by experimenting with objects in the environment. One difficulty an observer has in interpreting these experiences is in inferring the specific theme of the child's investigation from his nonverbal behavior. Another difficulty is in distinguishing these "scientific" enterprises from simple play-exploration. For example, if a child is observed playing with his toy cars . . . pushing the cars along, making engine sounds, crashing them against the furniture . . . this activity would not qualify as an intellectually valuable experience in our view. If, however, he *systematically* varies his actions on the cars, say, by changing how hard he pushed [sic] them or the inclines on which he rolls them, and carefully watches the results of his actions, the experience would then be regarded as a concrete-reasoning intellectual experience. . . .

Several examples in Carew's study depict the parent responding to or initiating informal "experiments" with their children in the home setting. She clearly believed that intelligence, as measured by the existing intellectual performance tests, is essentially coconstructed by parent and child, not simply with respect to vocabulary enrichment and verbal fluency, but also with regard to concept formation. She supported neither the view that nature determines the results of intelligence testing nor the view that intelligence is what the tests "test." She wrote in the tradition that there was nothing particularly special or magical about successful performance on IQ tests; rather, the home environment nurtured and enabled the child's construction of adaptive intelligence as we define it in Western thought.

Carew continued the previous excerpt with a particularly rich example, describing the behavior of an observed child, Brenda, whose solitary experiment was thought to, literally, stimulate the child's intellectual development:

> For example, flotation. [Brenda seems to be asking herself] Why do some things float and others sink? . . . Brenda (13 months) sips a glass of milk in her highchair. She pushes the glass away, sliding it along the table-top. Suddenly she drops a piece of meat into the glass and it sinks. She startles slightly and then deliberately puts a potato chip in and it floats. She looks puzzled. Brenda puts her hand deep into the glass and seems to be searching for the piece of meat at the bottom. She lifts the glass toward her, peers into it, then pushes it away. Brenda puts her hand in again and waves her fingers about in the milk several times as if trying to reach the meat. (Later, Brenda resumes her experiment, deliberately dropping in pieces of meat and chips alternately into the milk.) (Carew, 1980, p. 79)

During the publication of the *Monograph*, and at the occasion of her unexpected and untimely death in 1981,[1] Carew had been funded to study similar phenomena in the home and neighborhood environments of African American children (NIMH and National Day/Infant Care Home Study, Contract No. HHS 105-80-C-041). This project, the Toddler and Infant Experiences Study, was affectionately known as the TIES project (Massey, Milbrath, Hayes, Buchanan, David, & Rosenberg, 1996). The first *Newsletter of the Black Caucus of SRCD* (Spring, 1980, p. 6) described the purposes of that study, in which the co-principal investigators were Grace Massey and the late Marie Peters, as follows: "TIES' purpose is to examine the socioemotional, intellectual, creative language, and physical development of Black toddlers and the corresponding childrearing practices, attitudes, beliefs, and values of working-class and middle-class Black parents." The description emphasized a commitment to the study of the normative development of Black children, a scientific commitment from which Carew never wavered. Her long-range plans, as expressed informally to this author, were to extend her studies to include an international focus. Unfortunately, the loss of both Carew and Peters (in 1984)[2] devastated Massey and the research team, and the long-range promise of TIES was not realized.

Carew's focus on the contribution of human relationships to the elaboration of adaptive intelligence was compatible with findings in the earlier doctoral dissertation of my colleague at the University of Chicago, K. Alison Clarke-Stewart (1973). Clarke-Stewart's study was based on the results of factor analyses of discrete behaviors, rather than Carew's predetermined behavioral categories. Specifically, a mother who was judged warm, contingently responsive, stimulating, and enriching, from both visual and verbal perspectives, appeared to produce an intellectually competent, secure child, as observed from behaviors at home and elsewhere. Furthermore, the best single predictor of the child's overall competence score was the amount of maternal verbal stimulation, whether or not in direct response to children's vocalizations. In the Clark-Stewart study, whereas maternal behaviors appeared to determine childhood cognitive competencies, childhood social behaviors appeared to determine whether mothers and children at these ages (9–18 months) engaged in reciprocal interactions.

In summary, in the developmental field, descriptions of effective parenting have portrayed mothers as active and participatory in exchanges with their preschool children. Mothers set standards of excellence, structured learning experiences, were verbally stimulating, and were firm and consistent in their disciplinary practices. They appeared to use reasoning and persuasion and their knowledge of their children's personal interests to motivate them. They were neither extremely permissive nor severely punitive, but instead were contingently responsive to their children's needs in accordance with perceived developmental status.

These research findings were consistent with another academic tradition, in which I had been earlier mentored, established in the research of Hess and Shipman (1965) and augmented by the theoretical framework of the British scholar Basil Bernstein. Bernstein had noted the importance of language and speech for differentiating among communicative patterns of various British social classes (Hess, 1970). The research of Hess and Shipman, conducted with African American mother–child dyads of diverse Southside Chicago social status groups, emphasized that observed communicative patterns were always framed in the context of human relationships, in particular the earliest parent–child relationships. Hess and Shipman underlined the important role of the mother as the child's earliest "teacher." Success or failure in this role, they reasoned, could affect children's school readiness.

Whereas Hess and Shipman's (1965) research stressed mean differences between social status groups in mother–child interactions and child performance outcomes, my award-winning doctoral research (Slaughter, 1969) stressed individual differences in reported parenting styles within lower socioeconomic status groups. Hess (1970) had relied upon patterns of parental authority in relation to types of work roles experienced, given the adult family members' socioeconomic status, to account for the correlation of child achievement performance with social cultural context. In my dissertation, I studied 90 mother–child pairs and the linkages between parenting style differences and measures of school readiness. Following this research, I argued in my 1983 *Monograph* that the element of traditionalism associated with earlier, more rural patterns of childrearing had been sustained and perpetuated in urban Chicago, much to the academic disadvantage of many children. Individual differences in child achievement performance within lower socioeconomic families could be accounted for by the degree of traditionalism in familial patterns of interactions with children. If this were true, then changes in maternal and child behaviors in the direction of more "modern" approaches to childrearing, as encouraged by intervention programs such as Head Start, should be most pronounced in those families in which African American mothers are judged least "traditional" in childrearing beliefs and practices. My 1983 *Monograph* reported the results of the effort to test this hypothesis.

In defining "traditionalism" I sought support from the writings of cultural anthropologists (e.g., Kluckhohn & Strodtbeck, 1961) and sociologists (e.g., Smith & Inkeles, 1966). Summarizing some of this literature, I stated:

> Two lines of research have addressed cultural values and social mobility as reflected through the expressed value orientations of members of

the culture. The first line was developed by Kluckhohn and Strodtbeck, the second by Inkeles. Since each ... had serious conceptual and methodological problems, the two traditions were reformulated and integrated to meet present needs .... Ethnic cultures which possess similar values and traits are more likely to function effectively in American society, and therefore, experience more rapid assimilation and advancement .... The modernization position, developed by Inkeles, considered individual change within the context of cultural change .... The concept of psychological modernity ... emphasized the psychological adjustments and competencies required because of rapid modernization or industrialization of cultures .... Neither [researcher] ... focused on intra-societal urban contrasts ... [and both] failed to include women in their researches and they rarely specifically addressed the role of prejudice and racial discrimination. Therefore, I chose to develop a new measure of expressed values. The measure would incorporate: (a) an emphasis on the more familiar and traditionally adaptive styles within lower-status Black communities, as contrasted with styles which might be more characteristic of middle- or upper-status communities; (b) an expansion of the original Kluckhohn (1961) dimension categories to include Personal Control—the perceptions of desired control and influence over social others; and (c) a greater opportunity for each respondent to locate her own personal position relative to her perceptions of the position of African Americans and Other Americans .... Review of the historical and sociological literature, as well as discussions with our predominantly Black research team, led me to posit that some value preferences would be more characteristic of the respondent who was currently actively pursuing educational mobility than others. The "modern" and "traditional" ends of the value continuum for each [presented] situation were thus defined. (Slaughter-Defoe, 1996, pp. 146–147)

This long quotation indicates that I struggled with how to bring the then prevailing insights of sociology and cultural anthropology to the developmental psychology paradigm embraced by colleagues like Carew (1980) and Clarke-Stewart (1973). Mothers, I reasoned, were not just practitioner parents; they also had beliefs and values that resulted from the socializing influences of their own interpersonal environments and those of their subculture. Furthermore, some mothers were more committed and competent than others in using education as a vehicle for social mobility for themselves and their children. Knowledge of these beliefs and values would help to identify those families likely to be most responsive to early interventions, particularly those designed to support or buttress school readiness.

Support for this view was obtained from the study of early intervention with 83 Black mother–child dyads who resided in a Chicago Housing Authority complex.[3] Two parent-education models of intervention were introduced to the stratified random sample of dyads: the Levenstein Toy Demonstration (TD) model (Levenstein, 1970) and the Auerbach/ Badger Mothers Discussion (MD) group model (Auerbach, 1968; Badger, 1971). United Charities of Chicago, a social service agency, introduced both models, employing experienced social workers as parent education interveners. In the TD format, mothers observed as the social worker modeled how to use a new toy in participatory, interactive play. Afterwards, they tried the method themselves, and the toys were left as a gift. Controls received only the toys, with no special services in parent education. Discussion group mothers (MD) had their relationships with each other and (indirectly) with family members facilitated by a participating social worker, also available to mothers for special case services. Children in the three dyads ranged between 18 and 24 months at the start of the study.

My 1983 *Monograph* reported on this research. MD group participants were favored over the TD dyads and the no-treatment controls on all study outcome measures. Generally, mother–child dyads who were more participatory and interactive during a structured 20-minute play session in an experimental setting were also more likely to be "less traditional" with respect to maternal child rearing beliefs and values. Children in these dyads tended to continue to perform better—as measured by scores on traditional IQ tests, with advancing age over the 2-year time period of the study—than children in other treatment conditions.

Despite elaborate praise of the scientific merit of the *Monograph* by both commentators, Bettye Caldwell and Felton Earls, at the conclusion of the *Monograph* (Slaughter, 1983), I felt as if only a small group of informed devotees really appreciated the study and its utility. Social policy appeared to be made not by research findings, as had been hoped (and taught by Hess and colleagues), but at best by collaborative relations between researchers and persons in the practice and policy arenas. It seemed that the goals of my research were noble but naive. The larger society did not care about the beliefs and values of a group of Black women and their children. This interest in cultural context seemed to be a peculiar "affliction" of the author, raised in the 1940s and 1950s on Chicago's Southside in a predominantly working-class African American community in which four generations of "mothers," ranging from great-great maternal grandmother to mother, were available at birth. In contrast, the larger society seemed to care most about accounting for dysfunctional parents and families—those with multiple problems, who were also prone to child abuse and neglect. The dominant culture was not interested in defending the women who were attacked for not rearing children who could advance themselves through the public education system.

Various explanations to the dominant cultural view were offered. Some argued that the parents' childrearing practices had nothing to do with their children's failures in school, stating that focusing on mother–child relations was essentially "blaming the victim" instead of the sorry state of her child's school and its failure to educate children. Others pointed to the importance of the larger cultural context in shaping parental goals, subsistence goals that might or might not emphasize formal schooling but certainly included survival skills. Still others stressed that relationships with fathers, peers, and siblings—also important to children's development, were neglected in the narrow focus on mother–child relations. Thus, the constructive aspects of parent–child relations for childhood socialization and competence in Western schooling were devalued.

Since the publication of my 1983 *Monograph*, the emergence of the nation's desire for sustained global/international competitiveness and the arrival of newer immigrant—frequently impoverished—populations have kept this field vibrant and active. Yet none of the competing perspectives has offered a substantive alternative conceptual perspective on young children's learning and development. In fact, some of the most compelling research in recent years has shown how the adaptive characteristics of young African American children can be used to interact favorably with school curricula (e.g., Boykin & Allen, 1988). Nonetheless, despite lacking the full natural portrait so passionately desired by Carew, we have continued to "intervene" as I knew we would.

REFERENCES[4]

Principal Monographs

Carew, J. V. (1980). Experience and the development of intelligence in young children at home and in day care. *Monographs of the Society for Research in Child Development*, Serial No. 187, Vol. 45, 6–7.

Slaughter, D. T. (1983). Early intervention and its effects on maternal and child development. *Monographs of the Society for Research in Child Development*, Serial No. 202, Vol. 48, 4.

Other References

Auerbach, A. (1968). *Parents learn through discussion: Principles and practice of parent group discussion*. New York: Wiley.

Badger, E. (1971). A mothers' training program—the road to a purposeful existence. *Children*, **18**, 168–173.

Boykin, A. W., & Allen, B. (1988). Rhythmic movement facilitation of learning in working class Afro-American children. *Journal of Genetic Psychology*, **149**, 335–348.

*Carew, J. V., Chan, I., & Halfar, C. (1976). *Observing intelligence in young children: Eight case studies*. Englewood Cliffs, NJ: Prentice-Hall.

Clarke-Stewart, K. A. (1973). Interactions between mothers and their young children: Characteristics and consequences. *Monographs of the Society for Research in Child Development*, Serial No. 153, Vol. 38, 6–7.

Garrett, A. (Ed.). (1980, Spring). Newsletter of the Black Caucus of the Society for Research in Child Development. (Available from Diana Slaughter-Defoe, 3700 Walnut Street, Philadelphia, PA 19104-6216.)

Hess, R. (1970). Social class and ethnic influences upon socialization. In P. Mussen (Ed.), *Carmichael's manual of child psychology* (Vol. 2, pp. 457–558). New York: Wiley.

Hess, R., & Shipman, V. (1965). Early experience and the socialization of cognitive modes in children. *Child Development*, **36**, 369–386.

Kluckhohn, C., & Strodtbeck, F. (1961). *Variations in value orientations*. Evanston, IL: Row, Peterson.

Levenstein, P. (1970). Cognitive growth in preschoolers through verbal interaction with mothers. *American Journal of Orthopsychiatry*, **40**, 426–432.

*Massey, G. C., Milbrath, C., Hayes, W. A., Buchanan, A., David, J., & Rosenberg, J. (1996). Observation instruments of Toddler and Infant Experiences (TIES). In R. Jones (Ed.), *Handbook of tests and measurements for Black populations* (Vol. 1, pp. 19–30). Hampton, VA: Cobb & Henry.

*McCall, R., Eichorn, D., & Hogarty, P. (1977). Transitions in early mental development. *Monographs of the Society for Research in Child Development*, Serial No. 171, Vol. 42, 3.

*Piaget, J. (1952). *The origins of intelligence in children* (2nd ed.). New York: International Universities Press.

Slaughter, D. (1969). Maternal antecedents of the academic achievement behaviors of Afro-American Head Start children. *Educational Horizons*, **48** (1), 24–28.

Slaughter-Defoe, D. (1996). The expressed values scale: Assessing traditionalism in lower socioeconomic status African American women. In R. Jones (Ed.), *Handbook of tests and measurements for Black populations* (Vol. 2, pp. 145–167). Hampton, VA: Cobb & Henry.[5]

Smith, D., & Inkeles, A. (1966). The OM scale: A comparative sociopsychological measure of individual modernity. *Sociometry*, **29**, 353–377.

*White, B., Carew-Watts, J., Barnett, I. C., Kahan, B., Marmor, J., & Shapiro, B. (1973). *Environment and experience: Major influences on the development of the young child*. Englewood Cliffs, NJ: Prentice-Hall.

*White, R. (1959). Motivation reconsidered: The concept of competence. *Psychological Review*, **66**, 297–331.

NOTES

1. Jean Carew's death was reported in the Fall 1982 issue of the *NEWSLETTER of the Black Caucus of the Society for Research in Child Development* (Number 4):

Dr. Jean Carew (1936–1981)

> There have been many memorials to Jean. The Fall 1981 Newsletter of SRCD, Inc., had this to say: "Jean Carew's death will be felt by many in child development as a personal, as well as professional, loss. In a highly competitive field, she conducted her research and her private life with great integrity, courage, and warmth. She possessed intellectual qualities which distinguished her as an exemplary academician and were reflected in her incisiveness, originality, and exacting standards of scholarship. As a human being, she was invariably fair, generous and compassionate."

Aline Garrett

> "I admired and trusted her. She was the only consultant I've ever had to any of my researches, and the only Black woman who reviewed my work for promotion and tenure at Northwestern."

Diana T. Slaughter

"In June, 1981, a memorial service was held for Jean V. Carew in the garden of the Center for Advanced Study in the Behavioral Sciences at Stanford University where Jean had been a fellow. In June of 1982 a second memorial service was held for Jean in Radcliffe Yard of Harvard University where Jean had been on the faculty. Her recent research on the development of Black children was pioneering—breaking old patterns of thought and strategy in psychological research; defying deeply embedded and destructive stereotypes of Black families; and promising a new version of health and resilience in young children. In this work, Jean's heart, mind, and spirit came together, her ideology and intellect were joined."

Marie F. Peters.

2. The death of Marie Peters (1920–1984) was reported in the Spring 1984 issue of the *NEWSLETTER of the Black Caucus of the Society for Research in Child Development* (Number 6).

3. Margaret Beale Spencer was research project director of my study while still a graduate student at the University of Chicago's Committee on Human Development.

4. Key Sources to Jean V. Carew's monograph are starred in References (*); other listed items are key sources to Diana T. Slaughter's monograph.

5. In my monograph this reference was listed as "Slaughter, D., & Walcer, C. (in press). Expressed values of lower socioeconomic status black American women." It was scheduled to be a book chapter in the volume *Minority Women: Social and Psychological Perspectives*, edited by Reid and Puryear, which the publisher, Holt, Rinehart, and Winston, later chose not to publish. The information was later published in the prior cited 1996 two-volume handbook compiled by the late Regenald Jones, *Handbook for Tests and Measurements for Black Populations*.

IX. EFFECT OF AN OCCUPATIONAL SHIFT ON FAMILY LIFESTYLE: AN ECOLOGICAL APPROACH

In this chapter, I briefly describe the goals, research design, and findings of a study I undertook in 1974. At that time, before ecological approaches to studying families and communities were prevalent, I received a grant from the U.S. Department of Health, Education, and Welfare, Office of Child Development, to study the effect of an occupational shift on family lifestyle in a small Southern town, where I was a lifelong resident. In the 1970s, journal editors in the psychology field were considerably less friendly to a study design that, although contextually rich, had so many "uncontrolled" variables. Now that the climate is more favorable, I hope future generations of scholars will be inspired to pursue and report ecological studies of human lives in communities in need of economic and social empowerment. Reports should engage audiences that are more inclusive than scholars and scientists who read academic journals. I think they should also engage governmental officials and other public servants who are dedicated to improving their communities.

THE COMMUNITY I STUDIED

The community was a semi-rural town in Louisiana with a population of less than 10,000. The *Statistical Profile of Parishes* (Public Affairs Research Council of Louisiana, 1973) indicated a bleak economic picture for this community: 46% of the families in the parish (county) had incomes in the poverty range, and unemployment had reached nearly 13%. Compounding the problems that result from and poverty and unemployment was the low educational attainment of the parish—far below that of the nation. The median years of school completed was only 5.1 with 49% of the people in the parish having fewer than 4 years of formal education. Poverty, unemployment, and low educational attainment were especially prevalent among Black residents in the community, who made up 51% of the population.

The South, with its traditional agrarian economy, has sought to alleviate the problems of inflation, unemployment, and underemployment by attracting new industry to the area. This motivation and the bleak economic climate of the parish led its officials to conduct a labor survey in December 1968. Results from the survey indicated that the parish possessed may potential employees who were very interested in finding work. The officials took the necessary steps to secure and prepare a site for a new physical plant, and 2 years later a new textile plant located in the parish.

With the arrival of the new industry, the parish officials had as their major concern the economic impact of the new industry on the community. Data that reflected an increase in sales taxes, a decline in welfare rolls, and the opening of new bank accounts were all well received. The officials were less concerned with the ecological and psychological impact on changes in family life.

It is important to understand that this was a community where change came slowly. The typical life pattern for most residents was birth, attendance at the local public schools, work at a local job, marriage to someone from the community, children, retirement, and death, generally without ever leaving the community. A minority of the residents went on to college after high school. Those who earned education degrees usually returned to the community to teach. Graduates in other areas usually left the community to find jobs. Until 1970, those residents existing at the poverty level managed to survive economically, primarily through the few factories, which canned and processed the local agricultural products, such as sugar cane, potatoes, okra, and pepper. For many residents, this meant seasonal employment.

In 1970, a new kind of industry, a total process textile plant, located in the community. This plant took raw yarn and made it into ready-to-wear men's and boys' briefs, T-shirts, and athletic shirts. It had 140,000 square feet of floor space, and an additional 100,000 square feet was already being planned. The annual amount of new money going into the community was approximately 52 million dollars. The following facts indicate the size and capacity of the new plant—the world's largest bleacher and knitter: In 1 week 7,000 dozen T-shirts were made (192 shirts were cut at one time). The T-shirts, and the athletic shirts, were bleached and dyed into approximately 25 colors—a process involving 35,000 pounds of salt per week. Some 6 million yards of thread were used in a week. The new industry also sewed private labels in garments for customers including Sears, Roebuck & Co., Zayre, Target Stores, and T.G. & Y., Division of City Products. The plant provided over 1,000 new jobs, primarily to women and Blacks who previously had been employed in low-paying, unskilled jobs, or were unemployed.

As a participant observer, having lived in this parish for 30 years, I was keenly aware of the economic changes occurring in this community as a result of this new industry. For example, the number of new cars on the road increased. This condition inevitably led to long traffic lines, especially on payday. City officials were forced to study the problem of traffic flow; as a result, left turn lanes and "no left turns" signs at intersections were introduced. Two new banking institutions opened. White housewives in the community were busily calling around to find domestics to work, as so many ex-domestic workers were now employed by the new industry. In addition, two new day-care centers appeared. Throughout the community, people were talking about the new industry.

THE QUESTIONS I HAD

For me, the ecologically relevant concern was the nature of changes that might be occurring in the family and in the community as a result of this new form of employment. I wanted to study families where women experienced a significant change in occupation. As both a resident of this town and a researcher, I knew the potential for change that might accompany changing financial circumstances. The objective of my study was to determine, using an ecological approach, the impact on new employees, their families, and the community when a new industry locates in a small community. A family (however it is configured) resides in its own unique community, which views the occupational roles of adult family members in distinct ways. In general, major changes that occur to any member of the family affect all members, and ultimately the community.

Specifically, the following questions were raised: (a) What is the impact on the family when women, who are generally the primary socializing agents for children, have a new job with a daily financial earning capability equal to their former weekly salary, and with new working conditions and requirements, such as large numbers of coworkers, a large physical plant, and assembly lines? (b) Are there specific circumstances to which the new industry employee and her family must adjust? (c) How is the adjustment of the new employee affected by the length of employment? (d) What are the social and academic consequences for children whose mothers shift from low-paying, unskilled jobs to higher paying jobs? (e) Are there substantial social and economic changes in the lifestyle of the family?

TACKLING MY QUESTIONS

I designed a study that included 218 women reflecting local employment patterns. All were identified through their place of employment, except those in the domestic group; these women were identified through a nomination process, as this is the typical way in which domestics are hired. Of the 83 women (both Black and White) employed in the new industry, one third had been employed for approximately 1 year, and two-thirds for 3 years. The new industry workers were compared with three other groups of women who were employed in typical jobs in the community: the first comparison group was composed of 34 women employed by a local factory that provided traditional unskilled and low-skilled jobs; all women in this group were Black. The second comparison group was composed of 35 women employed in the domestic area (private households) in the local community; all women in this group too were Black. The third comparison group was composed of 66 professionals (teachers); this group included both Black and White women.

My psychology students interviewed all of the participants in their homes for approximately 1 hr. The structured questionnaire was designed to assess background data (age, marital status, children, education, etc.), the work situation (problems, pressures, satisfaction, motivation, reinforcement, etc.), effects on the lives of children (child care, school achievement, achievement motivation), social and leisure time activities, and the general use of the added income.

DEMOGRAPHICS

The majority (52%) of the new industry workers were young women, between the ages of 18 and 33; the percentage was higher for the Black workers, perhaps because it was the younger domestic workers who shifted to the new industry. Workers in the domestic comparison group were 42 years of age and older, with one person over 65. The majority of factory workers (61%) and professionals (74%) were younger than 42.

In this traditional community a large majority of the participants were married. Within the families of the 218 women, 462 children were identified, almost half of whom were 12 years of age or younger. Black workers accounted for a higher proportion of working mothers with children ages 5 years or younger. As expected, the data on educational achievement indicated that domestic workers had the lowest average grade level completed (4.97); factory workers had completed 8.32 grades, and the new industry workers 10.8 grades. Of course the professional workers had all completed college.

The academic achievement of elementary, junior high, and high school students in the areas of mathematics and reading was obtained from the Metropolitan Achievement Tests. Although both national and local percentile scores were provided, only local scores were used, as the primary objective of the study (regarding the academic performance of children) was to evaluate the group performance of children whose mothers work in differing occupations in the local community.

WHAT I LEARNED

As economic change comes to a community, the people there are also changed in some way. One aspect of this study was to look at the impact of change over time (1 vs. 3 years of employment in the new industry). In addition, comparisons of race, of new industry workers with workers in traditional jobs in the community, and of childrearing practices and family concerns were studied, 4 years after the textile plant had opened. Generally, the results indicated no real differences in the groups based on years of employment, except in a few areas. For example, the majority of the workers who had been employed for 3 years at the new industry earned higher salaries. Although both 1- and 3-year workers were satisfied with the job, the 3-year workers specifically complained about being "bored with doing the same job." The 3-year workers also reported more behavior problems with their children. Possibly the work at the new industry was more demanding and less flexible than domestic work. There was pressure on the workers to "make production," and the resulting stress may have been directed at their children. Mothers may have had less energy to interact with or supervise their children. Over time, problems with children increased.

The demographic data indicate that the new industry attracted young married women with school-age children, especially young Black women who previously had been employed in unskilled jobs. They viewed this job as an opportunity to earn more money and contribute to a better way of life for their families, and thereby empower themselves and their families. White women, who traditionally have not entered the labor force as readily, did so because they were not previously employed, and thus had available time to work. The new industry also attracted women who had completed only 2 years of high school; for women with so little education, it provided the only option for a higher wage.

White industry workers, the majority of whom had been housewives, were concerned with the job and its encroachment on their free time. Their specific job complaints centered around having to work extra hours and on Saturdays. Black workers had a different perspective: because of their previous work experience, they were most concerned about the fringe benefits. Their major complaint was having various personal leaves without pay. Despite the complaints, both Black and White workers stated that their husbands and children expressed satisfaction with their having this job.

A high level of similarity between Black and White industry workers was evidenced in areas concerned with children: their preschool children were cared for by relatives; discipline involved a variety of methods, especially verbal interaction; a number of responsibilities and duties were expected of children, as was educational improvement.

The children of the textile industry workers showed an improvement from 1973 to 1974 in their reading and mathematics scores, while the scores of the children whose mothers worked in the local factory declined. The improved scores may reflect the greater educational achievement of the industry worker parents relative to the local factory worker parents (10.8 vs. 8.3 years of school). In addition, a large majority of the industry worker families subscribed to newspapers and magazines. Both Black and White industry workers reported that their children aspired to professional careers. Children of White workers were more likely also to indicate marriage as a future goal.

The armed services were a more frequent career choice of the children of Black 3-year workers; traditionally, Blacks have been overrepresented there. The creation, in 1973, of the Volunteer Army (VA), with its bonuses, job security, and educational, health, and VA housing benefits, caused many young people to view military service as a viable career option. Having any career was important during this time of inflation and unemployment.

In the area of family relationships, the new industry workers appeared to be moving closer to the kinds of family activities typical of professional workers. For example, only the new industry workers and the professional workers were high on the Index of Family Togetherness measure. Black 3-year workers were especially likely to engage in many activities—such as eating out, going to athletic events, and going to movies—as a family unit; each of these activities requires financial resources. This reflected a change from women in the domestic group. Another change in the new industry workers was the much greater number who had both a checking and savings account (62%), compared with domestic workers (23%) and factory workers (10%). The new industry workers associated somewhat with other workers from their same unit, but in general spent their free time with family members. They reported visiting relatives either daily or weekly. They did not play card games at home, nor did they frequent nightclubs. Only the Black 1-year industry workers gave small house parties. This may reflect their pleasure at having additional income. The family members in all of the groups reported going shopping and attending church services together.

Because of the additional income, families now seemed to have a broader view of what was possible in their lives. All of the workers hoped for a better life, and were especially concerned about the future education of their children. They no longer seemed relegated to the traditional life pattern of this small community. As an observer of this community, I predicted additional positive changes in the future for the families and the community, as a result of the new economic empowerment.

REFLECTIONS

As I reflect on the community and the changes that occurred, I am impressed with the impact a positive economic change can produce. As I was so close to the community, my primary concern with conducting the research was not what positive impact this would have on my career (although it did), but rather what would be the local benefits of my research to the community. This position is one that is a consistent theme throughout this *Monograph*, specifically the commitments of Caucus members to using scientific research results for the overall, direct benefit of African American communities.

Given my beliefs, I directed much of my energies locally. I shared my research findings with the administration of the new industry and with government officials. I made several presentations to local and regional conferences on poverty. Area newspapers provided a great deal of publicity regarding the study. They were concerned about the causes of poverty and with the development of some positive solutions. I even received a congratulatory telephone call from the President of my university. Subsequent to release of the study results, I did receive my promotion to Associate Professor.

Although I no longer live in this community, I continue to be involved with public service projects designed to improve the economic conditions of the area, and to attenuate the psychological effects of chronic poverty. As a result of these collaborative efforts with other public servants, today industry in the community is flourishing and all segments of the community are benefiting.

Throughout this *Monograph*, the message is clear—members of this Caucus were, and are, concerned with the welfare of African American children, their families, and their communities. I personally think future generations of researchers should begin with this concern and let it guide their research.

REFERENCE

Public Affairs Research Council of Louisiana Inc. (1973). *Statistical profile of parishes*. Baton Rouge: Author.

X. THE "HISTORY" OF TWO MILESTONE DEVELOPMENTAL PUBLICATIONS ON BLACK CHILDREN

Several colleagues have been important to the viability, vitality, and virtual survival of a Black presence and perspective in the Society for Research in Child Development (SRCD). When considered from the perspective of the 21st century, a couple are now deceased, others have changed their priorities over the years, while several remain very highly invested in the initial mission of importing greater cultural diversity into SRCD. Considering the original group, the sensitivity and responsiveness of many of SRCD's often weary but resilient African American scholars, collectively, remain an integral part of the improved approaches to Black child development research specifically and the field of child development more broadly. This group of resilient Black scholars includes Diana Slaughter-Defoe (then Slaughter), the late John McAdoo, Harriette McAdoo, the late Jean Carew, Aline Garrett, Ura Jean Oyemade-Bailey (then Oyemade), Algea Harrison-Hale (then Harrison), and John Dill. Although not long out of the academy themselves, all portrayed a spirit of commitment and steady engagement to the task of insuring that the experiences of children of color would not be ignored in the written and spoken representations of developmental science. Their strong and unwavering message was that human development theorizing, empirical demonstrations of inherent processes, and interpretive frameworks should and would include African American children's experiences.

This is *not* to say that all were similarly endowed with a fighting spirit to push for the group's physical and full presence in the business of the Society. Nor were all equally persistent and hard nosed in pushing for a conceptual representation of inclusiveness in the literature at all cost, for broadly acquired lessons of raw competitiveness were not lost on this group, and an instinct for professional survival was strong. Nevertheless, there was a commitment to perpetuating and promoting integrated perspectives that focused on the lives of African American children specifically, and on the humanity of Black people and their contextually and historically linked

113

experiences more generally. That was the context of professional growth and development for graduate students and newly minted Ph.D. professionals in the early 1970s.

FIRST MILESTONE: *BEGINNINGS*

In 1973, at the urging of one of my professors, Diana Slaughter, I attended my first SRCD meeting in Philadelphia. I was then completing my second year as a doctoral student at the University of Chicago's Committee on Human Development. The 1973 meeting was the first in which Black developmentalists gathered as an organization. At the 1975 meeting, gathering as a "Black Caucus," we decided to present a slate of members who would be willing to participate in various roles within SRCD. My name appeared on the slate, and subsequently an invitation was extended to me for membership on the Summer Institutes and Study Group Committee, one of several standing committees of SRCD. I served three 2-year terms (1977–1983) on the Committee and used the knowledge accrued to familiarize myself and the Caucus membership with the Committee's important role in providing resources for specialized meetings, and thus promoting the publication and dissemination of developmental science.

During the 1975 SRCD Meeting in Denver, CO, it was suggested that a volume on social and affective processes of Black children was needed. I later used the experiences obtained from participation in the Summer Institutes and Study Group Committee to write a proposal for a Study Group Meeting on African American children. I invited the participation of two other young colleagues, a developmental psychologist, Geraldine Kearse Brookins, and a sociologist interested in Black families, Walter R. Allen. In the spring of 1979, following the San Francisco SRCD meeting, Geraldine Brookins and I met at Jackson State University (Mississippi) to plan for creating the Study Group Meeting. Later that year, Walter Allen consented to join the effort. We worked on a preliminary proposal that was submitted and funded ($2,400) to begin work on a two-part Study Group Meeting, and the writing process was begun.

An initial planning meeting, held in December 1979 at Emory University in Atlanta, was attended by the editors along with Glen Elder and Diana Slaughter. Given the importance and complexity of the issues to be addressed, we decided that the Study Group should meet over a 2-year period. We continued the process by phone and mail and produced a full proposal that was submitted and funded as a two-part Study Group Meeting in 1980 ($7,000).

Scholars representing multiple disciplines were invited to write chapters. Interest in participating was enthusiastic; no one declined the invitation. Finally, in 1985, our work was published in a volume entitled *Beginnings: The Social and Affective Development of Black Children* (Spencer, Brookins, & Allen, 1985): it explored the complex processes of Black child development in the area of social-affective functioning and as linked with maturational processes and social experiences in diverse contexts.

The funding from SRCD was augmented with support from the Carnegie Foundation and the Foundation for Child Development. In addition to financial support and the enthusiastic participation of the contributors (to be discussed later), substantial support was also obtained from several individuals. Donna Banks provided me with significant assistance on tasks ranging from preparing proposals to arranging meetings. University of Michigan-based support from graduate assistants such as Aisha Ray, Anne-Marie Debritto, Blondell Strong, and Angelle Cooper was invaluable. Ed Sammons and Nesha Haniff provided further support. Collectively, the coeditors had additional funded projects for work related to the publication of *Beginnings* from the National Institute of Mental Health, the Spencer Foundation, the Charles Stewart Mott Foundation, the Ford Foundation, and the Rockefeller Foundation. It was unmistakably a collaborative, non-competitive, and interdependent process that, more than likely, provided the foundation for the editors' extremely close relationship today—some 20 years later!

While we were in the throes of implementing and publishing this scholarly product, the SRCD Black Caucus lost a central member of its core: Jean V. Carew (1936–1981). Accordingly, the volume was dedicated to her memory: "Committed scholar, faithful colleague, and friend of Black children." Because of the seminal role of University of Chicago professor Edgar Epps in the professional development of two of the editors, he was invited to write the foreword to the volume. There Professor Epps proclaimed the foundational role of the volume for altering preconceived notions concerning Black children and families. In noting long-term conceptual shortcomings in the field, Epps acknowledged the important normative stance provided in the volume and its "rigorous examination of children and youth from a pluralist perspective while maintaining a developmental focus" (Spencer et al., 1985, p. xiii) Epps also observed that the questions pursued and issues highlighted in the book acknowledged the central theme of adaptive lifestyles (rather than the usual a priori assumptions of psychopathology and deviance) and recognized the volume's relevance to other populations.

Another important acknowledgement by Epps was the volume's linkage to earlier generations of Black scholars: E. Franklin Frazier, sociologist and expert on the Black family; Charles S. Johnson, sociologist and expert on

Black youth; Allison Davis, anthropologist and expert on childrearing practices and ability testing; and Kenneth Clark and Mamie Clark, experimental psychologists and experts on racial self-image. Epps also pointed out the debt to early scholars, including the historians W. E. B. Du Bois and John Hope Franklin, economist Vivian Henderson, and educator Horace Mann Bond. Epps concluded his foreword with thoughts on how the collection of essays would serve as an important addition to "knowledge concerning the ways in which racial experiences—experiences that are shaped by the societal patterns of subordination and superordination—affect childrearing patterns and family and individual coping styles" (p. xv). Epps posited that *Beginnings* was a good title because it reflects not only an emphasis on early childhood development but also the authors' perceptions that important work from a specifically "Black perspective is in its beginning phases" (p. xiv). Epps's conclusion represents the "heart" of many discussions the authors had concerning the need to express just that duality: the "newness" of the field and the emphasis on the early years of life. As indicated by Epps's foreword, the contributors were colleagues both known and unknown to one another. All were known by their ideas and became known personally through the process of collaboration.

After much serious thought and discussion, the book was organized in three parts, each of which represented particular issues and special needs. Part 1, "Orienting Issues for the Study of Black Children," described major conceptual concerns; these were viewed as powerful orienting perspectives, such as the changing social science perspectives on Afro-American life and culture, depicted by V. P. Franklin. Diana Slaughter, and Gerald P. McWorter tracked the impact of the University of Chicago school of thought on the views held by scholars and the general public about Black people. John U. Ogbu's chapter emphasizes a particular cultural ecological analysis of competence among inner-city Black youths, and Glen H. Elder's chapter offered his well-known perspective by emphasizing historical perspectives and analyses.

Part 2, "Research and Theory on Black Child Development," contained sections on (a) social competence (with contributions by Vonnie C. McLoyd, Elsie G. J. Moore, Bertha Garrett Holliday, Yvonne Abatso, John Dill, Ewart A. C. Thomas, and Urie Bronfenbrenner); (b) identity (contributions by William E. Cross, Jr., Leachim Tufani Semaj, Marguerite N. Alejandro-Wright, Bruce Robert Hare and Louis A. Castenell, Jr., Margaret Beale Spencer, and Morris Rosenberg); and (c) family (contributions by Velma LaPoint and colleagues, Geraldine Kearse Brookins, Walter R. Allen, and Aimee Dorr).

Finally, in Part 3 the editors provided a group synthesis of theories, policy implications, and recommendations (Chapter XVII). The richness of the book's content resulted in unusual success for an edited volume and the accrual of healthy royalties to SRCD. In sum, the volume was considered one of Erlbaum's great successes, having sold more than 2,400 copies since 1985. It went into a second printing, and was ultimately published in a soft-cover edition. Erlbaum editors indicate the volume is still in print.[1] This success and visibility had other unexpected outcomes.

SECOND MILESTONE: A SPECIAL ISSUE OF *CHILD DEVELOPMENT*

Between 1986 and 1994, I served on the Advisory Board of the W. T. Grant Foundation's Young Scholars Program. Also on the Board, along with anthropologists, medical researchers, cognitive scientists, and social workers, was another developmental psychologist, Willard (Bill) Hartup (Emeritus of University of Minnesota), who had maintained a long-term affiliation with the SRCD journal, *Child Development*. As we dined at lunch, between review sessions of the Board, Bill inquired why I was not submitting manuscripts to *Child Development*. To his astonishment, I responded in earnest that my experience (along with others') was that the journal lacked interest in my program of research, which integrated the role of race and the experience of racialized contexts. To his credit, Bill suggested that I submit a proposal for a special issue or partial issue of *Child Development*.

The partial-issue idea was based upon an assumption that there might not be sufficient research of the quality required for a full journal. I reassured Bill that there was no shortfall of projects—just an apparent lack of editorial interest. Because Vonnie McLoyd had editorial experience with the *Child Development*, Hartup suggested that I consider her as a coeditor. I then spoke with several Caucus members, including Professors Allen, Brookins, and Slaughter, who concurred that it would be an important opportunity for the Caucus. This project, however, lacked the collegial, interdependent, and collaborative effort that developed in the evolution of *Beginnings*: Vonnie McLoyd and I had no previous relational history as scholars, and our training experiences as graduate students, at the University of Michigan and University of Chicago, respectively, were apparently very different.

Despite our different perspectives and competitive styles, we forged a partnership and planned a strategy. A call for papers on the theme of "Minority Child Development" was published in *Child Development* in August 1987. Given the ongoing nondevelopmental, deficit oriented, and often psychopathological character of the published literature on minority children at the time, we chose to emphasize papers that focused on minority child development themes and family processes, peer socialization, ecological contexts outside the home, and economic conditions. McLoyd and

I each took responsibility for half of the submitted papers and solicited evaluations from, at minimum, three reviewers. As was typical for the journal, all submissions were blind reviewed. In each case, two of the three reviewers were chosen by one guest editor and the third was recommended by the other. For the most part, the review process was implemented in a parallel fashion. In all, 76 manuscripts were received for review with 45 (59%) focusing on African American children, 27 (35%) on Hispanic children, and only four (5%) on Asian children. Some manuscripts had a single ethnic focus (e.g., African Americans alone), whereas others embraced African Americans along with another group. As with *Beginnings*, we wished to include papers representing a particular viewpoint or issue in need of emphasis. Accordingly, three scholars were invited to submit papers, and each coeditor submitted a paper. The reviews for the coeditors were handled by the journal editor, Bill Hartup.

The process of implementing the production of this volume was also quite different from that of *Beginnings*, especially in terms of support. For example, although there was little or no institutional support at my home institution, McLoyd's activities were generally advised and supported by Harold W. Stevenson of the University of Michigan. Because of the nature of the blind review process, colleagues around the country, such as Slaughter, Allen, and Brookins, provided collegial support. The task benefited from over 200 reviewers participating at some level in the process! When published as Volume 61(2) of *Child Development* in April 1990, the special issue included an Introduction Section with two papers by the coeditors, a Review section with the solicited papers from Cynthia Garcia-Coll (focusing on minority infant developmental outcomes), Algea Harrison and colleagues (on minority family ecologies), Slaughter-Defoe and colleagues (on minority children schooling and achievement) and the coeditors (McLoyd emphasizing economic hardship on Black families and children, Spencer and colleague focusing on identity processes and racial and ethnic minority children. From the 76 manuscripts received for review, 19 were selected for publication, bringing the number of papers in the volume to 26. Thus this special issue presented over 326 pages of journal space on minority children and families, a topic that continues to be underaddressed. In terms of sheer volume, nothing like it has been published in a trade (organization based) journal since that time.

PVEST: A PATH TO THE FUTURE

Although *Beginnings* and the special issue of *Child Development* were very different, both provided important mechanisms for the distillation of ideas

118

generally underrepresented in traditional publishing venues, and both had a clear impact on the field. In many ways, the issues they addressed have become more complex since majority researchers have become accustomed to including more diverse samples; however, their interpretational perspectives remain myopic, at best, particularly when interpreting the behavior of culturally diverse children. This myopia may have been sustained by the recent pattern of large "collaborative research networks" still lacking senior minority perspectives. Certainly, given the increasing competitiveness of the social science research enterprise and the fierce competition for research funding, some minorities themselves have learned the benefit of virtual silence when "at the table" as a mechanism for securing professional rewards and recognition.

Most discouraging, of course, is the dwindling supply of minority social and behavioral scientists. The number of minority social scientists who graduated across multiple disciplines from the University of Chicago reached a peak between 1973 and 1983, and the same is true of similar research universities. A recent research report published by the *Journal of Blacks in Higher Education* (Ranking America's Leading Universities on Their Success in Integrating African Americans, 2002) indicates that the University of Chicago (where the author received her doctorate) received the lowest diversity ranking, virtually tied with Johns Hopkins University and California Institute of Technology.

Projects such as *Beginnings* and the *Special Issue of Child Development* served as important collegial processes for the coeditors, made significant impacts on the field more generally, represented notable achievements for the Caucus, and possibly illuminated paths to the future. For example, to be included in the sixth *Handbook of Child Psychology*, I have had the opportunity to expand and develop the phenomenological variant of ecological systems theory (PVEST), a new theoretical model I introduced in 1995 (Spencer, 1995).[2]

As indicated in both *Beginnings* and the *Special Edition of Child Development*, a priori assumptions of pathology continue to characterize theoretical assumptions of Black youths' development. PVEST is an identity-focused cultural ecological (ICE) perspective and a sensitive heuristic device capable of analyzing human development irrespective of race, ethnicity, social class, gender, immigration status, and any other human factor. As such, this framework, initiated during the first 25 years of the Black Caucus of SRCD should mark another milestone in the study of Black child development.

REFERENCES

Ranking America's Leading Universities on Their Success in Integrating African Americans. (2002). *The Journal of Blacks in Higher Education*, **36**, 87–98.

Spencer, M. B. (1995). Old issues and new theorizing about African American youth: A phenomenological variant of ecological systems theory. In R. L. Taylor (Ed.), *Black youth: Perspectives on their status in the United States* (pp. 37–69). Westport, CT: Praeger.

Spencer, M. B., Brookins, G. K. & Allen, W. R. (Eds.). (1985). *Beginnings: The social and affective development of Black children*. Hillsdale, NJ: Erlbaum.

Spencer, M. B., & McLoyd, V. (Eds.). (1990). Minority children [special issue]. *Child Development*, **61** (2).

NOTES

1. Lori Stone and Rebecca Larsen (personal communication, August 22, 2005). The information in this paragraph was provided by Stone and Larsen, who are current editors at Lawrence Erlbaum Associates Inc. in Mahwah, NJ. All royalties on the volume were directed to SRCD.

2. A recent invitation extended to me by Editors-in-Chief William Damon and Richard Lerner, for the sixth Edition of the *Handbook of Child Psychology* (expected to appear in 2006), suggests an additional and unique opportunity for impacting the field. The 100-plus-page manuscript I am preparing for the *Handbook* focuses on a theoretical framework of normal human development which was originally synthesized (Spencer, 1995) specifically to include minority *and* majority group human beings: a PVEST. The current project significantly expands the original paper. Among other improvements in the project are: explication and integration of historical and policy contributions such as the Brown versus Board of Education Decision on the field of child development; emphasis on the theory's application for diverse groups, including privileged individuals and immigrants; and the introduction of a dual-axis model of PVEST for more specifically demonstrating resilience and vulnerability.

XI. THE ROLE OF AFRICAN AMERICAN SCHOLARS IN RESEARCH ON AFRICAN AMERICAN CHILDREN: HISTORICAL PERSPECTIVES AND PERSONAL REFLECTIONS

First published in 1930, *Child Development* has been an official publication of the Society for Research in Child Development (SRCD) since 1936. It is distinguished by its preeminence, wide dissemination, and longevity as an outlet and repository for research and theory in child development. As such, *Child Development* exerts a major influence on what emerges as canons of the discipline. Three issues related to the journal have been of long-standing concern to African American scholars: the rate at which research on African American children and families appears there (i.e., the percentage of articles focusing on African American children of the total number of articles published in the journal during any 1 year), the nature of that research, and the involvement of African American scholars in the editorial process. This essay highlights some personal experiences and chronicles historical events of particular relevance to these issues.

The essay is divided into two major sections. The first focuses attention on changes in the field of child development within two broad domains: (a) the quantity and quality of research articles about African American children and (b) editorial policies relevant to the diversity of subject populations represented in *Child Development*. I begin with reflections about personal encounters that stimulated my interest in historical perspectives on the study of African American families and children. This is followed by a summary of findings from research studies examining secular changes in the rate and nature of research on African American children appearing in *Child Development*, and cohort differences in the professional lives of African American scholars in the field of human development. Several indicators, including recent efforts that track the race/ethnicity of research samples, editorial statements, and instructions to authors, are interpreted as evidence of heightened sensitivity to the race and ethnicity of research samples. This section concludes with an analysis of the role of the SRCD's Committee on Ethnic and Racial Issues (formerly the Committee on

121

Minority Participation (COMP), and the Black Caucus of SRCD in forging these changes. The second section of the essay is devoted to a discussion of the emergence of African American scholars as critics and arbiters of developmental theory and research. It chronicles appointments of African American scholars to the Editorial Board of *Child Development* and as Associate Editors of *Child Development*. I conclude that (a) notable progress has been made on several fronts, but it is measured in small steps, not major leaps; (b) advances are products of dynamic processes across distinct networks of researchers in the discipline, with their ultimate epigenesis lying in societal forces such as the civil rights movement; and (c) proactive strategies of scholars of color figure prominently as precursors of these advances.

RESEARCH ON AFRICAN AMERICAN CHILDREN AND FAMILIES

In 1976, Robert Guthrie, a psychologist then employed by the Psychological Sciences Division of the Office of Naval Research, published a provocative, well-researched historical analysis of the field of psychology in relation to the issue of race. Aptly entitled *Even the Rat Was White: A Historical View of Psychology*, Guthrie's treatise detailed the Eurocentric approach and racist themes that marked the early psychological and anthropological study of African Americans. He presented copious evidence of White researchers' obsession with cataloguing race differences, measuring human physical characteristics (e.g., skin color, hair texture, thickness of lips) as criteria for racial classifications, and mental testing of African Americans, especially children. Guthrie also focused attention on early African American psychologists in the academy (i.e., those awarded doctorates in psychology and educational psychology between 1920 and 1950), providing information about their training, professional achievements, career patterns, and roles as critics and professors of psychology at Black colleges and universities. Anticipating persistent criticisms and controversies that mark the study of African Americans to this day (Garcia Coll et al., 1996; Huston, McLoyd, & Garcia Coll, 1997; Jones, 1991; Rowe & Rodgers, 1997), these early scholars protested against invidious racial comparisons, the use of psychological tests normed with White samples only, and claims that genetic factors underlie psychological differences between African Americans and Whites (Guthrie, 1976).

Guthrie's book, published 1 year after I received my Ph.D., had a singularly profound impact on my sensibilities and academic pursuits as an African American psychologist. It psychologically and intellectually anchored me to these early, beleaguered pioneers, bestowing a stabilizing sense of historical place, continuity, and belonging. It also nurtured an enduring interest in historical trends in published research on African American children. What accounted for the personal poignancy and transformative powers of this book? As I reflect on this question, four factors stand out: (a) it was powerfully written, laying bare in copious detail the alliance between "science" and racism; (b) it was written by an African American scholar; (c) one of the early African American psychologists cited in the book was an inspiring and imposing man whom I held in high esteem, Herman Hodge Long, who was president of Talladega College (where I was an undergraduate) and had received his PhD from my graduate alma mater, the University of Michigan; and (d) it evoked childhood memories of African Americans' obsession with skin color and hair texture, born of racial discrimination and caste barriers, and all manner of ways in which those of us with dark skin and coarse hair were disadvantaged by the prevailing value system.

Several other forces, taken together, consolidated my interest in the treatment of race within psychology. Myers, Rana, and Harris's (1979) annotated bibliography of the research and writings published on African American children in the major social science journals between 1927 and 1977 underscored the importance of a firm grasp of prior research and its biases as essential to the advancement of the field. The thoughtful discussions at the Conferences on Empirical Research in Black Psychology gave top billing to new concepts and innovative, rigorous methodologies as gateways to insights about race and psychological issues (Boykin, Franklin, & Yates, 1979). Initiated in 1974 by a small group of young African American psychologists, these invitational conferences brought together 25 or so scholars to discuss and critique their empirical research on African Americans. The conferences were not affiliated with any professional organization. Supported by a variety of sources, including the National Institute of Mental Health, the conferences have been convened throughout the years, in rotation, by A. Wade Boykin, A. J. Franklin, J. Frank Yates, Harriette McAdoo, John McAdoo, Algea Harrison, and William Cross. With the exception of Franklin and Cross, all received Ph.D.s from the University of Michigan, foreshadowing the emergence of a comparatively large, active, and close-knit network of African American research psychologists with doctorates from this institution.

Graduate training at the University of Michigan (1971–1975) increased my knowledge about developmental research on African American children and how that research is linked to sociohistorical context and the characteristics and interests of the "knower." Much of the extant research struck me as sterile and pejorative, the product of scholars who lacked even rudimentary knowledge about the culture of African Americans. I began to comprehend that African Americans were especially well placed to make certain contributions to the field by virtue of perspectives, experiences, and knowledge that typically set them apart from their academic colleagues (e.g., experiences of legalized discrimination, intimacy with elements of African American culture, propinquity to economic hardship by virtue of their own life histories). Among these potential contributions were the identification of ethnocentric concepts, the proffering of alternative explanations of African American behavior, and the development of research informed by their duality of experiences in the Black community and in White society.

Any doubts I might have had about the importance of these contributions have long since been dispelled (McLoyd, 1994; Washington & McLoyd, 1982). Although contests of ideas are at the core of mainstream psychology, the issue of race can readily transform these contests into high-stakes intellectual battles that bear on both policy and practice. Ours is a nation that has been transfixed and transformed by race and racial oppression since its inception, where the visible marker of "race" is a major determinant of social location and economic opportunity, and where racial segregation is evident in virtually all contexts. It is no exaggeration to say that race *is* the prime American dilemma (Hacker, 1992; Moskos & Butler, 1996).

The context of my graduate training afforded experiences that engendered optimism and confidence in the collective capacities of African American psychologists to meet these intellectual challenges. By the early 1970s, a critical mass of African American students was pursuing graduate study in the Department of Psychology at the University of Michigan. These graduate students established a tradition of activism (e.g., vigorous recruiting of African American students from historically Black colleges, evaluating the credentials of African American applicants and making recommendations to admissions committees within the Department, developing and implementing community service projects) and regularized various mechanisms to support newcomers both intellectually and socially (e.g., study groups and orientations for entering graduate students). Most were enthusiastic and involved members of the Black Student Psychological Association, and many had backgrounds similar to mine (e.g., hailing from Southern states having graduated from small, historically Black, liberal arts colleges). These experiences fostered a collective sense of identity, efficacy, and destiny, while mitigating feelings of personal vulnerability and alienation in this new environment. My recollections of this unique period in my development are in full accord with data suggesting that a critical mass of students and faculty of color augurs well for morale because it reduces the perception of tokenism, gives voice to the concerns of people of color, and increases prospects that these concerns will be addressed in a productive manner (Jones, 1990; Stricker, 1990).

124

Appraising the Treatment of African Americans in Child Development Research

The work of Guthrie and others cited above raised for me the question of whether published research on African Americans had really changed over time. As a developmental psychologist who was now an Assistant Professor of Psychology at the University of Michigan, I decided to focus on the representation of African American children and their families in the preeminent journal in the field, *Child Development*. Super's (1982) analysis of secular trends in research published in *Child Development*, using 10 randomly chosen articles from each year between 1930 and 1979 (totaling 500 articles), solidified this plan of action and provided very helpful guideposts. To bring my project to fruition, I enlisted the assistance of Suzanne Randolph, an African American graduate student in Michigan's Developmental Psychology Program at the time, and several other African American graduate students from allied fields.

Using an explicit set of criteria, we identified 215 research articles published in *Child Development* between 1936 and 1980 that focused on African American children or adolescents. Each article was coded for over 25 variables concerning characteristics of the research sample, the topical focus of the study, the research methodology, and the nature of the discussion and interpretation of the research findings. In keeping with the observations of Guthrie (1976) and Myers et al. (1979), as well as findings from a content analysis of articles about African American children published in over 20 journals between 1973 and 1975 (McLoyd & Randolph, 1984), we found that the number of race-comparative studies in the selected *Child Development* volumes was almost twice that of race-homogeneous studies (i.e., studies with only African American children as research participants). Moreover, all race-comparative studies had White children as a comparison group (though several had children from other ethnic minority groups as a comparison group as well).

The rate of published articles concerning African American children was extremely low between 1936 and 1965, increased gradually between 1966 and 1970, rose sharply between 1971 and 1975, and declined thereafter. Notable changes over time in both directions also were evident in (a) the proportion of studies that were race-comparative, (b) the prevalence of methodological and interpretational problems in studies (e.g., confounding race and social class, nonspecification of children's social class background, nonspecification of experimenters' race, overgeneralization of findings), (c) authors' tendencies to explicitly espouse a deficit model to characterize or explain African American children's behavior, and (d) authors' tendency to discuss methodological factors that threatened the validity of the findings (McLoyd & Randolph, 1985). We speculated about the influence of social and political changes in American society and forces

125

within the discipline of psychology itself that gave rise to these changes. Following the completion of this study, and under the auspices of the Center for Afro-American and African Studies at the University of Michigan, I taught an advanced undergraduate seminar focusing on the history of social science research on African Americans.

Meanwhile, another African American graduate student in Michigan's Developmental Psychology Program with whom I worked closely, Shirley Aisha Ray, became interested in cohort differences in the professional development of African American scholars in the field of human development. This interest eventuated in a small-scale study that Ray (1983) carried out independently during 1981–1982. Informed by writings on the professional experiences and perspectives of African American psychologists and other social scientists (e.g., Bayton, 1975; Davidson, 1973; Mitchell, 1982; Wispe, Awkward, Hoffman, Hicks, & Porter, 1969), Ray's study provided a unique opportunity for a subsample of these scholars to speak for themselves. She used four sources to identify potential study participants: (a) Directory of Some Black Americans Interested in Child Development Research, prepared by Diana Slaughter (1975); (b) SRCD Directory of Minority Members, compiled by Algea Harrison, Bettye Caldwell, I. Heras, and Lee C. Lee (1979); (c) Directory of Professionals and Researchers in the Area of Black Families, compiled by Marie Peters (1980); and (d) the participants list for the Sixth Conference on Empirical Research in Black Psychology, held at Oakland University in November, 1981). Ray then mailed letters to 60 scholars, requesting a $1\frac{1}{2}$-hour telephone interview. Eighteen letters were returned as undeliverable, but another 18 scholars were successfully contacted in a follow-up telephone call. All agreed to participate in the study, but only 15 completed the interview.

Respondents had received their doctorates between 1950 and 1981 and had published research on African American children and/or their families. Two cohorts, defined by the date their doctorate was awarded (pre-1970 [$n = 6$] vs. post-1970 [$n = 9$]), were compared to determine if length of time in the field moderated the nature and psychological impact of their professional experiences. The interview, consisting primarily of open-ended questions, focused on respondents' strategies for coping with multiple role expectations, professional experiences in the academy, and experiences in graduate school.

Among the salient themes emphasized by respondents were the following: (a) the untenability of the deficit model applied to African Americans and optimism that their past, current, and future research would help undermine the model's hegemony; (b) the field's devaluation of research on African Americans, as reflected in the difficulty scholars working in this area experienced in their attempts to secure research funds and publish in mainstream journals; (c) sparse human resources (e.g., lack of mentors, advocates, and research collaborators), combined with excessive demands for university service, as factors that put African American scholars in mainstream universities at high risk of running aground professionally; (d) feelings of marginality and alienation in their academic departments; (e) the special challenges involved in conducting research with African Americans (e.g., traveling long distances at considerable expense because many major research universities are situated in small cities away from large concentrations of African Americans; overcoming African Americans' justifiable suspicions of researchers' motives); (f) feelings of guilt and frustration produced by respondents' desire to lend their skills and expertise to serve needs in the Black community, on the one hand, and the absorptive and demanding nature of academic roles and the lack of rewards in mainstream academia for community service, on the other; and (g) the need for African American scholars to continue to build supportive links among themselves and to take a more proactive, rather than reactive, stance towards mainstream research.

Few cohort differences were found, with the exception that as graduate students, the older cohort had fewer African American professors and mentors and had contact with fewer African American graduate and undergraduate students than did the younger cohort. In sum, whereas over time the degree of physical/cultural isolation experienced during graduate training diminished, the stressors that African American scholars encountered in their roles as professors and researchers were not appreciably tempered. This study, with its interesting, though preliminary findings, established a base on which future research on this topic can profitably build (Ray, 1983).

Serendipitously, the completion of Ray's study and Randolph's and mine coincided with the call for papers for the 50th anniversary meeting of SRCD in 1983 in Detroit, the theme of which was the history of the Society, childhood, and child development research. Findings from these two studies were presented at the meeting as a part of a symposium that I organized and chaired, entitled "The Study of Afro-American Children and Families: An Historical Analysis." All of the symposium participants were African American scholars. In addition to the papers by Ray ("The Professional Development of African American Psychologists") and McLoyd and Randolph ("Trends in the Study of Afro-American Children"), a third paper was presented by Gerald A. McWorter, Department of Sociology, University of Illinois ("Social Origins of the Scientific Study of Afro-American Children and Families"). This last paper identified four early developments that had a major influence on the study of Black child development, giving special attention to the social science tradition established at the University of Chicago. The symposium discussants were John Dill (Department of Psychology, Memphis State University) and Vincent Franklin (Department of

History, Yale University). McWorter's paper was based on work that he and Diana Slaughter had recently completed, but Slaughter's name was omitted from the symposium because she already had the maximum number of submissions allowed for the conference. It was through a study group meeting held at Emory University and organized by Margaret Spencer, Geraldine Brookins, and Walter Allen that I became familiar with the work of Slaughter, McWorter, and Franklin on the origins of social science research on African American children and families. The study group resulted in Spencer, Brookins, and Allen's (1985) edited volume, *Beginnings: The Social and Affective Development of Black Children*. Slaughter and McWorter's (1985) paper on the social origins of the study of African American children and families was published in this volume.

Subsequent to the SRCD biennial meeting in 1983, Alice Boardman Smuts, chair of the subcommittee charged with planning the historical program of the 1983 meeting, and John Hagen, chair of the 1983 Program Committee, edited a volume of the *Monographs of the SRCD* that contained about one quarter of the historical papers from the meeting (Smuts & Hagen, 1985a). According to Smuts and Hagen (1985b), of 25 historical papers submitted by developmentalists for presentation at the meeting, 8 were accepted for the program and 1 for the *Monograph*. The latter was the paper by McLoyd and Randolph (1985), described above. Following the first round of reviews, a paper by Marie Peters (a member of the SRCD Black Caucus) analyzing 50 years of research on African American children was provisionally accepted for publication in the *Monograph*, but regrettably could not be included because of Peters's untimely death (Smuts & Hagen, 1985c).

Heightened Sensitivity to the Race and Ethnicity of Research Samples

Recent years have witnessed increased focus on the race and ethnicity of samples in published studies and papers presented at professional meetings. This focus has underscored the paucity of research on children of color and the need for redress. Three types of evidence signify this trend: recent studies that systematically track the rate and nature of research focusing on populations of color, editorial statements, and instructions to authors.

Tracking of Research Samples

Investigations that track changes in the quantity and quality of research on African American children and other children of color are important as markers of progress and regression in the discipline and its publication

128

outlets. They also are indispensable as levers to bring perceptions and reputations into line with reality when disparities exist. A study by Hagen and Conley (1994) of articles published in *Child Development* between 1980 and 1993 found that the rate of research on African Americans remained extremely low through the 1980s. The publication of the special issue on minority children, coedited by Spencer and McLoyd (1990), resulted in an increase in 1990 in the percentage of articles focused on African American children, followed by a decline in 1991. The rate increased sharply during 1992 and 1993, but whether this marked a real growth trend or was simply random variation remains unclear. Rates of research on Hispanics and Asian Americans were abysmally low throughout the 14-year period.

Publications other than *Child Development* also have been the object of systematic tracking. In her impressive study examining secular trends between 1970 and 1989 in the rate of published research on African Americans, Graham (1992) focused on six journals of the American Psychological Association, two of which publish a high percentage of articles focusing on child and adolescent development (i.e., *Journal of Educational Psychology* and *Developmental Psychology*). She found a steady decrease in the number and percentage of articles about African Americans (defined as those articles in which the authors specifically stated that African Americans were the population of interest or analyzed their data by race) as well as widespread methodological and reporting problems similar to those found in our analyses of *Child Development* (e.g., confounding of race and social class, nonspecification of experimenters' race, unacceptable criteria such as subjective impressions for defining social class).

Editorial Statements

As articulations of policy entered into the public record, editorial statements became another signal of increasing sensitivity to issues surrounding research on children of color. In her editorial marking the publication of the first volume (62) of *Child Development* completed under her editorship, Somerville (1991) affirmed that

> We endeavor to publish descriptions of the populations under study that are as complete as possible with regard to race, ethnicity, social class, and other defining characteristics, even though we recognize that not all of the information will be available for every paper. (p. 874)

She ventured that several sociocultural, economic, and broad societal shifts would broaden our views of development and present distinct challenges and opportunities to enrich our understanding of the interplay of various processes in development. One of these shifts, noted Somerville, is growth in the population of children of color, such that "by the middle of the next century the majority of children living in the United States will belong to what now are termed 'minority groups'" (p. 873). Although not explicitly encouraging submissions that focus on children of color or illuminate race and ethnicity as they bear on development, these statements acknowledge the importance of understanding development in these children.

The problem of inadequate descriptions of subject populations alluded to in Somerville's editorial statement was subsequently revealed to be remarkably severe. Hagen and Conley (1994) found that 50–70% of studies published in *Child Development* each year between 1980 and 1991 did not reveal the ethnic/racial composition of the research sample! Owing to Somerville's (1991) guidelines, a striking decline began after 1990 and continued through 1993 in the percentage of articles published in *Child Development* in which this information was omitted (from approximately 50% in 1990 to approximately 25% in 1993).

Five years later, in an editorial marking the end of her term as editor of *Child Development*, Somerville (1996) provided a gauge, albeit crude, of the breadth and diversity of articles published in the journal during her editorship. She noted, for example, that of the 400 empirical papers appearing in volumes 65–67 of *Child Development* (the last three volumes produced under her editorship), 28% were based on ethnic minorities residing in the United States or non-Western countries, and 34% reported studies in which participants were below middle class in socioeconomic status. A number of Somerville's annual reports to the Governing Council and the SRCD Publications Committee on the activities of the journal focused on a broad range of diversity issues. For example, many included data on the ethnicity, social class, and nationality (American vs. non-American) of samples in research studies published in *Child Development*, as well as data on the academic disciplines represented by authors of articles appearing in the journal.

In a statement appearing in the SRCD Newsletter, William Hall (1992), Chair of the SRCD Publications Committee from 1991 to 1993, tacitly acknowledged that the journal's record of disseminating research on children of color was a legitimate concern. The statement affirmed the Society's commitment to publishing research on diverse populations and to maintaining diverse Editorial Boards. However, because it specified no particular categories of diversity (e.g., ethnicity, class, discipline, nationality), commitment to ethnic diversity, in particular, could only be inferred. The statement read:

> At its recent meeting in New Orleans, the Publications Committee reaffirmed its commitment to producing publications of high scientific merit. The Committee also reaffirmed its commitment to diversity in the content of its publications and the make-up of our editorial reviewing boards. Several

activities are underway that will facilitate both of these commitments: (1) the increase in publication of articles not dealing solely with traditional mainstream populations; (2) the preparation of a document on the perils and prospects of determining the social class membership of non-middle-class subjects; and (3) the publication of special editions and special sections of *Child Development*. In addition to the three activities listed, the Publications Committee continues to consider ways of handling issues of opinion as expressed by the readership within our publications structure. We would be interested in your ideas and suggestions. (p. 4)

Instructions to Authors

Another significant development reflecting heightened sensitivity to the race and ethnicity of research samples involved the guidelines for submission of papers for presentation at the 1993 biennial meetings of SRCD. Distinguished from previous instructions by explicit attention to issues of racial and ethnic diversity, the guidelines stated:

> We [the Program Committee and the Governing Council] welcome submissions that extend or replicate prior studies with reference to populations that may have been under-represented in the original empirical investigation. ... We encourage organizers to include presenters with data from diverse racial and ethnic groups. ... All data-based submissions should include information on age, gender, race, and ethnicity of subjects. (Instructions for Submissions, 1993 SRCD Biennial Meetings, pp. 2–6).

Synergistic Forces of Change: Role of the SRCD Committee on Ethnic and Racial Issues (Formerly the COMP) and the Black Caucus of SRCD

The research studies conducted by Hagen and Conley (1994) and Graham (1992) built on and extended in important ways McLoyd and Randolph's (1984, 1985) content analyses of research on African American children published in *Child Development* and other human development journals. However, among the more immediate impetuses for Hagen and Conley's appraisal of *Child Development* were concerns persistently voiced by members of the SRCD Committee on Ethnic and Racial Issues and the Black Caucus of SRCD. While maintaining separate identities, these two entities traditionally have enjoyed collaborative, cooperative relations and pursued similar as well as complementary goals. Fostering this symbiotic relationship is the overlap in membership of the two entities that has existed since the point of their coexistence. Both the Committee and the Caucus have lamented the paucity of research published in *Child Development* about

African American children and other children of color and the omission of information about the race, ethnicity, and social class of research samples in published studies. The Committee on Ethnic and Racial Issues requested systematic monitoring of progress or lack thereof in these areas, as evidenced in minutes of its meetings and communications to the SRCD Governing Council during the late 1980s and early 1990s.

Hagen and Conley's (1994) research documenting trends in the race and ethnicity of children in studies published in *Child Development* was first presented at a meeting of the Committee on Ethnic and Racial Issues held October 1–2, 1992. Reflecting the sentiments expressed during that meeting, the Committee on Ethnic and Racial Issues, in its report to the Governing Council (dated March 10, 1993), requested documentation of shifts that might have occurred in several other characteristics of articles published in *Child Development* not reflected in Hagen and Conley's preliminary report, including (a) number of articles specifying socioeconomic status; (b) number of articles with context as the main variable and/or as part of the explanatory framework; and (c) number of studies of racial/ethnic minority samples based on a normative versus deficit framework. The Committee suggested that this information be presented in the SRCD Newsletter "inasmuch as we think that any progress in this area should be highlighted and commended" (p. 2). (Hagen and Conley's findings *were* subsequently published in the SRCD Newsletter.) The Committee went on to assert that:

> The publication process in *Child Development* exemplifies the core of the issues that this committee has been addressing for a while. One is the issue of increasing the diversity of the subjects upon which "normative" processes of development are documented. It is our impression that most of the literature on ethnic and racial minorities tend [*sic*] to concentrate on deficits at the same time that most studies of normative processes tend to concentrate on white, middle class populations. The importance of documenting normative processes in other racial, ethnic, and cultural populations need [*sic*] to be recognized and the Society needs to make a clear stand, as was done in the call for submissions to the program, throughout its publications. What this implies is that new methodologies which might be more ecologically relevant, less traditional, less psychometrically sound, exploratory, etc. will be welcomed in our publications. Also, replication studies with underrepresented populations will be allowed. In order to invite such submissions, the instructions to authors would clearly make such a statement. In addition, the instructions to reviewers should include the parameters to guide such reviews. ... The instructions to authors that appear in *Child Development* should clearly encourage submissions that address issues of diversity, including race and ethnicity. (p. 2)

In a similar vein, the explicit encouragement by the 1993 Program Committee of diverse racial and ethnic perspectives was a direct response to admonishments and proposals from the Committee on Ethnic and Racial Issues. In a letter (dated November 10, 1991) to Joy Osofsky, Co-Chair of the SRCD 1993 Program Committee, on behalf of the Committee on Ethnic and Racial Issues, Susan Crockenberg asserted:

> The membership as a whole remains unexposed to research across a range of content areas that provides new information about children from understudied ethnic and racial groups. We believe that the consequence of this lack of exposure is a continued neglect of research on children from these groups. In an attempt to remedy this situation, we have developed several proposals we would like to see incorporated in the 1993 SRCD program. . . . Specifically, we would like submissions to include information on the ethnic and racial composition of samples, and to have the directions to all panel chairs and reviewers include consideration of sample composition as a significant feature in evaluating the contribution of the research to the field. We would also like to see the membership encouraged to submit posters of research carried out with "minority" children to the area panels that reflect the content of the research, and to organize symposia that include participants whose research on the topic of interest has been carried out with children from diverse racial and ethnic groups.

The turn of events during the late 1980s and early 1990s made it clear that the issues facing the Society concerning racial and ethnic diversity were of such complexity and sensitivity that more dialogue among the key principals was essential (see minutes of the meetings of the Governing Council, April 26–27, 1989; April 16–17, 1991; March 13–15, 1992). In her role as Chair of the Committee on Ethnic and Racial Issues, Cynthia Garcia Coll attended a meeting of the editors of *Child Development* and the SRCD Publications Committee in October 1991. As described in the Publications Committee's report to the Governing Council (March 1993), the meeting was convened to:

> . . . discuss ways in which the editorial staff of *Child Development* can response [*sic*] to issues of importance to the membership of SRCD. . . . Among the points raised at that meeting was the need for more thorough reporting by manuscript authors of demographic information about research subjects. . . . The Publications Committee discussed the possibility of preparing a publication describing techniques useful for gathering such data and favored a recommendation to Governing Council that such a publication be considered. Governing Council responded favorably to the recommendation and the Publications Committee asked one of its members, Doris Entwisle, Department of Sociology, The Johns Hopkins University, to

prepare a paper describing techniques useful for gathering demographic data on diverse populations. In the Publications Committee's view the paper would serve as a first step in preparing further publications on this topic. (pp. 1–2)

The paper referred to in the report presented guidelines for measuring children's race/ethnicity and socioeconomic status; it subsequently appeared in *Child Development* (Entwisle & Astone, 1994).

The shift toward more direct communication continued at the meeting of the Committee on Ethnic and Racial Issues held October 1–2, 1992. At that meeting, three non-Committee members were present: Robert Emde (President of SRCD), John Hagen (Executive Officer of SRCD), and Susan Somerville (Editor of *Child Development*). The primary mechanism for facilitating communication between the Governing Council and SRCD Committees is appointment of a representative from Governing Council to each Committee. Hence, the presence of these three individuals, all occupying key leadership positions in the Society, at a meeting of this Committee was highly unusual, if not unprecedented. Probably the leadership recognized the gravity of the issues involved and the need for responsive and vigorous action. As will become clear in the next section, a notable denouement of these dialogues was the appointment of the first African American as an associate editor of *Child Development*.

AFRICAN AMERICAN SCHOLARS AS CRITICS AND ARBITERS OF DEVELOPMENTAL THEORY AND RESEARCH

In addition to focusing attention on the need to increase the rate of published research about children of color, the COMP (Committee on Ethnic and Racial Issues) and the Black Caucus since their inception have advocated for increased involvement of African American scholars in the editorial process of *Child Development*. Competent, conscientious consultants are at the heart of the activities of any esteemed scholarly journal. They evaluate the merits of the research and/or theoretical work, using broad guidelines set forth by the editors, and make recommendations to editors as to whether a manuscript should be accepted, rejected, or revised and resubmitted for further consideration. Consultants also routinely suggest ways in which they believe the authors can strengthen the manuscript and/ or the research. The exemplary review identifies both strengths and weaknesses in the work, and is prompt, discerning, and constructive in tone. Among consultants' rewards for discharging this essential professional responsibility are opportunities to sharpen their analytic and technical skills, broaden their base of knowledge within and across disciplines, and keep current with new developments in the field. Knowledge often is acquired not only from the manuscript itself, but from the comments of the other consultants who evaluated the manuscript.

Reviewers bring conceptual, theoretical, methodological, and other kinds of perspectives/biases to this important task, and in the ideal circumstance, their collective biases provide the manuscript with an evaluation that is in the interests of the field and everyone concerned (Hartup, 1984). If the continued vitality of developmental psychology as a discipline is dependent on broadening its "mainstream" focus to include children from ethnically, racially, and culturally diverse backgrounds, so too should its course be influenced by the voice of scholars of color as arbiters of research and theory in the discipline. Their perspectives about what defines meritorious research, often wrought by experiences and social locations not shared by their White colleagues, *should* be reflected in the editorial process. To do so is in keeping with the principle of inclusion. Their perspectives *need* to be reflected in the editorial process because increased diversity in judgment can engender healthy tension and spirited discourse. This discourse is essential to the incubation and forging of perspectives that are more dynamic, complex, and deliberate in their efforts to grapple with the intricacies of race, ethnicity, culture, and class as they bear on behavior and development.

As an example, relentless criticism of the deficit model buttressing early childhood intervention for poor children was a major factor that triggered and sustained the evolution toward more sound, ecologically oriented approaches in early childhood intervention, such as family support programs (Oyemade, 1985; Powell, 1988; Washington, 1985). Interventions espousing ecological perspectives are distinguished by primary attention to improving the social and economic context of parenting and children's development, rather than changing the individual in isolation from his or her social environments. At the heart of this evolving direction is increased appreciation of stress, social support, and broader contextual factors as determinants of parenting behavior on the one hand, and as conditioners of parents' and children's ability to profit from an intervention program on the other (Powell). Scholars of color, especially African American scholars, led the frontal assault on the deficit model during the 1970s and early 1980s (e.g., Allen, 1978; Boykin et al., 1979; Hall, 1974; Jones, 1972; Ogbu, 1981), although some White scholars played critically important roles as well (e.g., Baratz & Baratz, 1970; Bronfenbrenner, 1975; Cole & Bruner, 1971; Labov, 1970; Tulkin, 1972).

In the sections that follow, I present an overview of trends in African American scholars' level of involvement in the editorial process of *Child Development* and an analysis of events and circumstances that forged these changes, the most crucial of which were instigated by the Committee on Ethnic and Racial Issues. Attention is devoted to two milestones in the racial/

135

ethnic diversification of the editorship of *Child Development*, first, the appointment of African Americans to the Editorial Board and, second, the appointment of African Americans as Associate Editors.

Appointments to the Editorial Board of Child Development

Each editor and associate editor of *Child Development* makes her or his own appointments to the Editorial Board, consulting each other as necessary to avoid making requests to the same individual. Appointees work primarily with the editor who invited them to serve on the Board. Board membership is determined by a complex set of factors, including visions and priorities of the editors, scholars' willingness to serve, editors' experience with individual scholars as ad hoc reviewers and members of the Board, trends in the nature and broad topical foci of manuscripts submitted to the journal insofar as they dictate essential domains of expertise, and changes in associate editors during an editor's 6-year term (a fairly common occurrence).

African Americans' membership on the Board is used here as the indicator of their involvement in the editorial process of the journal for two reasons. First, although the names of Board members and ad hoc reviewers are routinely published in *Child Development*, it is easier and less labor intensive to track the former than the latter. Second, compared with ad hoc reviewers, members of the editorial board of any journal, including *Child Development*, typically exert more influence on what manuscripts are published by the journal. During any time period, an editorial board member evaluates more manuscripts submitted to the journal, on average, than does an ad hoc reviewer. The focus here notwithstanding, it is important to point out that trends in the number of African American scholars on the Editorial Board of *Child Development* may differ from trends in the frequency with which African American scholars serve as ad hoc reviewers for the journal.

Prior to 1980, no African American scholar had been appointed to the Editorial Board of *Child Development*, although some had served as ad hoc reviewers for the journal. The editorial term of Mavis Hetherington (1978–1984) marked the first time that an African American was appointed to the Board. According to the list of Editorial Board members appearing in each issue of *Child Development*, John McAdoo was the first African American scholar on the Board, appointed in mid-1980. By December of that year, he was joined by other African American scholars, namely, Harriette McAdoo, Vonnie McLoyd, and Margaret Spencer, and three other scholars of color, Felicisima Serafica, Luis Laosa, and Daniel Kee. Two additional African American scholars, Juarlyn Gaiter and William Hall, were appointed during the next 4 years.

In comments marking the end of her editorial term, Mavis Hethering-ton (1984) noted that among the goals she held upon assuming the edi-torship of the journal was "to increase the number of talented young researchers, minority scholars, and nonpsychologists on the editorial board" and to increase the number of reviews (p. vii). As six African Amer-ican scholars (and three other scholars of color) were appointed to the Board during her editorship when none had been appointed hitherto, Hetherington was justified in judging herself to have been fairly successful on this count. As for the goal of increasing the number of reviews, Hetherington's editorial term marked a period of tremendous growth in the number of scholars appointed to the Board. At its close, the Editorial Board of *Child Development* consisted of 168 members, a dramatic increase from 57 members at the beginning of Hetherington's term, and 90 mem-bers at the end of the editorial term of her predecessor, Wendell Jeffrey.

The efforts of the COMP were pivotal antecedents of the appointment of African Americans to the Editorial Board of *Child Development*. In its report to the Governing Council in 1978 (dated April 26), the Committee, under the leadership of Algea Harrison, urged the Governing Council to take action in three areas to increase minority scholars' participation in the society, namely, governance, professional socialization, and professional in-tegration. With respect to professional socialization, three specific actions were recommended: "(a) Invite minority members to participate in the program planning of the Society's biennial meetings; (b) Invite young mi-norities to review journal articles for the Society's publications; (c) Invite minorities to serve on editorial boards of the Society's publications" (p. 3). To aid Governing Council members in achieving these goals, COMP as-sembled a directory of SRCD minority members and distributed it to SRCD committee chairs and editors of the Society's publications. As stated in the COMP's report to Governing Council 2 years later (dated February 1980),

> The first copy of the Directory was distributed in June, 1979 and an updated version was distributed in October, 1979. . . . The Publication Committee has been most responsive to the issue of minority participation in the reviewing process. Mavis Hetherington has distributed the Directory to the Associate Editors and has communicated with the Chair regarding her efforts. (p. 2)

From a broader perspective, growth in the number of African American scholars on the Editorial Board between 1980 and 1984 can be attributed to a confluence of factors that included (a) a steady campaign by members of COMP to have representation of African American scholars on the Board and in all the other central functions and activities of the Society, at both the committee level and general membership level; (b) cooperative efforts of the Editor of *Child Development* to advance toward this goal, including solicitation of recommendations of African American scholars to serve as reviewers; (c) increasing numbers of African American developmental psychologists moving up the ranks of the professoriate in universities with strong research traditions; and (d) broader societal forces (e.g., the civil rights movement, Equal Employment Opportunity statutes) that gave rise to, and began to normalize, ethnic scholars' increased access to employment and professional opportunities that hitherto had been denied them.

The editorial term of Willard Hartup (1984–1990) brought new developments and shifts in the makeup of the Editorial Board of *Child Development*. It was during this term that the special issue of *Child Development* on minority children was published, with Spencer and McLoyd (1990) as guest coeditors. (A discussion of this project is found in chapter XI of this volume). In addition to showcasing empirical research and critical review papers focused on children of color, this effort occasioned the involvement of a larger than usual number of African American scholars, per manuscript, as ad hoc reviewers of manuscripts submitted to the journal. Hartup's term marked a decrease in the number of scholars appointed to the Board, hovering somewhere between 85 and 110 in any one year. Likewise, the number of African Americans on the Board declined from six during Hetherington's editorial term to three during Hartup's term, although the percentage of African Americans of the total number of Board members was about the same during the two editorial terms (approximately 3.5%). African American scholars who served on the Board during all or part of Hartup's term were Algea Harrison, John McAdoo, and me. Cynthia Garcia Coll, another scholar of color, also was appointed to the Board during this time. Like the editorial terms of her two predecessors, Susan Somerville's editorial term (1990–1996) resulted in developments of particular relevance to the role of African Americans as critics and arbiters of research. A discussion of these developments is presented in the following section.

Appointments of Associate Editors of Child Development

As the final arbiters, editors bear ultimate responsibility for the quality, breadth, and diversity of articles that appear in a journal. They reserve certain prerogatives and exercise considerable discretion in the publication process. Editors' assertions of their authority, of course, occur within the confines of the journal's mission and the pool of the manuscripts submitted. But even here, they exert influence by decidedly and, in some cases, unwittingly encouraging certain kinds of submissions and resubmissions and discouraging others.

Consider the ways in which associate editors' imprints are made on *Child Development*. As noted previously, they appoint individuals to the

Editorial Board and select reviewers for manuscripts assigned to them by the Senior Editor. In the tasks of identifying consultants, securing reviews, and rendering decisions about the disposition of manuscripts, the editor and associate editors of *Child Development* function relatively independently of each other. Their editorial decisions are guided, but not dictated, by consultants' evaluations. That is, consultants' evaluations are "advisory rather than binding" (Hartup, 1984, p. 1969). Historically, strong sentiment has existed among editors of *Child Development* that editorial decisions should not be made on the basis of majority rule, even though consultant agreement may be high and even though editors tend to agree with the majority of consultants most of the time. This provides editors with the latitude that is needed when a fatal flaw or, conversely, important strengths in an empirical study or theoretical work are detected by only one reviewer or only by the editor (Hartup).

In August 1993, Somerville appointed me as the first African American associate editor of *Child Development*. The circumstances favorable to this development were multifaceted. First, the Committee on Ethnic and Racial Issues, during a committee meeting at Brown University on November 8, 1991, agreed that appointment of an associate editor with expertise in the area of development in children of color was needed. In a report to the Governing Council summarizing the minutes of that meeting, the Committee made a formal recommendation to this effect. It also (a) presented a list of scholars possessing expertise in the development of ethnic minority children in the United States and recommended that these scholars be invited to review manuscripts for the journal, and (b) recommended that the notice to contributors published in *Child Development* emphasize the Society's evolving commitment to address issues of diversity by explicitly encouraging submissions reporting findings from normative studies of ethnic and minority populations and studies employing a range of methodologies. In a subsequent meeting held at Wellesley College on October 1–2, 1992, the Committee on Ethnic and Racial Issues discussed these recommendations and several others with Somerville. (As noted previously, John Hagen, Executive Officer of SRCD, and Robert Emde, President of SRCD, also attended this meeting.)

Second, as Somerville noted in her annual report for *Child Development* (1992), several of the associate editors had informed her during 1992 that they could not continue with the customary manuscript load. Following a long series of discussions with the associate editors, potential new associate editors, the Chair of the Publications Committee (William Hall), the Executive Officer, and other key persons in the Society, Somerville increased the number of associate editors from four to seven (the ongoing discussions having involved several individuals partly because of the financial implications of a marked increase in the number of associate editors). In so doing, she responded to the need to broaden the expertise and perspectives represented among the associate editors, while also reducing the manuscript loads of certain editors.

Third, by the early 1990s, I had accrued considerable editorial experience. I had been on the Editorial Board of *Child Development* since 1980 and served on the editorial boards of several other journals (e.g., *Developmental Psychology, Journal of Black Psychology, Journal of Research on Adolescence*). In addition, I had been guest coeditor of the special issue of *Child Development* on minority children (published in 1990) and was coediting (with Aletha Huston and Cynthia Garcia Coll) its special issue on children and poverty (published in 1994).

Drawing on my experiences as guest coeditor and discussions with potential Editorial Board members and several other scholars, I appointed to the Editorial Board two African American scholars, Harriette McAdoo and Suzanne Randolph. (A number of other African American scholars could not serve on the Board because of heavy editorial responsibilities for other journals.) I also appointed two other scholars of color (Ana Marie Cauce and Suniya Luthar) and seven majority scholars (Gene Brody, Lindsay Chase-Lansdale, Geraldine Downey, Constance Flanagan, Doran French, Aletha Huston, and Ann Masten), all of whom had conducted exemplary research with African American children and families or had expertise in the study of poor or economically distressed families and children. Other African American scholars who served on the Board during all or part of Somerville's editorial term included Geraldine Brookins, Sharon Nelson-LeGall, and Angela Taylor. In sum, Somerville's editorial term brought an increase in the presence of African Americans on the Editorial Board that rivaled the increase during Hetherington's term. It is my impression that her term also resulted in a substantial increase in the rate of research published in *Child Development* on African Americans, specifically, and people of color, generally (exclusive of the special issue on poverty). Verification of this perception awaits systematic analyses.

At the end of Somerville's term, Marc Bornstein assumed the editorship of *Child Development*. His Board of 15 associate editors included one African American scholar, Diana Slaughter-Defoe. It also is noteworthy that two other African American scholars in the field of human development, Melvin Wilson and Diane Scott-Jones, have been appointed in recent years as associate/senior editors of major journals (*American Journal of Community Psychology* and *Journal of Research on Adolescence*, respectively). Both are members of the Black Caucus of SRCD and past SRCD Committee Chairs. I am cautiously optimistic that, together, these appointments bespeak a progressive trend in the academy that will gain momentum as we enter the 21st century.

CONCLUSION

During the course of their coexistence, the Committee on Ethnic and Racial Issues (formerly COMP) and the Black Caucus assiduously challenged the Society to take actions to stimulate, advance, and disseminate knowledge about children of color. They assumed a decidedly proactive stance, offering concrete suggestions and recommendations to the Governing Council, the Publications Committee, the Program Committee, and other committees of SRCD about ways to alleviate some of the problems they perceived to beset the journal *Child Development*, the organization, and the discipline itself.

Within the context of growing sensitivity to issues of diversity, broadly defined, the leaders of the Society and editors of its flagship journal have responded by affirming their commitment to these goals and searching for ways to meet the challenges they pose. As detailed in this paper, this affirmation has come in the form of editorial statements; instructions for preparing submissions of papers for presentation at biennial meetings; information appearing in the Society's newsletter about the rate of research on ethnic minority children; meetings that have brought together the leaders of SRCD, the Editor of *Child Development*, and the Committee on Ethnic and Racial Issues or its representative; and appointments of African Americans to the Editorial Board and as associate editors of the journal. The periods 1980–1984 and 1989–1993 stand out for their measured progress toward enhancing the racial and ethnic diversity of the organization, involving African American scholars in the editorial process of *Child Development*, and heightening the consciousness of the organization about the importance of progress on these fronts.

The preeminent challenge lying before us continues to be the production of stellar, ecologically valid research (basic, applied, and policy-focused) about development in children of color and strategic, timely dissemination of this knowledge to scholars, practitioners, and policymakers. Dramatic increases in the proportion of American children who are from ethnic minority backgrounds, combined with declines in the proportion of adolescents and young adults in the total American population, demand increased understanding of the pathways to both successful and problematic development in children of color. America's economic and social well-being will depend even more than at present on its ability to enhance intellectual and social competence and minimize problematic development in all its youth (Edelman, 1987; Wetzel, 1987). In the interests of continued enlightenment and betterment of American society, we must press ahead with all deliberate speed toward systematic study of these complex issues. I remain sanguine that our efforts can make a positive difference.

We also need monitoring of the professional lives of African American scholars, including their success in publishing their research in mainstream journals such as *Child Development* and experiences that foster such success (e.g., mentoring, quality of reviews, and the review process). Scholars of color in the field of human development typically evidence a steadfast commitment to research on children and families of color and often stake their professional careers and identities on their ability to contribute to knowledge in these domains. They bring unique perspectives and competencies to their work that enrich our understanding of development in these populations. Consequently, strategies that enable scholars of color to pursue productive research careers are crucial to any serious effort to diversify and improve our understanding of human development (McLoyd, 1994).

REFERENCES

Allen, W. (1978). The search for applicable theories of Black family life. *Journal of Marriage and the Family*, **40**, 117–129.

Baratz, S., & Baratz, J. (1970). Early childhood intervention: The social science base of institutional racism. *Harvard Educational Review*, **40**, 29–50.

Bayton, J. A. (1975). Francis Sumner, Max Meenes, and the training of Black psychologists. *American Psychologist*, **30**, 185–186.

Boykin, A. W., Franklin, A. J., & Yates, J. F. (Eds.). (1979). *Research directions of Black psychologists*. New York: Russell Sage.

Bronfenbrenner, U. (1975). Is early intervention effective? In M. Guttentag & E. Struening (Eds.), *Handbook of evaluation research*, (Vol. 2, pp. 519–603). Beverly Hills, CA: Sage.

Cole, M., & Bruner, J. (1971). Cultural differences and inferences about psychological processes. *American Psychologist*, **26**, 867–876.

Davidson, D. (1973). The furious passage of the Black graduate student. In J. A. Ladner (Ed.), *The death of White sociology* (pp. 23–51). New York: Vintage Books.

Edelman, M. W. (1987). *Families in peril: An agenda for social change*. Cambridge, MA: Harvard University Press.

Entwisle, D. R., & Astone, N. M. (1994). Some practical guidelines for measuring youth's race/ethnicity and socioeconomic status. *Child Development*, **65**, 1521–1540.

Garcia Coll, C., Lamberty, G., Jenkins, R., McAdoo, H., Crnic, K., & Wasik, B., et al. (1996). An integrative model for the study of developmental competencies in minority children. *Child Development*, **67**, 1891–1914.

Graham, S. (1992). Most of the subjects were White and middle class: Trends in published research on African Americans in selected APA journals, 1970–1989. *American Psychologist*, **47**, 629–639.

Guthrie, R. V. (1976). *Even the rat was White: A historical view of psychology*. New York: Harper & Row.

Hacker, A. (1992). *Two nations: Black and White, separate, hostile, unequal*. New York: Scribner.

Hagen, J. W., & Conley, A. C. (1994, Spring). Ethnicity and race of children in studies in *Child Development*, 1980–1993. *Newsletter of the Society for Research in Child Development*, 6–7.

Hall, W. S. (1974). Research in the Black community: Child development. In J. Chunn (Ed.), *The survival of Black children and youth*. Washington, DC: Nuclassics and Science Publishing.

Hall, W. S. (1992). Statement from chair of SRCD publications committee. *Newsletter of the Society for Research in Child Development*, p. 4.

Hartup, W. W. (1984). Editorial. *Child Development*, **55**, 1669–1670.

Hetherington, E. M. (1984). Editorial: A parting comment. *Child Development*, **55**, vii.

Huston, A., Garcia Coll, C., & McLoyd, V. C. (1994). Children and poverty [special issue]. *Child Development*, **65** (2).

Huston, A., McLoyd, V. C., & Garcia Coll, C. (1997). Poverty and behavior: The case for multiple methodologies and levels of analyses. *Developmental Review*, **17**, 376–393.

Jones, J. M. (1990). Who is training our ethnic minority psychologists, and are they doing it right? In G. Stricker, E. Davis-Russell, E. Bourg, E. Duran, W. Hammond & J. McHolland et al. (Eds.), *Toward ethnic diversification in psychology education and training* (pp. 17–34). Washington, DC: American Psychological Association.

Jones, J. M. (1991). Psychological models of race: What have they been and what should they be? In J. D. Goodchilds (Ed.), *Psychological perspectives on human diversity in America* (pp. 7–46). Washington, DC: American Psychological Association.

Jones, R. L. (Ed.). (1972). *Black psychology*. New York: Harper & Row.

Labov, W. (1970). The logic of non-standard English. In F. Williams (Ed.), *Language and poverty* (pp. 153–189). Chicago: Markham.

McLoyd, V. C. (1994). Research in the service of poor and ethnic/racial minority children: Fomenting change in models of scholarship. *Family and Consumer Sciences Research Journal*, **23**, 56–66.

McLoyd, V. C., & Randolph, S. (1984). The conduct and publication of research on Afro-American children: A content analysis. *Human Development*, **27**, 65–75.

McLoyd, V. C., & Randolph, S. (1985). Secular trends in the study of Afro-American children: A review of *Child Development*, 1936–1980. In A. B. Smuts & J. W. Hagen (Eds.), History and research in child development: In celebration of the fiftieth anniversary of the Society. *Monographs of the Society for Research in Child Development*, (Vol. 50, 4–5, Serial No. 211), 78–92.

Mitchell, J. (1982). Reflections of a Black social scientist: Some struggles, some doubts, some hopes. *Harvard Educational Review*, **52**, 27–44.

Moskos, C., & Butler, J. (1996). *All that we can be: Black leadership and racial integration the Army way*. New York: Basic Books.

Myers, H. F., Rana, P. G., & Harris, M. (1979). *Black child development in America 1927–1977*. Westport, CT: Greenwood Press.

Ogbu, J. (1981). Origins of human competence: A cultural–ecological perspective. *Child Development*, **52**, 413–429.

Oyemade, U. J. (1985). The rationale for Head Start as a vehicle for the upward mobility of minority families: A minority perspective. *American Journal of Orthopsychiatry*, **55**, 591–602.

Powell, D. (1988). Emerging directions in parent–child early intervention. In I. Sigel (Series Ed.) D. Powell (Vol. Ed.), *Advances in applied developmental psychology. Vol. 3. Parent education as early childhood intervention: Emerging directions in theory, research, and practice* (pp. 1–22). Norwood, NJ: Ablex.

Ray, S. A. (1983). *The professional development of Black social scientists who study children*. Paper presented at the Biennial Meetings of the Society for Research in Child Development, Detroit, MI.

Rowe, D., & Rodgers, J. (1997). Poverty and behavior: Are environmental measures nature and nurture? *Developmental Review*, **17**, 358–375.

Slaughter, D., & McWorter, G. (1985). Social origins and early features of the scientific study of Black American families and children. In M. B. Spencer, G. K. Brookins & W. R. Allen

(Eds.), *Beginnings: The social and affective development of Black children* (pp. 5–18). Hillsdale, NJ: Erlbaum.

Smuts, A. B., & Hagen, J. W. (1985a). History and research in child development: In celebration of the fiftieth anniversary of the Society. *Monographs of the Society for Research in Child Development*, **50** (4–5, Serial No. 211).

Smuts, A. B., & Hagen, J. W. (1985b). Introduction. In A. B. Smuts & J. W. Hagen (Eds.), History and research in child development: In celebration of the fiftieth anniversary of the Society. *Monographs of the Society for Research in Child Development*, (Vol. 50, 4–5, Serial No. 211), vii–ix.

Smuts, A. B., & Hagen, J. W. (1985c). Historical approaches to child development: Introduction to Part 2. In A. B. Smuts & J. W. Hagen (Eds.), History and research in child development: In celebration of the fiftieth anniversary of the Society. *Monographs of the Society for Research in Child Development*, (Vol. 50, 4–5, Serial No. 211), 41–43.

Somerville, S. (1991). Editorial. *Child Development*, **62**, 873–874.

Somerville, S. (1996). Editorial: Some closing thoughts. *Child Development*, **67**, 2605–2607.

Spencer, M. B., Brookins, G. K., & Allen, W. R. (Eds.). (1985). *Beginnings: The social and affective development of Black children*. Hillsdale, NJ: Erlbaum.

Spencer, M. B., & McLoyd, V. C. (1990). Minority children [special issue]. *Child Development*, **61** (2).

Stricker, G. (1990). Minority issues in professional training. In G. Stricker, E. Davis-Russell, E. Bourg, E. Duran, W. Hammond & J. McHolland et al. (Eds.), *Toward ethnic diversification in psychology education and training* (pp. 1–8). Washington, DC: American Psychological Association.

Super, C. M. (1982). Secular trends in child development and the institutionalization of professional disciplines. *Newsletter of the Society for Research in Child Development*, 10–11.

Tulkin, S. R. (1972). An analysis of the concept of cultural deprivation. *Developmental Psychology*, **6**, 326–339.

Washington, E. D., & McLoyd, V. C. (1982). The external validity of research involving American minorities. *Human Development*, **25**, 324–339.

Washington, V. (1985). Head Start: How appropriate for minority families in the 1980s? *American Journal of Orthopsychiatry*, **55**, 577–590.

Wetzel, J. (1987). *American youth: A statistical snapshot*. New York: William T. Grant Foundation.

Wispe, L., Awkward, J., Hoffman, M., Hicks, L. H., & Porter, J. (1969). The Negro psychologist in America. *American Psychologist*, **24**, 142–150.

XII. HEAD START: TRANSLATING RESEARCH INTO POLICY AND PRACTICE

This chapter chronicles some of the contributions of the Society for Research in Child Development (SRCD) Black Caucus scholars to Head Start research, programs, and policies, particularly during the period of 1970–1996, before the active engagement of SRCD members—and other academics—in Head Start research. Since the Black Caucus of SRCD was founded, one of its key areas of contribution has been Project Head Start. Through the Minority Scholars Interested in Head Start Research and other avenues, SRCD Black Caucus members have (a) engaged in research, program, and policy activities intended to enhance the parental involvement component of Head Start and to assess both the quality of Head Start programs and the overall educational component; (b) participated in Project Head Start as members of advisory panels, proposal reviewers, and principal investigators on research projects; and (c) engaged in the training of Head Start staff through credit and non-credit staff development programs.

Considered the most successful component of President Lyndon Johnson's War on Poverty, Project Head Start is a federally sponsored preschool program designed to enable disadvantaged children to cope better with traditional schooling and to help children and their families achieve economic self-sufficiency. Head Start is particularly important because it has provided a unique range of services to large numbers of poor and ethnic minority children. It combined child care with medical and dental treatment, emphasized the child's psychological development and school readiness, and introduced "social services into the child's home environment plus education of the parents" (Ross, 1979, p. 38).

Project Head Start was launched during the summer of 1965 with the expectation of spending about $17 million for about 100,000 children. The demand was far greater than anticipated, however, owing largely to the massive manner in which the program was advertised. In 1972, Head Start was transformed into a predominantly part-day, full-year program for

300,000 children. Since then, enrollment has increased to more than 905,000 children representing many different cultures and ethnic groups: 39% African American, 32% White, 22% Hispanic, 4% American Indian, and 3% Asian. In age, 63% of the children served are 4 years old, 23% are 3 years old, 11% are 5 years old or older, and 3% are under 3 years old. At least 77% of the children are from families whose yearly incomes are under $15,000. Over the years, Head Start has provided comprehensive developmental services to more than 20 million children and their families. Currently, it serves approximately 20% of eligible low-income children.

The overriding philosophy of Head Start programs is comprehensive and interdisciplinary: Foster the development of the whole child. Each program must have an educational component; a health component, including nutritional, dental, and mental health services; and a social services component. Services for special education children must be provided. Finally, parental involvement is one of the most distinctive features of Head Start; each program must attempt to actively involve the child's family.

Many SRCD Black Caucus members had links to Head Start at its creation. For example, Diana Slaughter-Defoe (then Slaughter) worked with Robert D. Hess and Virginia Shipman at the University of Chicago in pioneering research on the importance of parenting and early childhood experiences for later development. Slaughter-Defoe published her doctoral dissertation with data from the very first (summer 1965) Head Start population (Slaughter, 1969). Howard University, which employed several people who became Caucus members, hosted the Howard Preschool Center, the Head Start pilot site for the Children's Bureau during 1963–1965. After the SRCD Black Caucus was formed in 1973, the considerable breadth of Head Start-related research being conducted by minority scholars became apparent. Areas of focus included parenting, infant development, parent involvement, play, early childhood education, early childhood interventions, self-concept and self-esteem, substance abuse prevention, family studies, the Black family, Black men, childhood socialization, educational assessment and intelligence, cultural diversity, teen pregnancy, effects of poverty, infancy and infant development, ethnic identity, risk and resilience among African American children, and economic self-sufficiency.

MINORITY SCHOLARS INTERESTED IN HEAD START RESEARCH

Beginnings

Despite the number of Caucus members who were engaged in research related to Head Start in the 1970s, Clennie Murphy, an African American and Associate Commissioner of the Head Start Bureau, along with Trellis

Waxler, also an African American and Program Specialist in the Bureau, noted that there were few contributions from minority researchers to the Head Start research agenda and subsequent Head Start policy. This led, in 1982, to dialogue with Ura Jean Oyemade Bailey (then Oyemade), a Professor at Howard University, and Valora Washington, then Associate Dean in the School of Human Ecology at Howard, about convening a group that became the Minority Scholars Interested in Head Start Research. The first meeting took place in Atlanta, GA, in 1983, and there were biannual meetings thereafter until 1991. During the period 1983–1991, participating Minority Scholars included Lula Beatty, Andrew Billingsley, O. Jackson Cole, John Dill, Patricia A. Edwards, Eugene Garcia, Aline Garrett, Sadie Grimmett, Dominic Gullo, Robert B. Hill, Asa Hilliard, Priscilla Hilliard, Mildred Johnson, Shirley Jones, Luis Laosa, Rachel Lindsey, Vonnie McLoyd, Jose Oliva, Ura Jean Oyemade Bailey, Lillian Phenice, Diana Slaughter-Defoe, Margaret Beale Spencer, Joseph Stevens, Brenda Taylor, Valora Washington, Marvin Watkins, Trellis Waxler, and Robert Woodson. The Minority Scholars group included, in addition to minority researchers, federal and local representatives from the Head Start community: Sylvia Carter, Barbara Harrison, Carlethea Johnson, Richard Johnson, Clennie Murphy, Audrey Palmer, Donald E. Smith, Helen Taylor, and Edward Vaughn.

The recommendations resulting from the meetings of Minority Scholars stimulated further involvement in Head Start-related activities, particularly in the areas of parental involvement, policy and program advisory committees, research and program implementation, and staff training and development. This paper chronicles many of these early Black Caucus contributions.

1983 Meeting of Minority Scholars

At the first National Meeting of Black, Hispanic, and Asian scholars on "Minority Perspectives on the Future of Project Head Start," Minority Scholars grappled with three issues: the rationale for Head Start as a vehicle for upward mobility, the effects of Head Start on minority children, and the continuing appropriateness of Head Start for minority children. Washington and Oyemade (1985) summarized deliberations at the conference in terms of five priority issues:

> 1. *Define and enhance opportunities for parent involvement.* Because Project Head Start was formed as part of a comprehensive "War on Poverty" that sought to produce economic self-sufficiency for families, scholars asserted that the goal should be reaffirmed through efforts to document the extent of parent involvement, to recognize various kinds of parent involvement, to determine which type of Head Start climate best promotes parent

involvement, and to determine which types of parent involvement are most clearly related to pupil outcomes. In addition, the decision-making and process skills that enhance parental moves toward self-sufficiency and advocacy for themselves and their children should be explored.

2. *Assess the quality of Head Start programs and enhance the educational component of the Project.* Conferees had questions about variation in the quality of Head Start programs throughout the United States and concerns that, because of budgetary restraints, centers were offering some attendance options that might adversely affect pupil outcomes. Several recommendations were made to improve the educational component, among them calls to: inculcate ethnic values and heritage, facilitate the transition from Head Start to public schools, enhance the teaching of academic subjects, and examine more closely the results with respect to age of child, the impact of family involvement, and the type, duration, and intensity of intervention. There was also a concern about class size and staff–child ratios.

3. *Involve members of ethnic groups in Project Head Start as members of advisory panels, proposal reviewers, and principal investigators.* At the core of this recommendation was the lack of ethnic group representation in the research and evaluation of Project Head Start. This was of particular concern given that two-thirds of Head Start children were from racial minorities. The conferees recommended closer collaboration between federal and regional Head Start administrators and minority scholars.

4. *Address the issue of the training of Head Start staff, as well as their salaries and benefits.* Instead of improving the quality of training, and thus the quality of the educational component, many centers had had to cut budgets for staff development. This affected not only the quantity of available staff in training, but also the quality of teacher preparation (Zigler & Lang, 1983). Both the number of staff and the appropriateness of their training had a tremendous impact on the child outcomes. As improvements in curriculum, parent involvement, and outcomes for children were related to the quality of staff, it was suggested that the salary scale for Head Start personnel be reevaluated.

5. *Improve the Quality of Services that Regional Offices Provide to Grantees.* The Minority Scholars suggested that the number of community programs assigned to regional representatives should be reduced

so that the latter would not be overworked, could become familiar with individual programs, and could help maintain the quality of those programs (Zigler & Lang, 1983).

MINORITY HEAD START RESEARCH SCHOLAR ACTIONS TO ADDRESS RECOMMENDATIONS

Enhancement of Parent Involvement Component

Consequent to the recommendation from the Minority Scholars, a new major focus of research and program activities was parent involvement. Minority scholars were convinced that the effectiveness of Head Start programs was hampered by the relatively limited attention to family development. Furthermore, changes in family structures and functions since the founding of Head Start had altered the ability of many families to take advantage of traditional Head Start services. Six trends in family life were particularly evident (Washington & Oyemade, 1985): the feminization of poverty, the rise in teen parenting, the surging number of mothers of preschool children in the workforce, the increasing challenge for low-income families to attain economic self-sufficiency, substance abuse, and family and community violence. These trends were often interrelated: the female poor were frequently teen mothers who might abuse illegal drugs or be involved in community violence. Moreover, they created new demands on individuals and indicated an urgent need for complementary changes in the services Head Start provided.

Clearly, parent involvement in Head Start services was needed to address these problems. Yet effective parent involvement and empowerment strategies were increasingly difficult to plan and carry out for several reasons, including the rising number of multiproblem families enrolling in the program, the erosion of comprehensive services and intrafamily support, and greater poverty. Given these conditions, Minority Scholars focused on key areas related to Head Start parent involvement: economic self-sufficiency, substance abuse, and father involvement.

Parent Involvement and Economic Self-Sufficiency

As "welfare reform" initiatives at the time of the initial meeting of the Minority Scholars focused on the employment of public assistance recipients, a key issue was the impact of Head Start on economic self-sufficiency. In a national study of the long-term effects of Head Start, Collins (1983) reported that Head Start promoted self-sufficiency, for 7% of the parents indicated that Head Start had helped them to attain further education.

The low figure of the parents in the study obtaining jobs, however, suggested that these jobs were within Head Start. In fact, little was known about the relationship of parent involvement to family members' ability to obtain and maintain jobs, the impact of parent involvement on the career ladder movement of Head Start families, or the impact of Head Start on family income patterns and on family members other than Head Start children.

In an effort to address the paucity of research in this area, Oyemade, Washington, and Gullo (1989) sought to provide empirical information on the relationship of parent involvement to the economic self-sufficiency of Head Start families and children, specifically exploring the parents' Head Start experience, the level of Head Start center parent involvement activities, and the intensity of parental involvement. Their five major findings were as follows.

1. Overall, the Head Start parents in this study were significantly better off at the time of the study than at the beginning of their Head Start experience. The number of families receiving public assistance had been reduced from 49.2% to 33.1%. A significant number of parents reported improvements in their economic status; for example, the number of families above poverty level had climbed from 20.4% to 27.8%; there were similar improvements in home ownership and in numbers of both mothers and fathers working and earning college credit or degrees.

2. Although there were no significant differences between the subjects at low- and high-involvement Head Start centers at the beginning of their experience, after a few years the subjects at high-involvement centers were significantly ahead in terms of family income, employment of the mother, and employment of the father. Significantly more of the high-involvement parents (34% compared with 19%) were above the poverty level, too.

3. There was a significant positive relationship between intensity of Head Start parental involvement (i.e., the number of Head Start activities in which each parent was involved) and preferred daily activities, family income, occupation, and education of the mother. Parents with higher social status who responded both at the beginning of their Head Start involvement and when the interview was administered tended to have a greater intensity of involvement in Head Start activities. Similarly, parents with "higher education of mother" and "home ownership" had a greater intensity, including involvement in career- and job-related skill development activities.

4. The results suggested that Head Start, and particularly its parental involvement component, had a positive effect on the upward mobility of Head Start parents. A significant number of parents whose children attended high-involvement Head Start centers were economically better off than they were when their children began Head Start.

5. With regard to intensity of involvement, it appeared that parents who were more involved in Head Start tended to be relatively better off from the beginning. Even though their economic status improved through Head Start, the parents who took advantage of and benefited most from involvement opportunities appeared to have been those with higher incomes.

Overall, these findings clearly suggested that Head Start parental involvement was an appropriate and effective way to advance the skills and knowledge of parents far beyond the area of child development. Because Head Start had been successful in helping families climb the socioeconomic ladder, expanded efforts to involve parents might result in more significant gains. For example, though a significant number of Head Start families moved out of poverty, more than 70% remained in poverty; it was recommended that Head Start target the latter group.

Parent Involvement as a Means of Personal Growth

In another study, "Who Gets Involved? Head Start Mothers as Persons" (Slaughter, Lindsey, Nakagawa, & Kuehne, 1989), Minority Scholars investigated parents' opinions of typical parental involvement activities. Specifically, they sought to determine which activities were reported effective for personal growth and whether parents chose activities based on the type of program in which they participated.

The study also investigated the personality of the parent as an important component in the level of participation. The literature on possible "internal effects" of Head Start parent program activities suggested that self-esteem and parental involvement would be related, but prior to this exploratory study there was no research data on this topic. The three major findings were (a) evidence that the Head Start center may contribute significantly to the level of parental involvement by increasing the range of options available to them; (b) a significant relationship existed between involvement at high level and ego development, suggesting that parents experienced personal development through participation in these program activities; and (c) support for the literature that assumed that parental involvement in Head Start benefited the parents' personal growth and development. Such literature was important because it described how entire families ultimately could be enriched through their child's participation in a good educational program.

In view of the findings, Slaughter et al. (1989) stressed the urgent need for a systematic and thorough national evaluation of the parental involvement component of Project Head Start. Such an evaluation should include diverse but complementary measures of parental involvement and assess the parent's own perceptions; it should also include direct observations of Head Start centers with differing patterns and rates of participation. Special attention should be paid to parental personality development in addition to long-term external effects. The authors emphasized the need for more research into the self-perceptions of Head Start parents as adolescent and adult men and women who live and rear families in an extremely challenging and complex society. Given the current mandate for Head Start to be responsive to the changing needs of American families, what better way to begin than to discover Head Start parents as persons?

Unfortunately, the goal of a comprehensive assessment of the Head Start parent involvement component has not been achieved. Nonetheless, the research initiated by SRCD Black Caucus members and other minorities, concluding in the early 1990s, was followed by intense and ongoing involvement of the SRCD parent organization with Head Start. SRCD majority members, with the support of the Governing Council and Executive Director, John Hagen, have been strong supporters of the revitalized Head Start Research and Evaluation Division. Since 1991, this body has held biennial conferences (on the off-year of the biennial SRCD conferences) in which SRCD minority and majority researchers participate.

Addressing the Challenge of Substance Abuse

A significant barrier to parent involvement in Head Start was family involvement in substance abuse. Drug abuse had become one of the most serious and perplexing problems facing the Head Start community. Not only had increased rates of addiction placed the Head Start population at greater risk for dropping out of high school, unemployment, crime, incarceration, and continued poverty, but children exposed to substance abuse prenatally were entering the Head Start system at an alarming rate (Oyemade & Washington, 1989). In response, Head Start practiced two of the most effective techniques for preventing drug abuse: teaching in appropriate programs and working with parents.

The Elements of a Model Drug-Abuse Prevention Program

Minority scholars identified two critical components of an effective drug-abuse prevention program.

1. *The program had to be targeted to young children and their families.* The key to preventing drug abuse was suggested to clearly lie in family childrearing practices and teaching techniques in early childhood programs. Unless enough was known about the families (e.g., their approaches to discipline, management and communication styles, and causes of stress) to tailor the program to their needs, the program probably would never have been implemented effectively.

2. *The program had to address families' basic needs.* Effective early childhood programs such as Head Start already had a strong parent involvement component upon which to build expanded services in stress management, resource identification, family support, and family education. A primary prevention program, however, needed to assist families by building on these elements: showing how to avoid stress; teaching more about local, state, and federal agencies that offer assistance; providing opportunities for parents to build on their parenting skills; educating parents about the likely effects of different childrearing practices; and designing or adapting specially focused programs that encourage parents to make changes in their family relationships.

Parents and Children Getting a Head Start Drugs Curriculum

Carter and Oyemade (1990), along with other Minority Scholars, teamed with the National Head Start Association to develop a "Model Substance Abuse Prevention Program" for Head Start parents and children. The program, funded by the Office for Substance Abuse Prevention, is based on data gathered from Minority Scholars Interested in Head Start Research (Washington & Oyemade, 1987). The curriculum, "Parents and Children Getting a Head Start Against Drugs," is culturally responsive and based on accepted principles of child development and family support. The program has been implemented in Head Start programs in all 50 states.

Development of the curriculum was guided by research which identified family risk and protective factors related to children's involvement in substance abuse (Oyemade & Washington, 1989). Specific curriculum content focused on factors such as drug information, self-esteem, communication skills, stress, drugs in the community, health issues, values and peer

153

pressure, family management and relations, and developing support networks. The curriculum used discussion/experience rather than a didactic approach, and activities were based on knowledge about the specific culture.

The first model program was implemented in Head Start programs in Baltimore, MD. It was then replicated by several SRCD Black Caucus members and supporters, including Aline Garrett, Lillian Phenice, Rachel Lindsey, and Sadie Grimmett. The curriculum was published by the Center for Substance Abuse Prevention (CSAP). Since this initiative, CSAP, NHSA, and the Head Start Bureau have launched major substance abuse initiatives. Ura Jean Oyemade Bailey continues research with substance abuse in Head Start families through the Center for Drug Abuse Research at Howard University.

Data from a user survey indicate that more than 3,000 parents have been trained in the substance abuse curriculum. Participant evaluation of the curriculum has been very positive, and preliminary evidence suggests that the curriculum had a significant impact on reducing the family risk factors associated with substance abuse (Washington & Oyemade, 1995).

Fathers' Involvement in Head Start

The last of the Minority Scholars' key areas related to Head Start parent involvement is an emphasis on fathers' roles in child nurturance during the early childhood years. Interest in this area continues among SRCD Black Caucus members; for example, by 1997 Vivian Gadsden, of the University of Pennsylvania, had become the Director of the National Center on Fathers and Families (NCOFF).

Fathers' Roles in Child Nurturance

The late John McAdoo, an SRCD Black Caucus member, was one of the first to emphasize the need for research and programs addressing the roles and contributions of African American fathers to children's learning and healthy development. He and others, such as Lawrence Gary and colleagues at Howard University (e.g., Gary, Beatty, & Weaver, 1987), stressed that the father's role in child care and socialization has undergone changes. No longer were fathers exclusively responsible for the family's economic and material comfort. Maternal employment was only one of many reasons for the father's increased role in the nurturance and socialization of children (McAdoo, 1981). McAdoo also suggested that fathers' increased interactions with their children may have reflected their desire to have a larger part in their children's development. In African American families especially,

154

fathers were providing significant child care and household task assistance (McAdoo).

Male Participation in Head Start Programs

In the current national Head Start program, fewer than 10% of participants in the parent involvement component are male. In one of the first studies of male involvement in Head Start, a Minority Scholar, Lula Beatty (1989), interviewed 118 fathers from the Washington, DC, Head Start programs and found that nearly three fourths stated that they participated in Head Start activities only a few times a year or not at all.

When Beatty asked mothers, fathers, and staff to rank the reasons for low father participation in Head Start programs, four factors emerged as major barriers: the need for information (mothers did not tell fathers about, or encourage them to participate in, Head Start activities); father's absence from the home; the predominance of female staff and female-related activities; and frequent scheduling of activities at times inconvenient for fathers. Neither lack of interest nor lack of ability were cited as major barriers to father involvement in Head Start by the surveyed groups.

MINORITY SCHOLAR PARTICIPATION IN NATIONAL ADVISORY COMMITTEES AND OTHER HEAD START ACTIVITIES

Social Policy Issues Related to Head Start

Minority Scholars, in collaboration with Trellis Waxler, Clennie Murphy, and other Head Start Bureau officials, also endeavored to address the problem of inadequate representation of minorities in the program and policy areas of Head Start, including the Social Policy Committee of SRCD, Head Start advisory committees, and the Head Start Research Conference. Because of their efforts to increase minority involvement in Head Start research, Diana Slaughter, Valora Washington, Ura Jean Oyemade Bailey, and Rachel Lindsey were invited in 1988 by the SRCD Committee on Child Development and Social Policy to develop a Social Policy Brief on Head Start. Their report, "Head Start: A Backward and Forward Look," reviewed issues related to the evaluation of the effectiveness of Head Start, parental involvement in Head Start, the multicultural component of Head Start, and Head Start reauthorization issues.

The authors highlighted criticisms of contemporaneous evaluation efforts: narrowly focused outcome measures; failure to address potential selection biases in who attends Head Start; and failure to consider the respective impacts of (a) the lack of program continuity through the primary and elementary grades, (b) the variety of curricula across the various Head Start programs, and (c) family process variables.

The review of parental involvement in Head Start focused on the need to evaluate systematically its three components: (a) participation in the child's education and development; (b) participation in development of, and even administration of, the Head Start Program itself; and (c) participation in services and skills development for parents, apart from services to children. Moreover, the authors suggested that enhancing the parental involvement component to emphasize more services for parents would help to achieve the goal of economic self-sufficiency.

The authors also suggested that Head Start should be commended for taking steps to incorporate the sociocultural background of the children and families in the program and to develop curricula that focused on the varying cultures of the groups served by the program. They noted, however, a major weakness—the paucity of Head Start research on the sociocultural context in which ethnic minority children were socialized—and suggested that future efforts should focus on gathering data for a database on ethnic minority children, for use in developing multicultural programs. Finally, consistent with the recommendations of the Minority Scholars, the authors highlighted several key issues to be considered during the 1990 reauthorization of Head Start: changing family needs; expansion of services; monitoring and service delivery; space, insurance, and class size; and staff salaries, benefits, and training.

The *Social Policy Report* written by SRCD Black Caucus members (Slaughter, Washington, Oyemade, & Lindsey, 1988) was circulated to the membership of the parent organization. Issued when the Head Start Research and Evaluation Division was being revised, the report helped to forge close ties among the larger SRCD research community, SRCD's social policy initiatives, Project Head Start, and the new Head Start National Evaluation Advisory Panel, established by President George H. Bush in 1989 as Head Start readied for major program expansion. SRCD Black Caucus member Diana Slaughter-Defoe served on the Advisory Panel, which presented the first opportunity in more than a decade and a half for systematic analysis of research needs relevant to the future of Head Start. The panel addressed past research and evaluation findings, Head Start's information needs, and the Administration for Children, Youth, and Families' emerging strategy for expanding enrollment, upgrading quality, and introducing program changes.

The panel's initial charge was to recommend a series of options for evaluating the Head Start program. It soon became apparent, however, that the panel should instead focus on defining an overall strategy and a set of guiding principles for selecting and conducting future Head Start research

156

and evaluation efforts. The panel strongly stressed that to reach the nation's goals for Head Start, there must be established an integrated program of research and a supporting research infrastructure. The *Blueprint Report* of the panel has guided research and evaluation directions of Head Start since its publication (U.S. Department of Health & Human Services, 1990).

Advisory Committee on Head Start Quality and Expansion

The Advisory Committee on Head Start Quality and Expansion was created in June 1993 to review the Head Start program and make recommendations for improvement and expansion. Its 47 members, including SRCD Black Caucus members Diana Slaughter-Defoe and Valora Washington, sought to open a new chapter in the history of the program.

Reviewing existing data and reports on Head Start and consulting with a wide variety of individuals and groups across the country, the Committee found that, after a period of rapid expansion, Head Start should be proud of many successes yet still needed to address quality problems and to refocus on meeting the challenges of a new age. The Committee recommended three broad principles: (a) ensure that every Head Start program strives toward excellence in serving both children and families; (b) expand the number of children served and the scope of services provided in a way that is more responsive to the needs of children and families; and (c) encourage Head Start to forge partnerships with key community and state institutions and programs in the areas of early childhood, family support, health, education, and mental health, and ensure that these partnerships are constantly renewed and reconfigured to meet changes in families, communities, and state and national policies.

Head Start Transition Study

In 1990, the U.S. Congress authorized a major program designed to enhance the early public school transitions of former Head Start children and their families. This new program was launched—via 31 local Transition Demonstration Programs—to test the value of extending comprehensive, Head Start-like supports "upward" through the first four years of elementary school. In a follow-up to her participation on the National Evaluation Panel, Diana Slaughter-Defoe served on the National Advisory Committee for the Transition Study, providing direction to the project directors, Craig and Sharon Ramey, as they organized and implemented the evaluation of this innovative program.

In 1991, the Head Start Bureau, in collaboration with SRCD, initiated a biennial conference series to highlight and share research conducted on Head Start populations and related topics. The themes of the conference have included "New Directions in Child and Family Research: Shaping Head Start in the Nineties," "Implications for Serving Families with Young Children," "Making a Difference for Children, Families, and Communities," "Children and Families in an Era of Rapid Change," "Developmental and Contextual Transitions of Children and Families," and "The First Eight Years: Pathways to the Future." SRCD Black Caucus member Suzanne Randolph has served on the conference planning committee since its inception, representing both SRCD and its Black Caucus.

Following the 1990 report, *Head Start Research and Evaluation: A Blueprint for the Future*, the Commissioner for Children, Youth, and Families established a follow-up panel on "Research and Evaluation: Implementing the Blueprint." Diana Slaughter-Defoe and Luis Laosa served on this panel. One of its major tasks was to recommend studies on the Head Start population that could be undertaken over the next few years. At both the 1991 and 1993 Head Start National Research Conferences, members of the Head Start Minority Scholars Conference presented a panel to assess the evaluation activities of the Head Start Bureau in the context of recommendations generated at the Minority Scholars conferences.

During three of the Head Start Research Conferences, members of the Minority Scholars—Sadie Grimmett, Margaret Beale Spencer, Ura Jean Oyemade Bailey, Valora Washington, Diana Slaughter-Defoe, Luis Laosa, and Ethel Hall—critically assessed the priority areas identified by the National Evaluation Panel in relation to the perceived needs of minority children and families in Head Start. These areas included (a) bilingual/bicultural children and Head Start, (b) health care and children with disabilities in Head Start, (c) Head Start's influence on families, (d) Head Start and the community, and (e) the effect of the amount and intensity of participation in Head Start.

Of particular concern to Minority Scholars were issues such as: How is quality defined in evaluation? How is the interplay of program outcomes and diversity being addressed? To what extent has the differential impact of the program within groups been considered? What is the impact of Head Start parent involvement on relationships with the schools? What is the impact of Head Start on retention in the public schools? What is the impact of individual characteristics of parents on Head Start outcomes? What consideration is given to the role of community and societal factors in determining outcomes for children? What specific research strategies are employed in current evaluation studies and projected for future studies?

For each of the Head Start Research Conferences in which the Minority Scholars panel was held, there was much interest by minority and non-minority researchers and Head Start staff. Minority Head Start staff were keenly aware of the issues raised by the Minority Scholars and encouraged their future involvement in monitoring the evaluation programs. Although Minority Scholars continued to participate in advisory committees, the level and intensity of their involvement in overall Head Start research and evaluation remains minimal.[1]

HEAD START STAFF DEVELOPMENT AND TRAINING INITIATIVES FACILITATED BY SRCD BLACK CAUCUS MEMBERS

Minority Scholars emphasized the need for enhancing the skills of Head Start staff, particularly teachers. Because many minority scholars were at Historically Black Colleges and Universities (HBCUs), this problem was addressed by the Head Start Bureau through the HBCU Partnership Initiative. By 1999, 17 HBCUs had been awarded training grants.

In 1993, to address the need for administrative staff training, the National Head Start Association began its "Partnership Project" with funding from the W. K. Kellogg Foundation and the Ford Foundation. Under the leadership of Valora Washington, this project was designed to increase local collaborative efforts with public schools, child-care programs, health providers, family support services, special needs services, and the private sector.

EPILOGUE

As Head Start has expanded in various directions, minority scholars from many disciplines have become involved on multiple levels. For example, wide citation of the Head Start model as an international approach to alleviating the adverse effects of poverty on children and their families has stimulated the interest of the World Bank and the international community. New research on the importance of brain development during the early years has emphasized the prenatal to 3-year-old period, thereby expanding the Head Start research arena to public health and other interdisciplinary fields.

As Head Start expands and new researchers enter the field, it is clear that the original impetus for convening the Minority Scholars in Head Start Research (i.e., the relative paucity of minority researchers in the Head Start research literature) remains a critical factor. Although significant improvements have been made, many of the criticisms and concerns raised earlier by Minority Scholars are still relevant and need to be monitored vigilantly. Minority participation in the Head Start Research Conferences is unusually small. There remains a need to engage more minority researchers in proposal review committees, Head Start advisory committees, national evaluation and research studies, and overall policy and direction. Quite possibly, reconvening Minority Scholars, thus engaging a new generation of national and international scholars and researchers from diverse disciplines, is still the most viable strategy for stimulating renewed networking to address the many pressing issues facing minority children and families in poverty.

REFERENCES

Beatty, L. (1989, March). *Involvement of Black fathers in Head Start*. Paper presented at the Annual Meeting of the American Educational Research Association, San Francisco, CA.

Carter, S., & Oyemade, U. J. (1990). *Parents getting a head start against drugs: A primary prevention curriculum*. Rockville, MD: U.S. Department of Health and Human Services, Office for Substance Abuse Prevention.

Cole, O. J., & Washington, V. (1986). A critical analysis of the effects of Head Start on minority children. *Journal of Negro Education*, **55**, 91–106.

Collins, R. C. (1983). *Head Start: Foundation for excellence*. Washington, DC: U.S. Department of Health and Human Services, Administration for Children, Youth & Families.

Gary, L. E., Beatty, L., & Weaver, G. (1987). *Involvement of Black fathers in Head Start*. Washington, DC: Howard University, Institute for Urban Affairs and Research.

McAdoo, J. L. (1981). Black father and child interactions. In L. E. Gary (Ed.), *Black Men* (pp. 115–130). Beverly Hills, CA: Sage.

Oyemade, U. J. (1985). The rationale for Head Start as a vehicle for the upward mobility of minority families: A minority perspective. *American Journal of Orthopsychiatry*, **55**, 591–602.

Oyemade, U. J., & Washington, V. (1989). Drug abuse prevention begins in early childhood. *Young Children*, **44** (9), 6–12.

Oyemade, U. J., Washington, V., & Gullo, D. F. (1989). The relationship between Head Start parent involvement and the economic self-sufficiency of Head Start families. *Journal of Negro Education*, **58** (1), 5–15.

Ross, C. J. (1979). Early skirmishes with poverty: The historical roots of Head Start. In E. Zigler & J. Valentine (Eds.), *Project Head Start: A legacy of the war on poverty* (pp. 21–42). New York: Free Press.

Slaughter, D. (1969). Maternal antecedents of the academic achievement behaviors of Afro-American Head Start children. *Educational Horizons*, **48** (1), 24–28.

Slaughter, D., Lindsey, R. W., Nakagawa, K., & Kuehne, V. S. (1989). Who gets involved? Head Start mothers as persons. *Journal of Negro Education*, **58** (1), 16–29.

Slaughter, D., Washington, V., Oyemade, U. J., & Lindsey, R. W. (1988). Head Start: A backward and forward look. *Social Policy Report*, **3** (2). [Available from the Society for Research in Child Development, University of Michigan, 3131 S. State St. Suite 302, Ann Arbor, MI, 48108].

U.S. Department of Health and Human Services, Administration for Children, Youth & Families, Head Start Bureau. (1990). *Head Start research and evaluation: A blueprint for the future (DHHS Publication No. ACY91–31195)*. Washington, DC: Author.

Washington, V., & Oyemade, U. J. (1985). Changing family trends: Head Start must respond. *Young Children*, **40** (6), 12–15–17–19.

Washington, V., & Oyemade, U. J. (1987). *Project Head Start: Past, present and future trends in the context of family needs*. New York: Garland.

Washington, V., & Oyemade, U. J. (1995). *Project Head Start: Models and Strategies for the Twenty-First Century*. New York: Garland.

Zigler, E., & Lang, M. E. (1983). Head Start: Looking toward the future. *Young Children*, **38** (6), 3–6.

NOTE

1. As Minority Scholars engaged in research, we believed it was critical to document the findings and recommendations in order to maximize the impact on Head Start programs and policy as well as the overall field of early childhood development and intervention. Publication of the proceedings of the first Minority Scholars' meetings in the *Journal of Orthopsychiatry* (Oyemade, 1985) and the *Journal of Negro Education* (Cole & Washington, 1986) was a major milestone. Later, Garland Press published two books by Minority Scholars: *Project Head Start: Past, Present and Future Trends in the Context of Family Needs* (Washington & Oyemade, 1987) and *Project Head Start: Models and Strategies for the 21st Century* (Washington & Oyemade, 1995). Similarly, Diana Slaughter-Defoe edited a major volume in 1988, *Black Children and Poverty: A Developmental Perspective* (Jossey-Bass). Other publications by Minority Scholars with specific relevance for Project Head Start are available upon contact with the first author.

SECTION IV. SUPPORTIVE ACADEMIC INSTITUTIONS

The accomplishments of a group of African American scholars and their dedication to actions beneficial to Black children would not have been possible without the training and cultural milieu of educational institutions. Although African American members of the Society for Research in Child Development (SRCD) were educated at a variety of institutions, two universities stand out for their impact on the process—Howard University and the University of Michigan. There is an overlap between these institutions in faculty and students, which contributes to a continuous cross-fertilization of ideas and projects: many undergraduates from Howard University attend graduate school at the University of Michigan, and persons connected with Michigan often teach at Howard. Each university, however, has uniquely impacted the process of conducting social science research on Black children.

Algea O. Harrison-Hale writes in Chapter XIII about the University of Michigan and its pervasive influence on social science research on Black children. She addresses how the university has come to fulfill an important role in the professional research community, and how that role has been shaped by the activism of African Americans and Caucasian cohorts at the institution. Because of Michigan's tradition as a notable research institution, African American scholars who have studied, been mentored, or taught there have contributed outstanding research to the dialogue on Black children. Scholars elsewhere have noted the qualities of the design, the depth of the investigation, and the breadth of inferences from Michigan scholars. Harrison-Hale explains why the educational and cultural milieus at the University of Michigan are important to the broader community, the research and scholarly community, and policy and decision makers.

In Chapter XIV, Velma Lapoint and Veronica Thomas discuss the unique contributions of Howard University to social science research on Black children. The authors emphasize how the racial and cultural identity of scholars at this historical Black college informs scientific knowledge on Black children, and how these scholars' intimate knowledge of the Black community influences the ways in which they conceptualize, implement, and summarize their research. La Point and Thomas also note outstanding contributions of scholars from Howard University, beginning with the seminal work of Mamie Clark and Kenneth Clark, which revolutionized the educational system in America.

These two extraordinary universities and their excellent scholars have had tremendous impact on social science on Black children, advancing our understanding of both the development of Black children and their contexts.

XIII. CONTRIBUTIONS OF AFRICAN AMERICANS FROM THE UNIVERSITY OF MICHIGAN TO SOCIAL SCIENCE RESEARCH ON BLACK CHILDREN AND FAMILIES

The University of Michigan, a prestigious American institution of higher learning, has provided a tradition of scholarship for a dynamic cadre of African American scholars. This chapter explains how this union of scholarship and African American scholars occurred and its importance to social science research. Included also is a brief discussion on the contributions of some African American members of the Society for Research in Child Development (SRCD) who have a connection to the University of Michigan—as students, interns at one of its research centers, or faculty. Their residence at Michigan was fertile ground for fostering an empirical-based scientific approach to social issues and, not surprisingly, led to publications in SRCD's main journal, *Child Development*, a major source of information for policy makers, practitioners, and influential decision makers. Although *Child Development* has an 80–85% rejection rate, a survey of just six African American members of SRCD associated with Michigan found 13 articles published therein between 1973 and 1997, as well as two contributions to SRCD's *Monograph* series and two contributions to SRCD's *Review of Child Development Research* series. This suggests that Michigan provides both excellent research training and a supportive context for African American scholars interested in investigating the experiences of Black children and families. This environment was created from two social forces: the historical emphasis on research at Michigan and the activism of its African American students and faculty, along with Caucasian peers, colleagues, and faculty.

SOCIAL FORCES

Michigan Traditions

The University of Michigan was established in 1817 in Detroit, and later moved to its present location in Ann Arbor, where classes were first offered in the fall of 1841. In the 19th century, most educational institutions offered a traditional classical curriculum of recitations and lectures. Michigan challenged this tradition by offering its students a seminar on conducting research. The academic leaders of the university began to see its mission as adding to the pool of knowledge in the learned fields and envisioned this new knowledge being generated by empirical research. Thus by 1890 graduate students and faculty were conducting research in the university's laboratories, libraries, and museums. Graduate students had to undertake research projects supervised by faculty who were also involved in empirical studies. Also prevalent was the belief that the university must give service to the state that helped maintain it and aid citizens who were not enrolled at the school. By the end of the 19th century, the University of Michigan had become one of the most successful examples of a nonsectarian, state-supported university—a model for other state universities (Peckham, 1994).

As at most universities, psychology was first taught as part of the curriculum in the Philosophy Department. Scholars interested in issues relevant to psychology as it is known today were called moral philosophers. The naming of Henry Tappan and Erastus O. Haven, scholars in the moral philosophy tradition, as the first two presidents of the University of Michigan suggests that psychology was a valued field of study at the institution (Peckham, 1994).

Empirical work in psychology began when John Dewey came to the university in 1884, having received his Ph.D. from the Johns Hopkins University under the guidance of G. Stanley Hall. Dewey's legacy at Michigan was to continue the empirical approach of Hall and begin experimental work in psychology. He encouraged the founding of the first psychological laboratory at the university by James Tufts in 1890.

Through the years Michigan's reputation as an eminent research institution grew, and psychology became a department on its own in 1929. Since the 1960s Michigan's Department of Psychology has been consistently judged one of the five strongest in the country.

Black Action Movement (BAM)

When the University of Michigan opened its doors, it was available to all who could afford to pay. At that time, higher education was mainly a privilege of sons of the elite and wealthy, but Michigan admitted women and minorities in small numbers even in the early years. Nonetheless, progressive and concerned persons noted in 1969 that the number of African Americans enrolled at Michigan was only 1,000—in a student population of some 30,000. (I finished my master's degree there in 1959 and my Ph.D. in 1970, and had very few African American peers.) Thus a group of social activists on campus created the second force that shaped the relation between the University of Michigan and African Americans, the emergence of the BAM. I was a member of the group, as were Harriette McAdoo, John McAdoo, Vonnie McLoyd, and Suzanne Randolph, all of them also active in the Black Caucus of SRCD, eliciting more positive interactions between the SRCD's governing structure and its African American members.

BAM designed a plan of action for increasing African American enrollment at the university and approached the administration and the Board of Regents for financial support. The plan called for increasing financial aid, support services, and minority staff to address the needs of African American students; supporting a Center of Afro-American Studies; and increasing the percentage of African American students from 3% to 10%. When, in March 1970, the Regents of the university refused to meet BAM's demands for financial guarantees to meets its goals, BAM called for a campus-wide strike, which was supported by many members of the university community.

Although BAM had varying degrees of success in persuading the administration to meet its demands, the social movement resulted in the creation of a critical mass of African American faculty and students. Today BAM, having morphed into an organization known as By Any Means Necessary (BAMN), continues its tradition of social activism supporting the goals of the original movement. After Michigan's policies for affirmative action in admission to undergraduate educational programs and the Law School were challenged in court, the legal issues reached the level of the Supreme Court. In 2002, BAMN was instrumental in getting university students and others across the nation to demonstrate in front of the Supreme Court for this historic decision. Recently BAMN has reached out to Detroit, its closest urban area, for support, and has worked to stop the movement of Ward Connelly and others to put a referendum on affirmative action on a statewide ballot in Michigan.

The support at the university for the activism of its African American faculty and students, merged with its historical tradition of an empirical approach to psychology, created and continues to create a strong research-oriented group of African American social scientists. No other university has produced such a large alumni of African American scholars who are supportive of their peers from the university. This increasingly large group of scholars, who dominate empirical studies with Black participants, is affectionately known by the moniker "Michigan Mafia."

CONTRIBUTORS

Many Michigan associates brought their skills and training to the study of African American children and families, making contributions to the pool of knowledge and advancing the directions of studies of the Black experience. It is impractical to discuss the contributions, honors, publications, and professional positions of all members of the Black Caucus from the University of Michigan, and I apologize to those I have omitted. The focus here is on a handful of members who have had leadership roles in the Black Caucus and SRCD and made major contributions to the journal *Child Development*: Oscar Barbarin, Algea O. Harrison-Hale (the author), Harriette McAdoo, John McAdoo, Vonnie McLoyd, and Suzanne Randolph. The discussion makes clear that African American members of SRCD, trained to use the exacting scientific standards demanded by the University of Michigan, have made a unique and substantial contribution to social science research.

Oscar Barbarin was at the University of Michigan from 1979 to 2000, serving on the faculty of the Department of Psychology, School of Social Work, and Center for Afro-American and African Studies. Currently he is the L. Richardson and Emily Preyer Bicentennial Distinguished Professor for Strengthening Families in the School of Social Work, and Senior Investigator at the Frank Porter Graham Child Development Center at the University of North Carolina Chapel Hill. His research, begun during the first 25 years of the Black Caucus, focused on African American children and families, especially the effects of social risks on mental health. Barbarin (1999) investigated stress, coping, and socio-emotional development in families of children with life-threatening illnesses such as cancer, sickle cell disease, hemophilia, and AIDS, and tested the effects of a preventive, home-based, family-focused intervention. The intervention program was one of the first culturally sensitive projects for this special group of participants. Barbarin also collaborated on research with international colleagues and developed research and training exchange programs intended to nurture the next generation of South African scholars and prepare American students for scholarly work in Africa (Barbarin, 1999; Barbarin & Richter, 2001).

Algea O. Harrison-Hale received her Ph.D. from the University of Michigan in 1970 and is currently Professor of Psychology at Oakland University. She was senior editor of a *Child Development* review article on ethnic families of color, which summarized the literature and offered suggestions for future research (Harrison, Serafica, & McAdoo, 1984), and coauthored an article in *Child Development* on family ecologies of ethnic minority children (Harrison, Wilson, Pine, Chan, & Buriel, 1990). The latter was one of the first manuscripts in which the writers on the social science literature of an ethnic minority group were scholars from the same ethnic minority group.

Harriette McAdoo also received her Ph.D. from the University of Michigan and is currently University Distinguished Professor at Michigan

State University. Her skills in empirical approaches, research design, and statistics were learned from Michigan faculty, especially Lorraine Nadelman. McAdoo was coauthor of a major theoretical article on minority children which reflected current concepts and empirical findings (Garcia Coll et al., 1996). Presenting an integrative model for the study of developmental competencies in minority children, this article shaped future research designs in which minority children were subjects.

McAdoo was also one of three Associate Editors (with Ross Parke as Editor) of the seventh volume of the *Review of Child Development Research: The Family* (Parke, 1984). She is best known for publishing a series of books on Black families (H. P. McAdoo, 1981, 1988, 1997) and children (1985), which are still in print (one was reprinted in 2002).

The late John McAdoo, who also received his Ph.D. from Michigan, was one of the first researchers to identify, through empirical investigation, the positive influence of African American fathers on their children (J. L. McAdoo, 1979, 1981, 1988). Earlier social science literature on father absence had created a negative stereotype for African American fathers. McAdoo's untimely passing left a void in the activities of the Black Caucus, and his colleagues sorely miss him; at the time of his death, he was Professor in the Department of Family and Child Ecology at Michigan State University.

Vonnie McLoyd was Professor of Psychology at the University of Michigan and now holds the same position at the University of North Carolina-Chapel Hill. She was coeditor for two special issues of *Child Development*, which focused, respectively, on minority children (Spencer & McLoyd, 1990) and children and poverty (Huston, Garcia Coll, & McLoyd, 1994). The research that earned McLoyd an award from the MacArthur Foundation, however, was her illumination of the impact of poverty on the development of African American children. McLoyd's work (1990a, b; McLoyd, Jayaratne, Ceballo, & Borquez, 1994) illustrated, with empirical documentation, the connections between two trends in developmental literature—writings on developmental processes and writings on the impact of poverty on children. Her identification of the psychological processes involved in the impact of poverty on development has led to stronger policy positions (Huston, McLoyd, & Garcia-Coll, 1994).

Suzanne Randolph received her M.A. and Ph.D. in psychology from the University of Michigan and is currently Associate Professor at the University of Maryland. Randolph's examination, with coauthor Vonnie McLoyd, of the quality and quantity of research on African American children in *Child Development* from 1936 to 1980 was a major contribution to the field as a criticism of the scholarship of manuscripts selected to appear in SRCD's principal journal (McLoyd & Randolph, 1985). The authors' well-documented findings forced an examination of the validity and reliability of data in articles in *Child Development* in which African American children were participants. Their criticism of major shortcomings, such as the confounding of social class and race in research designs and suggestions that the lower scores of African American children were primarily because of their racial background, were appropriate and timely.

SIGNIFICANCE

All scholars need a supportive university environment, with established professionals as mentors, colleagues who share research interests, and graduate students to serve as research assistants. Financial and administrative support is also important. These are minimum qualifications for building a research tradition in an area of study. Since the 1970s, African American scholars have enjoyed such conditions at the University of Michigan and have continued to contribute to the social science literature on Black children and families. This is important to the field for several reasons.

Shared Expertise and Knowledge

The willingness of these African American scholars from Michigan to share their expertise and knowledge with minority students and peers has helped to expand the number of minority scholars who are well trained in research skills. Moreover, these scholars are becoming the voice for the Black experience in professional literature and applied areas relevant to the Black community, such as aging, education, clinical settings, and health issues. Following are some of the means or opportunities that have facilitated the spreading of the Michigan connection.

During the 1970s University of Michigan African American graduate students Frank Yates and A. Wade Boykin established a series of Empirical Conferences on Black Psychology to underpin the emerging area of Black psychology with sound empirical investigations of the Black experience. The five persons on the planning committee for the conferences included Michigan graduates Algea Harrison-Hale, Harriette McAdoo, and John McAdoo; Boykin, who became a graduate; and A. J. Franklin, who attended Michigan with an internship at the Institute for Social Research. The first 11 conferences, funded by foundation and government monies, were designed to convene a small group of Black social scientists whose primary interest was research. The small size of the group permitted a profound exchange that improved the participants' research projects and assisted them in preparing data for publication. Over approximately 30 years this conference series has facilitated the establishment of a network among Black social scientists across the nation. The conferences still take place, although not every year.

Another means of connecting persons to the Michigan traditions has been the Program for Research on Black Americans, at the university's Institute for Social Research. The African American Mental Health Research Program and the Michigan Center for Urban African American Aging Research are also at the Institute. The Center for Research on Ethnicity, Culture, and Health and the Program on Poverty, the Underclass, and Public Policy are located elsewhere at the university. These programs provide opportunities for internships, graduate and postdoctoral studies, scholarly research, and, especially, a free flow of ideas among scholars.

Exceptional Researchers

A second reason why the University of Michigan's supportive environment for African American scholars is important to the field is the development of an exceptional group of researchers to address issues and concerns of the Black community. Given the history of the field of psychology and the long tradition of a racist trend in its literature (Richards, 1997; Winston, 2004), scholars are needed who know the community and can describe the Black experience, explain behaviors with innovative conceptual frameworks, predict environmental conditions conducive to positive or negative experiences, and design constructive programs relevant to the culture. Scholars who possess these academic tools and understand the culture of the participants in their study can generate conceptual frameworks and empirical investigations to combat the taint of racism in developmental psychology, where the majority of studies are conducted by White middle- and upper-class scholars on White middle-class participants.

Progressive Education for All Students

A third reason why the presence of so many African American students and scholars on Michigan's campus is important to the field is its impact on a progressive education for all students nationally. The University of Michigan has traditionally made a commitment to including and advancing African Americans. In recent years affirmative action has come under attack by a well-financed group that opposes its purpose and results. The group has selected as battle grounds major public research universities that are mainly supported by tax dollars. The University of Texas, Austin, and the University of California, Berkeley, both flagships for their state's higher education, gave in to the pressures without a fight, resulting in a tremendous drop in enrollment by minority students.

When this same group filed a lawsuit against Michigan concerning its affirmative action, the university actively defended its programs. There were a number of strategies in play to win the final favorable ruling from the Supreme Court, but the most important one came from its research tradition. A team of researchers led by Patricia Gurin, Chair of the Psychology Department, conducted a major empirical investigation (Gurin, Dey, & Hurtado, 2002) that demonstrated the value of affirmative action for all students. Using the theoretical framework of cognitive development and social psychology, the team investigated the effects of classroom diversity and informal interaction among African American, Asian American, Latino/a, and White students on learning and democracy outcomes. The data analysis illustrated the educational and civic importance of informal interaction among different racial and ethnic groups during the college years. The article enlightened the nation, giving empirical evidence of how affirmative action contributes to the cognitive and social growth of all students. Thus other colleges and universities whose affirmative action programs are threatened can use the empirical investigations of scholars from Michigan as a justification for their efforts.

In summary, the social forces that welded together Michigan's academic tradition of empirical verification and the activism of its African American students and faculty produced a phenomenon that has contributed to the social science literature and promoted a progressive educational agenda.

REFERENCES

Barbarin, O. (1999). Social risks and psychological adjustment: A comparison of African-American and South African children. *Child Development*, **70**, 1348–1359.

Barbarin, O., & Richter, L. (2001). *Mandela's children: Child development in post-Apartheid South Africa*. New York: Routledge.

Garcia Coll, C., Lamberty, G., Jenkins, R., McAdoo, H. P., Crnic, K., & Wasik, B. H., et al. (1996). An integrative model for the study of developmental competencies in minority children. *Child Development*, **67**, 1891–1914.

Gurin, P., Dey, E. L., & Hurtado, S. (2002). Diversity and higher education: Theory and impact on educational outcomes. *Harvard Educational Review*, **72**, 330–366.

Harrison, A., Serafica, F., & McAdoo, H. (1984). Ethnic families of color. In R. D. Parke (Ed.), *Review of Child Development research: Vol. 7. The family* (pp. 329–371). Chicago: University of Chicago Press.

Harrison, A. O., Wilson, M., Pine, C. J., Chan, S. Q., & Buriel, R. (1990). Family ecologies of ethnic minority children. *Child Development*, **61**, 347–362.

Huston, A., Garcia Coll, C., & McLoyd, V. C. (Eds.). (1994). Children and poverty [special issue]. *Child Development*, **6** (2).

Huston, A., McLoyd, V. C., & Garcia Coll, C. (1994). Children and poverty: Issues in contemporary research. *Child Development*, **65**, 275–282.

McAdoo, J. L. (1979). A study of father–child interaction patterns and self-esteem in Black preschool children. *Young Children*, **34** (1), 46–53.

McAdoo, H. P. (Ed.). (1981a). *Black families*. Beverly Hills, CA: Sage.

McAdoo, J. L. (1981b). Black father and child interactions. In L. E. Gary (Ed.), *Black men* (pp. 115–130). Beverly Hills, CA: Sage.

McAdoo, H. P. (Ed.). (1988a). *Black families* (2nd ed.). Beverly Hills, CA: Sage.

McAdoo, J. L. (1988b). The involvement of Black fathers in the socialization of Black children. In H. P. McAdoo (Ed.), *Black families* (2nd ed., pp. 257–269). Beverly Hills, CA: Sage.

McAdoo, H. P. (Ed.). (1997). *Black families* (3rd ed.). Beverly Hills, CA: Sage.

McAdoo, H. P. (Ed.). (2002). *Black children* (2nd ed.). Thousand Oaks, CA: Sage.

McAdoo, H. P., & McAdoo, J. L. (Eds.). (1985). *Black children* (1st ed.). Beverly Hills, CA: Sage.

McLoyd, V. C. (1990a). The impact of economic hardship on Black families and children: Psychological distress, parenting, and socioemotional development. *Child Development*, **61**, 311–346.

McLoyd, V. C. (1990b). Minority children: Introduction to the special issue. *Child Development*, **61**, 263–266.

Mcloyd, V. C., Jayaratne, T., Ceballo, R., & Borquez, J. (1994). Unemployment and work interruption among African American single mothers: Effects on parenting and adolescent socioemotional functioning. *Child Development*, **65**, 562–589.

McLoyd, V. C., & Randolph, S. (1985). Secular trends in the study of Afro-American children: A review of *Child Development*, 1936–1980. In A. B. Smuts & J. W. Hagen (Eds.), *History and research in child development: In celebration of the fiftieth anniversary of the Society. Monographs of the Society for Research in Child Development* **50** (4–5, Serial No. 211), pp. 78–92.

Parke, R. D. (Ed.). (1984). *Review of child development research: Vol. 7. The family.* Chicago: University of Chicago Press.

Peckham, H. (1994). *The making of the University of Michigan, 1817–1992* (Rev. ed., M. L. Steneck & N. H. Steneck, Eds.). Ann Arbor: University of Michigan Press.

Richards, G. (1997). *"Race," racism and psychology: Towards a reflexive history.* London: Routledge.

Spencer, M. B., & McLoyd, V. C. (Eds.). (1990). Minority children [special issue]. *Child Development*, **6** (2).

Winston, A. S. (2004). *Defining differences: Race and racism in the history of psychology.* Washington, DC: American Psychological Association.

XIV. CONTRIBUTIONS OF HOWARD UNIVERSITY TO SOCIAL SCIENCE RESEARCH ON BLACK CHILDREN

This chapter highlights the significant contributions of Howard University to the history and development of social science research on Black children from 1973 to 1997. These contributions were made by various Howard University professors, many of whom were members, affiliates, or supporters of the Black Caucus of the Society for Research in Child Development (SRCD), as well as Black Caucus SRCD members who were professors from other universities and professionals from research organizations affiliated with Howard University's undertakings. This chapter does not detail the full research career of Howard University faculty who were also SRCD members. Rather, it cites these members' work within various academic and research units at the University, as well as conferences that they collaboratively organized about Black child development.

As coauthors of this chapter, we are both long-time Howard University faculty members in disciplines related to child development and education. Over the years, much of our work has had particular application to Black children's development. Velma LaPoint has been a member of the SRCD Black Caucus since the mid-1970s, and Veronica Thomas has held numerous key positions at Howard University that allow for intimate knowledge of the university's policies and programs that support social science scholarship related to Black children's development. As faculty members, we recognize the reciprocal influence of professional organizations, especially those that serve the needs of African American researchers and other professionals who work to promote Black children's development. These organizations contribute immensely to the development of the faculty and, of course, the faculty contribute to the development of the organizations and, ultimately, to the discipline. This reciprocal role is clearly illustrated in the history of the SRCD Black Caucus.

In Section I of this chapter, we provide a brief history of Howard University and its support of multidisciplinary research on Black children's development. In Section, II we document early and recent activities in various Howard University Departments, Centers, Institutes, and other programs. Faculty from Howard University and other institutions who were or are SRCD Black Caucus members are highlighted for their contributions to the history and development of social science research on Black children. As it was not feasible for us to provide a full citation of all the relevant faculty/staff publications and other works, readers are encouraged to refer to other chapters and Appendix A in this volume as well as available reference retrieval systems to obtain additional information. In the last section, we offer concluding remarks regarding the University's contributions to social science research on Black child development in the past, present, and the future.

Howard University's long tradition of focusing on the strengths of people of African descent as well as the vitality and intellectual tradition related to Black child development taking place at Howard University from 1970 to 1997 (and beyond) had a significant impact on the SRCD Black Caucus. In our review, four predominant yet overlapping themes emerged in relation to the research of Howard University social science researchers, including those early and remaining SRCD Black Caucus members. These themes are evident in the faculty members' published work and in reviews of conferences at Howard University relating to research on Black children's development. The first theme is the role of the researchers' cultural or racial identity in informing scientific knowledge. The cultural and racial identity of Howard's (Black) faculty significantly influenced their social science research perspectives on Black children: their intimate knowledge of Black institutions, values, religious ideals, and patterns of social and interpersonal relations has helped determine how they conceptualized (what they studied), implemented (how they studied it), and summarized (the conclusions and implications) their research. The second theme relates to Howard University researchers' emphasis on the nexus of culture, poverty, race, and empowerment (or perceptions of the lack thereof) on the psychological and behavioral outcomes of children. In other words, Howard researchers took into consideration both the macro- and microdynamics impacting Black child development. A third theme relates to the issue of cultural deficit versus cultural difference. In studying Black children, Howard University researchers moved away from the cultural deficit approach that was prominent in the existing literature related to this population. Instead, they emphasized respecting and acknowledging the cultural diversity that often results in different behaviors and practices among Black children and families. The fourth theme is advocacy versus objectivity. As social science researchers, Howard University faculty sought to conduct objective and sound research, yet as Black scholars they saw that advocacy played a major role in the meaning of their work. These researchers did not believe that advocating for Black children was antithetical to good social science research; instead they promoted applying sound research on behalf of Black children.

Our major sources of information for this chapter include both diverse archival records and published materials: (a) institutional reports from Howard University units such as the Moorland Spingarn Research Center, (b) annual and interim reports from selected departments, colleges/schools, and center/institutes, and (c) information on Howard University activities in refereed journal articles, book chapters, books, and other professional publications. In addition, we examined written and verbal reports from various SRCD Black Caucus members, such as Ura Jean Oyemade (Bailey), William Curtis Banks (deceased 1998), Diana Slaughter-Defoe, Albert Roberts (deceased 2004), John (deceased 1994), and Harriettee McAdoo, who were Howard faculty or who participated in Howard conferences related to research on Black children's development.

HOWARD UNIVERSITY: AN OVERVIEW, PAST, AND PRESENT

An Act of Congress (S529) established Howard University, a comprehensive, research-oriented, predominately African American university, in Washington, DC, in 1867. As one of the nation's most pre-eminent historical Black universities, Howard University has a mission to provide an educational experience of exceptional quality to students of high academic potential, with particular emphasis on educational opportunities for promising Black students, and to attract and sustain a cadre of faculty who are, through their teaching and research, committed to the development of distinguished and compassionate graduates and to the quest for solutions to human and social problems in the United States and throughout the world. The university has sought to remain true to its mission as a center of excellence, leadership, truth, and service. Today, Howard University is comprised of 12 schools and colleges offering degree programs in more than 120 specialized subjects and doctorates in more than 25 areas. Its students, numbering approximately 11,000, come from all 50 states and at least 115 countries.

Historically, Howard University has been a national repository of the African American cultural experience and a recognized center of African American thought, critical analysis, and leadership. It currently stands as the nation's only true comprehensive university with a predominately Black constituency, with a faculty engaging in a wide range of intellectual pursuits. Many faculty are renowned for expertise in their chosen discipline and have been on the cutting edge of this country's major social and political developments. As a Carnegie Foundation Research I Institution, Howard University has placed high priority on the active involvement of faculty in research activities. Over the years, the university has experienced a dynamic history, replete with tensions and triumphs relating to several issues, such as (a) its founding and administration by Black and White professionals, (b) its annual Congressional funding appropriation, (c) diversity in faculty research and advocacy that emphasized the nexus of race, culture, and social class and their role in the Black community's empowerment and resiliency, (d) student protests relating to their role in institutional governance and the need for Afro-centric curricula, and (e) strategies to position the institution for the future in the context of changing national and global priorities (Dyson, 1941; Henry, 1997; Holloway, 2002; Logan, 1969; Salzman, Smith, & West, 1996).

DEPARTMENTS, SCHOOLS, INSTITUTES, CENTERS, AND CONFERENCES

Howard University's presence in the history and development of social science research on Black children has been evident through work emerging from a number of academic departments, institutes, centers, conferences, and other projects. Many of these conferences and projects were organized or co-organized by SRCD members who were Howard University faculty. These and other significant initiatives have contributed to Howard University's continuing legacy—its quest for finding solutions to social problems and its effort toward improving the human condition. The following sections highlight significant contributions and activities of individual units in the advancement of social science scholarship on Black child development.

The Department of Psychology

The Department of Psychology faculty, through teaching and research, have historically sought to create opportunities for students to learn a rigorous scientific discipline and to pursue an extensive analysis of the Black experience—one of the hallmarks of the training program. Both faculty and students have strived to bring the science of psychology to bear on bettering the lives of minorities and other underserved populations. The faculty, students, and alumni in the department have contributed immensely to our understanding of Black child development. This is evident through the ongoing scholarship of departmental faculty in research on the cognitive, motivational, social, and emotional development of Black children, as well as their sustained involvement in professional associations, such as the SRCD Black Caucus, that promote work in this area.

Overview Prior to the 1980s

Howard University's Department of Psychology was created in 1928 within the College of Liberal Arts. The department quickly placed Howard as the leading Black university providing both undergraduate and graduate training in psychology. An excellent history of the Department of Psychology is chronicled in an article in the *Journal of the Washington Academy of Sciences* (Hopkins, Ross, & Hicks, 1994), and Guthrie (1998) provided a historical overview of the department in a chapter on the "Production of Black Psychologists" in his seminal book *Even the Rat Was White: A Historical View of Psychology*. Much of our discussion in this section is based on these two sources as well as personal communications with selected faculty members in the Department of Psychology.

Albert S. Beckham was the first person to teach psychology at Howard University, first as an instructor and later as an assistant professor. While there, Beckhman founded a psychological laboratory, the first of its kind at a Black institution, and taught all the courses in psychology. The courses focused on applied psychology, mostly in the service of teacher education. The relationship between psychology and teacher education was similar at many colleges and universities during the early history of the discipline (Hopkins et al., 1994). After 4 years at Howard, Beckham left to pursue a doctorate in psychology at New York University; his dissertation was one of the earliest studies of the intelligence of Black children conducted by a Black psychologist. Beckman continued to publish works on Black children and, parenthetically, was the husband of Ruth Howard Beckham, the first African American to receive a Ph.D. in developmental psychology from the Institute of Child Development, University of Minnesota.

In 1928, Francis C. Sumner, referred to as the "Father of Black American Psychologists" (Guthrie, 1998), joined the department as Acting Chair. Also joining the department were Max Meenes and Fredrick Watts, who, along with Sumner, formed the core departmental faculty, teaching and directing master's theses for the next 15 years. One notable master's thesis directed by Meenes was that of Mamie K. Phippes (later Clark), completed in 1939: *An Investigation of the Development of Consciousness of Distinctive Self in Pre-School Children*. Her work laid the foundation for the Clark (Mamie) and Clark (her husband, Kenneth B.) "doll studies," which ultimately played a critical role in the 1954 Supreme Court's *Brown v. the Board of*

Education decision to reverse the "separate but equal" doctrine and to declare racial segregation in schools unconstitutional. Both Mamie and Kenneth (who later went on to become the first, and still only, African American President of the American Psychological Association (APA)) had long and distinguished careers in psychology, with much of their work focusing on Black children's development. Notably, their work began with their bachelor's and master's degrees from Howard University. Excellent overviews of Clarks's contribution to the field of psychology can be found in several journals (Benjamin & Crouse, 2002; Keppel, 2002; Lal, 2002; Phillips, 2000).

The 1980s and Beyond

In 1980, a time of expansion, William Curtis Banks (social psychology, developmental), A. Wade Boykin (developmental), Alfonso Campbell (neuropsychology), Jules Harrell (personality), and Stanley Ridley (clinical) joined the faculty. Each of these scholars developed programs of research focusing on Black populations. Boykin is best known for his work on Black children's cognitive and motivational styles, continuing with an applied emphasis related to education and schooling. William Curtis Banks (deceased 1998), formerly Editor of the *Journal of Black Psychology*, was recognized as a leading researcher on Black children's racial identity, self-concept, and personality. Serge Madhere (developmental psychology) and Hope Hill (clinical), who joined the faculty later, conducted research related to Black children's development, with Hill's work focusing on violence and violence prevention, and Madhere's scholarship exploring cognitive development. Both were actively involved in the work at the Center for Research on the Education of Students Placed as Risk (CRESPAR), each heading a program of research that included a study of Black children's development.

Several members of the department's faculty became intricately involved in the work of the SRCD Black Caucus. Leading this effort, beginning in 1973, were Ura Jean Calhoun (later Oyemade Bailey), a founding member of the SRCD Black Caucus, and Albert Roberts (deceased 2004). Both were involved in curriculum development in the department and in a major federally funded training program for early child-care professionals in Washington, DC. In 1974, Roberts, along with psychologists James F. Savage and Alvis V. Adair, was awarded a multiyear grant from the U.S. Office of Child Development to study the socialization of children of incarcerated mothers. The grant employed many graduate students in Howard's Department of Psychology and School of Social Work, and afforded students the opportunity to collect data for thesis and dissertation research (Roberts, 2002). Other departmental professors who contributed to the

SRCD Black Caucus were Pamela Trotman Reid and John Chambers, currently at Roosevelt University and Florida A&M University, respectively. Both spent their formative years as assistant professors in Howard's Developmental Psychology Program before transitioning to other institutions and making their marks on the field of developmental psychology (Roberts, 2002).

Many talented students have been taught and mentored by psychology professors, who have collaboratively directed more than 100 master's theses and doctoral dissertations relating to Black children's development. A number of these students became or remain members of the SRCD Black Caucus. In addition, a number of undergraduates, who later received their doctorates from other institutions (e.g., Suzanne Randolph, Cynthia Winston, and Lisa Richardson) and graduate students (e.g., Brenda Allen, Caryn Bailey, Lula Beatty, Peggy G. Carr, Constance M. Ellison, Robert Jagers, and Forest Toms), who received their terminal degree from the department, have actively conducted social science research on the development of Black children. In sum, the psychology departmental faculty's contribution to the social science research on Black child development was significant, dramatic, and sustained. The programmatic research of A. Wade Boykin and the late William Curtis Banks was especially vital in their scholarship and training of students (Roberts, 2002).

The School of Education

The School of Education experienced numerous name changes and mergers within existing university units over its early history, while offering diverse programs. It has been the Normal Department, Department of Pedagogy, Teachers College, and Department of Education (Dyson, 1941; Logan, 1969). Teacher education and pedagogy was originally housed in the Normal Department, and has been part of the mission of Howard University since it opened its doors (Dyson, 1941; Logan, 1969). Over the years, the mission of pre-K through 12 teacher preparation has expanded to include training for a wide variety of education- and human development-related professions.

The School of Education in its present form dates from 1971, when the Department of Education in the College of Liberal Arts (now the College of Arts and Sciences) was awarded separate status as a School. It currently consists of three academic departments: (a) Department of Curriculum and Instruction, (b) Department of Educational Administration and Policy, and (c) Department of Human Development and Psychoeducational Studies. Each of these departments, either directly or indirectly, has some emphasis on Black child development through its curriculum, programmatic efforts, and research activities. In addition to these academic units, various co-academic units are operated by the School of Education: (a) the Center for Socioeconomic and Disability Policy Studies, a major training, technical assistance, research, and demonstration unit that focuses on minority disability issues as they affect both children and adults; (b) the Center for Academic Reinforcement, which provides academic support services to students; (c) the Center for Research on the Education of Students Placed At Risk (CRESPAR), a research and development center focusing on enhancing student academic achievement and social competence, schooling environments, and the quality of life for students, teachers, and family members; (d) Early Learning Programs, including a preschool and kindergarten; (e) the *Journal of Negro Education*, a quarterly peer-reviewed publication published continuously since 1932, designed to stimulate and publish work about the education of Black people and others; and (f) TRIO Programs, including Upward Bound, Student Support Services, and the Mathematics/Science Initiative Program—all focused on enhancing the educational outcomes of low-income students.

Although many professors in the School of Education's three academic departments have been actively involved in research on Black children's development, we will highlight the two Departments (Curriculum and Instruction, and Human Development and Psychoeducational Studies) that have had SRCD Black Caucus members on the faculty both early on and currently. The primary mission of the Department of Curriculum and Instruction is to prepare teachers for employment in school systems, but emphasis is also placed on educational research. Rosa Trapp Dukes (Dail), faculty member and current department chair, was an early member of the SRCD Black Caucus, and continues to work in the area of Black early childhood development.

The Department of Human Development and Psychoeducational Studies seeks to prepare educators, psychological and human development practitioners, and researchers for leadership roles and challenging careers involving research, service, and policy, as related to individuals and their families. Faculty members in the Human Development Program (both before and after relocation to the School of Education) with membership in the SRCD Black Caucus include Ura Jean Oyemade Bailey (cognitive and social development, early childhood development, nutritional factors and pregnancy outcomes, substance abuse), O. Jackson Cole, now a Howard University administrator and member of the Department of Psychology (cognitive and social development, early childhood development, nutritional factors and pregnancy outcomes), Velma LaPoint (education and academic achievement of Black youth, influences of commercialism on child development, children of incarcerated parents, social policies, and child development), Hakim Rashid (early childhood development, professional development, educational leadership and student outcomes, influences of commercialism on and child development, Muslim child development), Valora Washington, former full-time faculty member (early childhood development, education of Black youth, adoption, social policies, child development, and family life), and Quida E. Westney (early childhood development, adolescent pregnancy and parenting, child development and family life, and nutritional factors and pregnancy outcomes). Juarlyn Gaiter, formerly of the National Institute of Child Health and Human Development, National Institutes of Health, was also an adjunct professor in the Department, teaching courses in infancy, and an early member of the SRCD Black Caucus.

When the School of Human Ecology was created in 1974, having evolved from the Department of Home Economics, the preschool and parent education components of the Department of Home Economics were incorporated into the Human Development Program; this later became the Department of Human Development, and Ura Jean Oyemade (later Bailey), then an Associate Professor of Human Development, was named Chairperson of the new department. From the 1970s to 1993, the Howard University Nursery School was formally renamed the Howard University Laboratory Preschool (HULP), under the aegis of the School of Human Ecology. During this time, the HULP expanded its programmatic offerings and hours, garnering the interdisciplinary involvement of Howard University students and faculty. Non-Howard University scholars, such as Vonnie McLoyd, from the University of Michigan (also an SRCD Black Caucus member), served as visiting research fellows in the HULP.

The School of Social Work

The School of Social Work at Howard University was formally created in 1935, although instruction was offered in the social services as early as 1914. Lucy Diggs Slowe, the university's first Dean of Women, and Edward Franklin Frazier, Chairman of the Department of Sociology and former Director of the Atlanta University School of Social Work, helped establish instruction in social services and social work at Howard. The first general curriculum in social work was offered in the Department of Sociology and was directed by Frazier, a leading American sociologist and later author of classic publications such as *Negro Youth at the Crossroads* (1940/1967) and *Black Bourgeoisie* (1962). The impetus for the School of Social Work's creation included societal events such as the Great Depression, the Social Security Act in 1935, the emergence of large-scale public social services, and various events leading to World War II. Another strong impetus for social work education at Howard came from local constituents—African Americans employed in the District of Columbia's New Deal programs. Finally, there were few recognized programs in social work in the United

States, and none in Washington, DC, that were open to qualified African American applicants. Having started with an undergraduate curriculum in social work and expanding to graduate study, the School of Social Work currently offers both the master's and doctoral level graduate programs.

Professors (past and current) in the School of Social Work involved in research on Black children's development, who were or are members of the SRCD Black Caucus, include Gladys Hall (child mental health), the late John McAdoo (racial attitudes and self-esteem of Black preschool children, Black father–child interaction), Harriette Pipes McAdoo (racial attitudes and self-esteem in young children, Black family mobility patterns, coping strategies of single mothers, racial identity and self-concept development of African children); and Fariyal Ross-Sheriff (Black adolescent pregnancy and parenting). Ross-Sheriff, John McAdoo, and Harriette McAdoo (presently a faculty member at Michigan State University) assisted in the early development of the Black Caucus of SRCD: Harriette McAdoo was the first African-American to serve on SRCD's Governing Council (1979–1985), and John McAdoo served on SRCD's Committee on Minority Participation and was the first African American appointed to the editorial board of the premier SRCD journal, *Child Development*.

Research Institutes, Centers, and Selected Major Conferences

During the 1970s, Howard University began its transition to a research institution, with the creation of various centers, institutes, and other institutional supports to develop and sustain faculty research. This enhanced the capacity of faculty to pursue a concentrated program of research in the social and behavioral sciences. In the following sections, we briefly describe several Centers and Institutes, and highlight some of the work related to Black child development that emerged from these units. The research institutes and centers also provided a venue for non-Howard University scholars (e.g., Diana Slaughter-Defoe, Margaret Beale Spencer, Vonnie C. McLoyd, Grace [Massey] Carroll) to discuss their research related to Black child development, to review the research of Howard University scholars, and to develop collaborative work in this area.

Institute for Child Development and Family Life (ICDFL), 1972–1985

The ICDFL was established to provide a university-wide mechanism for coordinating interdisciplinary research, service, and training programs related to children and families—and especially Black Americans, locally, nationally, and globally within several activity areas (Institute for Child Development and Family Life, 1972). The ICDFL comprised a network of

Howard University scholars, staff, and programs from several disciplines (e.g., education, medicine, psychology, social work, human ecology, and communications). SRCD Black Caucus members (identified by their name at the time) were Ura Jean Oyemade (Associate Director for Research Development), Harriette Pipes McAdoo (School of Social Work), Albert Roberts (Department of Psychology), Fariyal Ross-Sheriff (School of Social Work), and Rosa Trapp Dukes (Center for the Study of Handicapped Children and Youth, School of Education).

The ICDFL convened two symposia at Howard. The 1978 meeting focused on identifying (a) Howard University faculty's published research and demonstration projects related to Black children and families and (b) future research, policy, and program needs for promoting the development and well-being of Black children and families. Of the 15 members of the Ad Hoc Committee, three were SRCD Black Caucus members/supporters: Ura Jean Oyemade of the School of Human Ecology, Albert Roberts of the Department of Psychology, and Rosa Trapp Dukes of the School of Education. Outcomes of the symposium included intra-university networking for potential research collaboration and a publication, *Research on the Black Child and Family at Howard University 1867–1978* (Rosser & Hamlin, 1979).

The 1981 symposium, "The Study Conference on Black Child Development," focused on the status of research on Black children's development (Institute for Child Development and Family Life, 1981). The conference agenda covered theoretical and methodological issues and challenges, research gaps, and implications for future research. The conference presented immense opportunities for networking and discussing African American and ethnic minority group perspectives in research. Several SRCD Black Caucus members—researchers and professors at Howard University (e.g., the late William Curtis Banks, A. Wade Boykin, Ura Jean Oyemade, Albert Roberts, Fariyal Ross-Sheriff, and Rosa Trapp Dukes) and other institutions (e.g., Walter Allen, William Hall, Diana Slaughter, and Margaret Beale Spencer)—participated in this meeting.

The Institute for Urban Affairs and Research (IUAR), 1972–1992

The IUAR served as a vital link between the Howard University community, the local community, and the nation, through its commitment to studying and solving social problems, particularly those affecting underserved, poor, and urban communities. IUAR had several goals, among them conducting social and behavioral science research, providing research opportunities for students, faculty, and other professionals, and providing technical assistance to community groups, public and private agencies, and professional communities. Over the years, the IUAR research staff was composed of a multi- and interdisciplinary cadre of scholars. Lawrence Gary (mental health, Black families) served as the Director of IUAR for most of its history, though Veronica G. Thomas (Black youth career aspirations, Black families) was Acting Director from 1990 to 1992. IUAR directed various research projects that focused on understanding and advancing Black children's development in areas such as mental health, child abuse and neglect, the use of social workers in schools, unwed fathers, father involvement in preschool education, substance abuse prevention, and minority male socialization. Through efforts to understand and promote Black child development, institute staff collaborated with faculty members in various Howard University schools/colleges and departments as well as scholars from other institutions. IUAR staff published several final reports, monographs, occasional papers, scholarly journal articles, book chapters, and books.

E. Franklin Frazier Center for Social Work Research: 1995 to Present

This center, named in honor of the sociologist and social work educator cited above, was created in the School of Social Work to generate knowledge for solutions to human, organizational, and societal problems, particularly those affecting African American and other ethnic and cultural populations. Two primary goals of the center are to advance knowledge of social work theory and practice that can influence public policy and to facilitate interdisciplinary research collaboration among School of Social Work faculty and staff, both within the university and with local, national, and international organizations. The center operates several government- and foundation-funded projects on topics such as child and family permanency planning, family homelessness, domestic violence, child welfare, teen pregnancy, housing, and welfare-to-work.

The School of Social Work Family and Community Resource and Research Center (FCRRC): 2001 to Present

The FCRRC is an outgrowth of the Baker's Dozen organization, incorporated in 1945 by 13 African American professional women who were all members of Delta Sigma Theta Sorority (some members being alumnae of Howard University and the School of Social Work). In a building near Howard University (purchased in 1945 and later deed to the University), the Baker's Dozen operated a youth center to reduce juvenile delinquency, from 1947 to 1962. After being dormant for many years, the Baker's Dozen building was extensively renovated and dedicated with a reopening and renaming celebration in 2001. The FCRRC plans to expand its current focus on training and intervention programs for the elderly to encompass research and intervention programs for Black children and adolescents.

Center for Research on the Education of Students Placed at Risk (CRESPAR)/ Capstone Institute: 1994 to Present

CRESPAR is a collaborative research and development effort between Howard University and The Johns Hopkins University, with directorships by A. Wade Boykin and Robert Slavin, respectively. It was established in 1994, with initial funding from the U.S. Department of Education's Office of Educational Research and Improvement (OERI). CRESPAR's mandate is to pursue a basic and applied research agenda, collaborative intervention projects, program evaluations, and scale-up and dissemination activities—all aimed at transforming schools, especially schools for children who have been placed at risk of educational failure. Howard University's CRESPAR founding team members included A. Wade Boykin (Department of Psychology), Kriner Cash (former Associate Dean, School of Education and Department of Curriculum and Instruction), Hope Hill (Department of Psychology), the late Sylvia T. Johnson (Department of Human Development and Psychoeducational Studies), Serge Madhere (Department of Psychology), and Portia Shields (former Dean, School of Education and Department of Curriculum and Instruction). Several SRCD Black Caucus members (e.g., Margaret Beale Spencer and Vivian Gadsden, both of the University of Pennsylvania) have served as members of CRESPAR's advisory board and reviewers.

During its second 5-year cycle, Howard University CRESPAR became subsumed under the auspices of the Capstone Institute and included the following areas with principal investigators: (a) The Talent Development Elementary School/Asset-Based Education Project: Principal Investigator, A. Wade Boykin; (b) Talent Development Secondary School Project: Principal Investigators, Velma LaPoint and Veronica G. Thomas; (c) Talent Development Professional Development Program: Principal Investigator, Constance Ellison; (d) Contextual Enhancements to Promote Children's Developmental Competencies: Principal Investigator, Robert J. Jagers; and (e) Talent Development Classroom Assessment Project: Principal Investigators, Gerunda Hughes and Michael Wallace.

The Howard University CRESPAR staff have presented at national conferences such as the American Educational Research Association (AERA), APA, Congressional Black Caucus Foundation (CBCF), National Association of Black School Educators (NABSE), National Black Child Development Institute (NBCDI), National Association of Secondary School

Principals (NASSP), National Commission on Educating Black Children (NCEBC), and SRCD. Conference involvement included coplanning and cohosting, along with the Center for Drug Abuse Research, the 1997 SRCD Black Caucus Pre-Conference in Washington, DC on "The Pursuit of Talent Development: An Approach to Optimizing Child Development." In 2000, several CRESPAR researchers gave a roundtable discussion at the University of the Western Cape, Cape Town, South Africa. CRESPAR staff have also presented at local and national meetings sponsored by school systems, individual schools, and non-profit research, policy, program, and advocacy organizations—many focusing on the status and needs of African American children and families served by public schools. Recently, through CRESPAR's professional development in-house Brown Bag lecture series, several members of the SRCD Black Caucus (e.g., Margaret Beale Spencer and Diana Slaughter-Defoe, both of the University of Pennsylvania) have presented their research relating to African American children's academic achievement and social competence.

CONCLUSION

Clearly, Howard University faculty and other researchers have played a significant role in the history and development of social science research on Black child development. Such work has supported the university's historical legacy of articulating solutions to social problems and improving the human condition, especially for people of African descent. Many Howard University scholars worked within the aegis of the SRCD Black Caucus, holding major leadership positions, and other individuals' work was consistent with the mission of the SRCD Black Caucus. Although Howard University activities related to Black child development occurring since 1997 were not the focus of this chapter, it should be noted that such work has continued into the present. We are experiencing significantly more interdisciplinary and multidisciplinary research related to Black children's development, a trend we hope will thrive as Howard University continues in pursuit of its core values of leadership, truth, excellence, and service.

REFERENCES

Benjamin, L. T., & Crouse, E. M. (2002). The American psychological association's response to Brown v. Board of Education: The case of Kenneth B. Clark. *American Psychologist*, **57**, 38–50.

Clark, M. K. P. (1939). *An investigation of the development of consciousness of distinctive pre-school children*. Unpublished master's thesis, Howard University, Washington, DC.

Dyson, W. (1941). *Howard University: The capstone of Negro education—A history: 1867–1940*. Washington, DC: Howard University.

Frazier, E. F. (1962). *Black bourgeoisie*. New York: Collier.

Frazier, E. F. (1967). *Negro youth at the crossways: Their personality development in the middle states*. New York: Schocken (originally published by the American Council on Education, 1940).

Guthrie, R. V. (1998). *Even the rat was white: a historical view of psychology* (2nd ed.). Needham Heights, MA: Allyn & Bacon.

Henry, C. P. (1997). Ralph Bunche and the Howard school of thought. In B. Nikongo (Ed.), *Leading issues in African American studies* (pp. 271–290). Durham, NC: Carolina Academic Press.

Holloway, J. S. (2002). *Confronting the veil: Abram Harris Jr., E. Franklin Frazier, and Ralph Bunche, 1919–1941*. Chapel Hill: University of North Carolina Press.

Hopkins, R., Ross, S., & Hicks, L. H. (1994). A history of the Department of Psychology at Howard University. *Journal of the Washington Academy of Sciences*, **82**, 161–167.

Institute for Child Development and Family Life, Howard University. (1972). *The Institute for Child Development and family life [Brochure]*. Washington, DC: Author.

Institute for Child Development and Family Life, Howard University. (1981). *The study conference on Black Child Development [Brochure]*. Washington, DC: Author.

Keppel, B. (2002). Kenneth B. Clark in the patterns of American culture. *American Psychologist*, **57**, 29–37.

Lal, S. (2002). Giving children security: Mamie Phipps Clark and the racialization of child psychology. *American Psychologist*, **57**, 20–28.

Logan, R. W. (1969). *Howard University: The first hundred years—1867–1967*. New York: New York University Press.

Phillips, L. (2000). Recontextualizing Kenneth B. Clark: An Afrocentric perspective on the paradoxical legacy of a model psychologist-activist. *History of Psychology*, **3**, 142–167.

Roberts, A. (2002). *The Department of Psychology*. Unpublished manuscript, Howard University.

Rosser, P. L., & Hamlin, J. F. (1979). *Research on the Black child and family at Howard University: 1867–1978*. Washington, DC: Howard University, Institute for Child Development and Family Life.

Salzman, J., Smith, D. L. & West, C. (Eds.). (1996). *Encyclopedia of African American culture and history*. New York: Macmillan.

187

XV. AFFIRMING FUTURE GENERATIONS OF ETHNIC MINORITY SCIENTISTS

In the Introduction we discussed early and continuing challenges to mentoring ethnic-minority scientists. We acknowledge, however, that there are important new challenges that our generation did not confront. First, the standards for scholarly science are more rigorous than ever before, in part because public confidence about the utility of scientific research for informing social and public policies is presently so low. Questions have been appropriately raised about the generalizability of earlier research on respected childcare programs and on solely Black–White populations to the more recent culturally and linguistically diverse Head Start populations (e.g., Woodhead, 1988). These questions challenged the credibility of the most enduring national child policy program we have. At the time, the implications of the challenge of cultural and linguistic diversity within impoverished child and family poverty populations seemed to be missed by even the most eloquent spokespersons for good child-care interventions and services (e.g., Edelman, 1992; Schorr, 1988). Standards for developmental research—standards endorsed by bipartisan political groups in the United States, such as the Head Start Blueprint for Research Advisory Panel (1990, September), minimally included knowledge of (a) systemic, ecological theories of human behavior, (b) multivariate and longitudinal research strategies, (c) extant theories of how cultural characteristics can impact behavior, (d) issues related to the challenges of research design and measurement development within a socially diverse nation of peoples, and (e) advances in computer technology relevant to this profession. With regard to ethnic minority people, the standards also included knowledge and understanding of (f) the existing body of literature generated by the earlier minority and majority scientists and researchers of the relevant populations.

Second, ethnic minority students today recognize that competition with nonminority students of majority scholars is especially keen, both in the academy and on the job market. Many of the majority scholars themselves absorbed and acted upon the advice and counsel of earlier, more senior, ethnic minority scholars. The impact of both intergenerational and peer mentoring has been to create a well informed, although small, cadre of majority scholars who have a much better understanding of the issues we addressed over a quarter century ago.

As professors in majority-dominated research academies for the past 30 years, we observe that since the 1980s (and in contrast to the generations of ethnic minority students in the 1960s–1970s) many majority students and young scholars in the behavioral and social sciences have no longer had to be convinced of the relevance of studying available research on ethnic minority populations, or even of producing it themselves. Indeed, today serious majority students and young scholars are eager to exploit all sources of information in their legitimately ambitious efforts to advance their own careers and related professional options in a tight job market. Furthermore, given these perceived markets, they are decidedly not eager to share limited resources with ethnic minority students and young scholars. Consequently, ethnic minority graduate students and younger scholars continue to confront special challenges, challenges that inform their behavioral attitudes and their apparent continued solicitation of special "assistance," even when it would appear that many majority attitudes are more progressive.

Third, and finally, we think the future also promises strong interethnic minority competition for available professional opportunities and resources. Therefore, all beginning ethnic minority graduate students in the social and behavioral sciences should prepare themselves for expertise in at least three American "cultures": their own, the perceptible "majority" culture, and another perceived "ethnic minority" culture. In the 1960s–1970s, when we obtained our graduate educations, expertise in the first two cultures was sufficient; this is no longer the case because of the considerable cultural diversity in America's child and youth populations.

MENTORING ETHNIC MINORITY SCHOLARS BEYOND 1997

The needs and requirements for professional mentoring of ethnic minority scholars and the related institutional adjustments include (a) culturally appropriate and diverse instruction; (b) suitable role models from similar cultural backgrounds who are knowledgeable about academic content in the area; (c) institutional forms of support, including financial assistance and infrastructures supportive of student life styles and goals as well as student visibility and participation; and (d) continued development of institutional norms for selection and retention, relative to the academic performance(s) of such students. Since 1954, many academies have had the opportunity to generate and share, with similarly situated schools and departments, normative data on the profiles of ethnic minority students and young scholars most likely to be academically and socially successful within them. For example, the Committee on Institutional Cooperation (CIC) network of the "big ten" schools, including the University of Chicago, has ample data on the profiles of successful matriculates to their institutions upon entry—if only newer faculty and departments were conscientious and determined enough to solicit them. Trends in American society should, indeed, be motivation enough for such efforts.[1] Furthermore, it would be easier to insure retention of the students if the faculty and scholars committed to enabling and training them would seek to establish liaisons and contacts with available outside networks, such as the Black Caucus of the Society for Research in Child Development (SRCD) and the Standing Committee on Ethnic and Racial Issues of the same organization. Contacts to this point have too frequently been narrowly limited to academic searches and recruitments for "minority faculty," and even this contact is endangered.

For many reasons, the SRCD has been exemplary in its contribution to the mentoring, socialization, and training, as well as its encouragement of hiring and promotion, of ethnic minority professionals. As one important recent example of SRCD's contributions, we note the introduction of the Millennium Fellows Program in 2001. This program targets minority undergraduate students who have not yet decided on a career path. By providing travel funds, registration fees, graduate and professional mentors, and meetings with some of SRCD's leaders at the biennial meeting, SRCD hopes to encourage these students to enter careers in the field of child development. Given its Standing Committee on Ethnic and Racial Issues, its ongoing support of the Black Caucus, and its commitment to the participation of ethnic minorities at every level of the governance structure, SRCD is in many respects a model for other mainstream scientific and professional organizations.

In summary, mentoring scholar-scientists is as much an art and an interpersonal adventure as it is a process of teaching research techniques and tools, particularly when the utility of these techniques and tools is not immediately obvious. Many ethnic minority graduate students lose respect for faculty when the faculty cannot help them build theoretical and practical bridges between their communities of origin and the academic and professional careers they wish to pursue.[2]

Students are fortunate when mentors find a way to include them in ongoing research, giving them tasks that articulate with their community and families of origin in a way that students perceive as worthwhile. Students are likewise fortunate when mentors let themselves be seen as real people, with academic and scientific interests, aims, and goals. If we had not experienced mentors like that, we could not have edited this *Monograph*.

CONCLUSION

We think that Algea O. Harrison-Hale's comments after reading the first complete manuscript draft of this monograph best capture the spirit of what the three of us as editors have learned from reviewing this quarter century process:

It has been an interesting journey to review the history of the Black Caucus and its relation to SRCD. What became most salient to me during the process was the amount of energy that was put into the efforts of impacting the [parent] organization. [Today] young African American scholars are finding it easier to get their work considered for presentation on the program at the biennial meetings and published in the Society's journals. Our generation saw the challenges through our experiences. We were overwhelmed in our training and our exposure to the social science literature with the "deficit model" of interpreting data about African American children and yet our realities did not correspond to the offered interpretations. We responded with our activism and our research. Consequently, African Americans are more involved in the governance of the Society, the Society has a process in place for professional socialization of young scholars, and African American scholars are integrated into the Society.

Importantly, I think there are trends within the field that reflect in some small measure the influence of our writings and activism. For example, our emphasis on interpreting data from the perspective of the culture of Black children gives credence to the larger trend of the importance of context in doing research about children. We objected to the field always presenting what is wrong with Black children rather than speaking to their strengths and identifying the characteristics of children that succeed although their lives defy the traditional theoretical concepts. Currently, there are many research programs designed to identify, describe, and explain resilient children. Our writings and research on the importance of Head Start to African American children have helped modify and preserve that important social program. Finally, our insistence on the importance of designing studies that illuminated within-group differences, rather than repeatedly comparing our children with children from another race, is crucial. As a result there is a body of literature about African American children completed by African American social scientists for young scholars to explore. When we embarked on our careers, there were such a limited number of studies and a scarcity of work completed by African Americans.

Times are changing, however, and the next generations of scholars have their own challenges from their experiences. From their view they may see more work to be done in the areas of governance, professional socialization, and professional integration. They may see the need for new and different research. I cannot view the world from their perspectives just as my father could not from mine. I am reminded of the lines from "Lift Every Voice and

Sing" that refer to having arrived at a place for which our fathers sighed. May future generations pick up the banner from where we laid it down.

In conclusion, we will continue our involvement in the Society for Research in Child Development and in the Black Caucus of SRCD as long as possible. However, as monograph editors, we also hope 2006 and beyond brings renewed racial and ethnic minority membership support and strength to both groups.

REFERENCES

Crosby, F. J. (2004). *Affirmative action is dead: Long live affirmative action*. New Haven, CT: Yale University Press.

Edelman, M. W. (1992). *The measure of our success: A letter to my children and yours*. Boston: Beacon Press.

McDaniel, M., & Slaughter-Defoe, D. (2003). *The Chicago School: Contributions to social research on Black children: Margaret Beale Spencer as Exemplar*. Unpublished manuscript, December.

Schorr, L. (1988). *Within our reach: Breaking the cycle of disadvantage*. New York: Doubleday.

Slaughter-Defoe, D., Kuehne, V., & Straker, J. (1992). African-American, Anglo-American, and Anglo-Canadian grade 4 children's concepts of old people and of extended family. *International Journal of Aging and Human Development*, **35** (2), 161–178.

U.S. Department of Health and Human Services, Administration for Children, Youth & Families, Head Start Bureau. (1990). *Head Start research and evaluation: A blueprint for the future (DHHS Publication No. ACY91-31195)*. Washington, DC: Author.

Woodhead, M. (1988). When psychology informs public policy: The case of early childhood intervention. *American Psychologist*, **43**, 443–454.

NOTES

1. We were aware, as we initially drafted this chapter, that the Supreme Court anticipated review of the ability to consider "race" in higher education applications. The issue had been previously discussed on the front page of an issue of the *Chronicle of Higher Education* (Vol. XLIX [No. 16], December 13, 2002). Fortunately, this serious challenge was defeated on June 13, 2003 (Crosby, 2004, p. xi).

2. A paper by Marla McDaniel (McDaniel & Slaughter-Defoe, 2003) nicely illustrated how important it was for Marla to encounter the research of Margaret Beale Spencer early in her graduate studies. In addition, one of Diana Slaughter-Defoe's best students was Canadian, and planned to return to live and work in that nation. Given the principles Diana wished to see applied to ethnic minority students in this country, she felt obligated to network this student as best she could, with Canadian academics with similar research interests, as well as the Canadian Psychological Association, where jointly authored papers are presented. An article was published in an internationally recognized journal that was eventually acknowledged by the academic institutions where the student would apply for work, be hired, and eventually be reviewed for promotion and tenure (Slaughter-Defoe, Kuehne, & Straker, 1992). During the mentoring and training, Diana made a point of listening, learning about, and respecting the student's social origins, and perceived-related special academic needs, none of which were devalued simply because she did not initially know of them or immediately understand them.

INTRODUCTION

This appendix was drafted using (a) information from Black Caucus newsletters, (b) the notes of the three authors, including a $22\frac{1}{2}$-page single-spaced Black Caucus Inventory of letters and similar documents for this time period, and (c) the collective memories of the authors. It is intended as an important reference, which readers will return to again and again. In this volume we are sharing a story, but it is a story from the perspective of several visionaries. This appendix attempts to give objective facts around which the stories have been constructed. After addressing the early history prior to elected Caucus Chairpersons, we describe the accomplishments of these Chairpersons between 1977 and 1997, and then provide additional details of key events under each Chairperson's tenure.

A. 1973–1976	Early History Before the Elected Caucus Chairpersons
1973, March	The first formal meeting of what was to become the Black Caucus of SRCD is convened by attendees of the 1971 Minneapolis meeting and the 1973 Philadelphia meeting. The Philadelphia meeting agenda is determined by Ura Jean Oyemade, Aline Garrett, John Dill, Evelyn Moore, Diana Slaughter, Joseph Hodges, Ido Rice (graduate student), and Graham Matthews (graduate student). Hodges, then a colleague of Ira Gordon at the University of Florida, leaves this meeting with a charge to investigate the relationship between Blacks and the organizational structure of SRCD. According to the agenda, Hodges leads the group discussion on this topic, and it is revealed that as we have now reached a critical mass, SRCD should be more responsive to us as a group. Hodges also

	determines that if we are to effect change, we need representation on the Governing Council.
1973, December	Diana Slaughter compiles the first "Directory of Blacks Interested in Child Development Research," listing 68 names, of which fewer than one third are SRCD members.
1974, Summer	Aline Garrett receives a grant from the U.S. Department of Health, Education, and Welfare, Office of Child Development, to conduct a research project entitled "Effects of Occupational Shift on Family Life Style," which employs an ecological approach, examining the impact of a new industry in a small community on families, parenting, and children's school achievement.
1975, April	An informal meeting of Jean Carew, Joseph Hodges, Harriette McAdoo, Arthur Mathis, and Algea Harrison results in the designation of Mathis and Harrison to make contact with SRCD's Executive Director, Dorothy Eichorn, and the other members of the Council to discuss Black representation on the Council.
	Attendees at the April 13th meeting also include President Francis Graham; Past President Leon Yarrow; Richard Bell, Chair of the SRCD Committee on Interdisciplinary Affairs; and Norman Livson, member of the Committee on Interdisciplinary Affairs.
	Evelyn Moore may have suggested the name "Black Caucus of SRCD."
	Algea Harrison provides Dorothy Eichorn with a list of 22 Black members of SRCD and other Blacks who are willing to serve on SRCD committees.
1975, June	Diana Slaughter compiles the second "Directory of Blacks Interested in Child Development Research," listing 91 names.
B. 1977–1997	Accomplishments of Elected Caucus Chairpersons During 2 Decades
Jean V. Carew	1977–1979. Graduate School of Education, Harvard University.
	She kept a clear focus on our need to engage the parent organization and have a meaningful

presence on the Governing Council and other standing committees of the Society; she nurtured the commitment to the naturalistic study of normative development among ethnic minority children and youth.

Diana T. Slaughter
1979–1981. School of Education, Northwestern University.

She conducted the first empirical survey of the action preferences and needs of Caucus members. Comments solicited from members were restated as 26 priorities; the top 7 focused Caucus directions from that point forward. The tradition of a steering committee that served to guide and counsel the Chairperson was created as an effort to begin to address the identified priorities.

Margaret B. Spencer
1981–1983. Department of Psychology, Emory University.

She continued the focus on the importance of research, publishing, and supportive mentoring of the next generation of scholars. The last was accomplished by the salient emphasis on reaffirming the legitimacy of African-American-focused developmental science.

Vonnie McLoyd
1983–1985. Department of Psychology, University of Michigan.

She focused her attention on trying to set up a system to provide future graduate students of color with relevant information about different graduate school programs (e.g., developmental psychology, human development, family studies), so that they could make informed decisions about which program would best serve their purposes.

Suzanne Randolph
1985–1987. Family and Community Development, University of Maryland.

She updated the Caucus membership directory. With her tremendous creative ability, she kept the Caucus in the forefront of the parent organization by producing artwork for the biennial meetings. She provided funds to the Caucus through the sale of copies of her poem, "When You Hear The Children Cry."

Valora Washington
1987–1989. Vice President/Dean of Faculty, Antioch College.

195

She was responsible for the first Pre-Conference of the Black Caucus. Thereafter, Black Caucus pre-conferences became a regular part of the SRCD biennial meeting. Under her leadership, Caucus dues were raised by the membership to a level that supported all Caucus activities.

Sherryl B. Graves
1989–1991. Department of Educational Foundations & Counseling Programs, Hunter College.
She fostered both internal and external goals for the Caucus. Internally, she was concerned with strengthening the Caucus as an organization through the establishment of various committees, including the Oral History Committee. Externally, she suggested that the Caucus establish ties to other Black professional groups and practitioners working with and for African American children.

Deborah J. Johnson
1991–1993. Child and Family Studies, University of Wisconsin-Madison.
She articulated a stronger, more purposeful mentoring philosophy and process for the Caucus, and opened the Pre-Conference to the entire membership of SRCD, leading to the best attended pre-conference ever. She commissioned the logo for the organization.

Melvin N. Wilson
1993–1995. Department of Psychology, University of Virginia.
He was the first male Chairperson of the Caucus. The 1995 Pre-Conference brought together senior and young researchers to discuss vital issues of African-American family life. The Black Caucus became an important vehicle for involving a greater number of its members in leadership roles and key positions throughout the large organizational structure of SRCD.

Ura Jean O. Bailey
1995–1997. Center for Drug Abuse, National Institute on Drug Abuse, Washington, DC, Howard University.
She chaired the 25th anniversary celebration of the Caucus. Under her leadership, there was a renewal of the commitment to see that the Caucus continues to carry out its mission of networking with other African American organizations, mentoring graduate students, conducting appropriate

research on Black children, and increasing the involvement of Caucus members in SRCD.

C. 1977–1997   Black Caucus Events

1977–1979, Jean V. Carew, Chair

1977   SRCD's Governing Council establishes the Committee on Minority Participation (COMP) as a new standing committee in the Society; Algea Harrison is designated as its first Chair. Other members are Ivonne Heras, Bettye Caldwell, and Lee C. Lee.

The SRCD Black Caucus is formally convened, and Jean V. Carew is chosen first Black Caucus Chairperson at the 1977 SRCD biennial meeting; at each biennial meeting thereafter, beginning in 1979, a new Chairperson is designated.

Appointments of Jean Carew, Diana Slaughter, and Margaret Spencer to standing SRCD committees—Program (Carew), Social Policy (Slaughter), and Summer Institute/Study Group (Spencer)—are made in an informal meeting with incoming SRCD President, Mary Ainsworth. Algea Harrison notifies Caucus members of the newly established SRCD Standing Committee on Minority Participation.

1978   The Committee on Minority Participation reports to the Governing Council on recommendations for increasing the participation of minority members in SRCD. These recommendations reflect three areas: governance, professional socialization, and professional integration. COMP also provides the Governing Council with Minority nominations for Governing Council and for each SRCD committee.

1979–1981, Diana T. Slaughter, Chair

1979   The Committee on Minority Participation is reappointed for 1979–1981 by Governing Council: members are Bettye Caldwell, Bill Burgess, Felicisima Serafica, Raymond Yang, and Algea Harrison as Chair.

Harriette McAdoo is appointed to the SRCD Governing Council (1979–1985).

Aline Garrett becomes newsletter editor.

Governing Council responds to the recommendations of the Committee on Minority Participation by making the following committee appointments: Lee C. Lee (Nominations), Harriette McAdoo and Charles Nakamura (Publications), William Hall, Chair, and Jean Carew (Program), James Comer and Luis Laosa (Social Policy). Carew, Slaughter, and Spencer are nominated to continue in their appointments.

1980   Jean Carew's monograph "Experience and the Development of Intelligence in Young Children" is published in *Monographs of the Society for Research in Child Development*, 45(1–2, Serial no. 183). K. Alison Clarke-Stewart, SRCD majority member, is the commentator.

John McAdoo becomes the first African-American appointed to the Editorial Board of the premier SRCD journal, *Child Development*.

The first SRCD Black Caucus newsletter is published, from the offices of the Department of Psychology, University of Southwestern Louisiana, Aline Garrett, Editor (Through spring 1997, 40 newsletters are issued.).

John Dill is appointed to the SRCD Interdisciplinary Affairs Committee.

Harriette McAdoo, Vonnie McLoyd, and Margaret Spencer are appointed to the Editorial Board of the SRCD journal *Child Development*.

The first and second sessions of the SRCD Study Group on the "Social and Affective Development of Minority Group Children" are convened by Margaret Beale Spencer, Geraldine Kearse Brookins, and Walter Allen at Emory University, Atlanta, Georgia. At both sessions, majority and minority scholars are present.

Diana Slaughter, Luis Laosa, and Lee C. Lee are nominated by SRCD's Nominations Committee in July 1980 to run for two Members-At-Large positions on the SRCD Governing Council. They are nominated together with three majority members, for a total of six nominees.

1981   William Hall is SRCD Program Chair for the biennial meeting in Boston, Massachusetts.

The SRCD Black Caucus is first listed as an organization in the SRCD Program in a "Conversation Hour" entitled "Some SRCD Black Caucus Perspectives on Directions in Developmental Research with Black Children and Families: Past, Present, and Future," organized by Diana Slaughter.

Teach-In on the Atlanta Child Murders and Resolution is presented at the SRCD Business Meeting by incoming Black Caucus Chairperson, Margaret Beale Spencer.

At the SRCD Black Caucus Business Meeting, the first dues structure is created; also, William Hall, Diana Slaughter, and Aline Garrett receive special commendation gifts for services rendered.

Diana Slaughter is elected to the SRCD Governing Council (1981–1987). The first ethnic minority member of SRCD to be elected to Council, she receives notice in January 1981, while Black Caucus Chairperson. The Second Teach-In on the Atlanta Child Murders is presented at the National Center for Child Abuse and Neglect by Ura Jean Oyemade and Diana Slaughter.

1981–1983, Margaret Beale Spencer, Chair

Jean Carew, First Caucus Chairperson, and CEO of her own private contract research firm based in Oakland, California, dies. Carew, Grace Massey, and Marie Peters are co-principal investigators of a naturalistic observational study of African-American children.

In a volume edited by Harriette McAdoo, *Black Families* (Beverly Hills, CA: Sage), John McAdoo publishes a chapter entitled "Involvement of Fathers in the Socialization of Black Children," possibly the first scholarly writing on this topic.

1982   William Hall is nominated for membership on the Governing Council of SRCD.

1983   Algea Harrison, Local Arrangements Chairperson for the SRCD biennial meeting in Detroit, Michigan, appoints local ethnic minorities to all committees of the Local Arrangements Committee where possible, and contracts local ethnic vendors for services to the SRCD biennial meeting.

1983–1985, Vonnie McLoyd, Chair

Diana Slaughter's monograph "Early Intervention, Maternal and Child Development," is published in *Monographs of the Society for Research in Child Development 48*(4, Serial No. 202). Commentators are SRCD majority member Bettye Caldwell and African American physician Felton Earls.

1984

Marie F. Peters, a faculty member at the University of Connecticut, Storrs, dies.

The Family, edited by Ross D. Parke, is published as Volume 7 of *Review of Child Development Research* (Chicago: University of Chicago Press). The three Associate Editors selected by the SRCD Publications Committee are Harriette P. McAdoo, Algea Harrison, and Felicisima Serafica. They publish a chapter in this volume, entitled "Ethnic Families of Color" (pp. 329–371).

1985–1987, Suzanne Randolph, Chair

1985

Margaret Beale Spencer, Geraldine Kearse Brookins, and Walter Allen publish the edited volume originating from the first Study Group devoted to consideration of African American children and families: *Beginnings: The Social and Affective Development of Black Children* (Hillsdale, NJ: Erlbaum). Contributing majority SRCD members are Glen Elder, Urie Bronfenbrenner, Morris Rosenberg, and Aimee Dorr. All publication royalties go to SRCD.

Vonnie McLoyd and Suzanne Randolph publish "Secular Trends in the Study of Afro-American Children: A Review of *Child Development*, 1936–1980," in History and Research in Child Development: In Celebration of the 50th Anniversary of the Society (Eds. Alice Boardman Smuts and John W. Hagen), *Monographs of the Society for Research in Child Development, 50*(4–5, Serial no. 211), pp. 78–92.

Diana Slaughter is a member of the first SRCD delegation to China, visiting childcare centers and meetings with Chinese psychologists in Beijing. The largest social development research initiative in China involved research into the effects of "only child" status in the family.

The SRCD Committee on Minority Participation (presently Committee on Ethnic and Racial Issues) becomes a standing committee of SRCD.

1987–1989, Valora Washington, Chair

Diana Slaughter is presented a plaque by the Caucus instituting the Black Scholar Achievement Award for "Scholar, Mentor, Advocate, and Friend." This award can be given at each biennial meeting.

Lee C. Lee is the first minority female developmental researcher to give an invited address at the Society's biennial meeting. She is introduced by Diana Slaughter.

Valora Washington and Ura Jean Oyemade publish *Project Head Start: Past, Present, and Future Trends in the Context of Family Needs* (New York: Garland Press).

John Ogbu is appointed to the Governing Council of SRCD (1987–1993).

1988

Bertha Holliday enumerates the three intellectual traditions that have influenced the SRCD Black Caucus—the University of Chicago, Howard University, and the University of Michigan—to Aline Garrett and Diana Slaughter in Washington, DC.

Diana Slaughter, Valora Washington, Ura Jean Oyemade, and Rachel Lindsey publish one of the earliest SRCD Social Policy Reports: "Head Start: A Backward and Forward Look." *Social Policy Report*, *3*(2) (available from SRCD Executive Director's Office, University of Michigan, Ann Arbor, MI).

Diana Slaughter publishes the edited volume initially based upon a 1987 SRCD Symposium: *Black Children and Poverty: A Developmental Perspective*, Volume 42 of *New Directions for Child Development* (Series Editor, William Damon; San Francisco: Jossey-Bass). The SRCD Symposium had been organized at the request of Program Committee member Valora Washington as a Social Policy Module.

Valora Washington and Velma LaPoint publish *Black Children and American Institutions: An Ecological Review and Resource Guide* (New York: Garland).

| 1989 | First Pre-Conference of the SRCD Black Caucus: "Raising the Next Generation of Black Children: Our Roles and Our Goals," in Kansas City, Missouri (Geraldine Kearse Brookins, Program Chair; Co-sponsor, SRCD Committee on Minority Participation). |
| | Session II of the first Pre-Conference is devoted to "The SRCD Black Caucus: The Founding Meeting in Philadelphia, 1973." The Session Chair is Sherryl Browne Graves, Hunter College, and other Panelists include Ura Jean Oyemade, Howard University; Aline Garrett, University of Southwestern Louisiana; and Diana Slaughter, Northwestern University. At this session the idea of doing an oral history of the Caucus's early years was born. |

1989–1991, Sherryl Browne Graves, Chair

1990	Margaret Spencer and Vonnie McLoyd publish the Special Issue of *Child Development*: Minority Children, Vol. 61(2).
	Vonnie McLoyd publishes the edited volume *New Directions for Child Development, Volume 46. Economic Stress: Effects on Family Life and Child Development.* (Series Editor, William Damon; San Francisco: Jossey-Bass).
1991	Second Pre-Conference of the SRCD Black Caucus: "Ethnicity and Diversity: Implications for Research and Policies," in Seattle, Washington (Geraldine Kearse Brookins and Margaret Beale Spencer, Program Co-Chairs; Co-Sponsor: SRCD Committee on Minority Participation). Acknowledgments are extended to the University of Minnesota and Emory University for their support of the Pre-Conference.
	At the Black Caucus Business Meeting, framed certificates are presented to Margaret Spencer and Vonnie McLoyd in recognition of the publication of the Special Issue of *Child Development*.
	An electronic mail group is set up by Robin Soler, a graduate student.
	Vonnie McLoyd is elected to Governing Council (1991–1997).

1991–1993, Deborah J. Johnson, Chair

1991   Membership explicitly approves a motion to open Black Caucus membership to persons of non-African-American descent (only implicit before).

Valora Washington of the Kellogg Foundation endorses the idea of an oral history project focusing on the SRCD Black Caucus, offering help in a letter to Diana Slaughter, Chair, SRCD Black Caucus History Committee.

Joseph H. Stevens, Jr., of Georgia State University, dies. An expert in early childhood, Stevens had been consulting on variables to be included in large-scale longitudinal data sets then being established.

1992   A.B. Nsamenang publishes *Human Development in Cultural Context: A Third World Perspective* (Newbury Park, CA: Sage). Nsamenang is a former student/colleague of a majority member of SRCD, Michael Lamb. Melvin N. Wilson, as a member of the SRCD Committee on Minority Participation, serves as liaison with the Black Caucus.

The Graduate Network of the Black Caucus (GNBC) section is introduced to the newsletter.

Geraldine Kearse Brookins is a candidate for at-large member of SRCD Governing Council.

An "Open Letter" is published in the Black Caucus newsletter from Caucus member Jacquelyn Faye Jackson to William Hall, Chair, SRCD Publications Committee, regarding Hall's solicitation for ideas and suggestions on how to promote diversity in the content of SRCD publications and on editorial review panels while maintaining the scientific merit of SRCD publications.

1993   Diana Slaughter organizes a meeting of Oral History Committee members: Ura Jean Oyemade, Valora Washington, Algea Harrison, Harriette McAdoo, Aline Garrett, and Melvin Wilson, the nucleus of the group engaged in writing this history. The History Committee is to have a three-part focus: (a) Washington and McAdoo would develop a working outline for an edited monograph or booklet on early Black Caucus history;

(b) the raw data of the Caucus's 20-year history would eventually be archived at Howard University, The University of Southwestern Louisiana (presently University of Louisiana, Lafayette), and the SRCD Archives at the National Institute of Medicine; and (c) finally, ongoing oral histories of Caucus members as they pertain to SRCD and their careers in child development would be collected as part of the ongoing responsibility of the Oral History Committee.

The SRCD Black Caucus Inventory, a 22-page annotated single-spaced listing of all documents presently held by Diana Slaughter in reference to the Caucus from 1973 through 1993, is developed and shared with History Committee members by Diana Slaughter. The documents, in addition to Caucus newsletters and pre-conference brochures, form the core of the factual basis of the present historical account.

Third Pre-Conference of the SRCD Black Caucus: "Reviewing Black Child Survival: Old Issues, New Directions," in New Orleans, Louisiana (Deborah J. Johnson, Program Chair; Co-Sponsor: Center for Family Studies, School of Family Resources and Consumer Sciences, The University of Wisconsin).

Twentieth Anniversary Reception honors past Chairpersons of the Black Caucus; each Chairperson receives a plaque listing dates of service, and the date of the duration of the Caucus.

Suzanne Randolph designs the official SRCD Conference poster. The design is also used for T-shirts and note cards on sale at the conference.

The SRCD Standing Committee on Minority Participation is renamed the Ethnic and Racial Issues Committee.

Commemorative buttons of the 20th Anniversary of the Black Caucus and videos of the 1993 pre-conference are on sale.

1993–1995 Melvin N. Wilson, Chair

1993   Jacquelyn Faye Jackson publishes "Human Behavioral Genetics, Scarr's Theory, and Her Views on

Interventions: A Critical Review and Commentary on Their Implications for African-American Children," *Child Development, 64*, pp. 1318–1332, in partial response to Sandra Scarr's 1991 Presidential Address.

1994   Sociologist A. Wade Smith dies; he was married to Caucus member, Elsie Moore, an early researcher on the effects of transracial adoptive home environments on Black children's cognitive styles and achievement. Patricia Greenfield and Rodney Cockling publish an edited volume entitled *Cross-Cultural Roots of Minority Child Development* (Hillsdale, NJ: Erlbaum).

Diana Slaughter-Defoe's biographical sketch appears in *American Psychologist* as she receives the Award for Distinguished Contribution to Research in Public Policy by the American Psychological Association. The sketch identifies the Black Caucus of SRCD, including several founding members: Ura Jean Oyemade-Bailey, Aline Garrett, Algea Harrison, Harriette McAdoo, John Dill, and the late Jean Carew. Althea Huston, Vonnie McLoyd, and Cynthia Garcia Coll publish "Children and Poverty," a Special Issue of *Child Development, 65*(2). The Margaret Beale Spencer Symposium on "Psychological and Physiological Dimensions of Black Child Development" reviews the progress made in the area of Black child development research over the 12 years since the publication of *Beginnings*. Many Caucus members, including co-editor Geraldine Kearse Brookins, attend and participate in the Symposium at the University of Pennsylvania, in Philadelphia.

John McAdoo, a faculty member at Michigan State University, dies.

1995   Fourth Pre-Conference of the SRCD Black Caucus: "The Family and Ecological Challenges: Community and Social Issues," in Indianapolis, Indiana (Melvin N. Wilson, Program Chair; Co-Sponsor: Department of Psychology, the University of Virginia).

Valora Washington and Ura Jean Oyemade publish the 2nd edition of *Project Head Start: Past,*

Present and Future Trends in the Context of Family Needs (New York: Garland Press).

Sadie Grimmett is honored at a Pre-Conference luncheon on the occasion of her retirement from Indiana University. Harriette McAdoo gives the keynote at the luncheon.

SRCD Governing Council Award to organizations outside of SRCD who work for the benefit of children is presented to Valeria Lovelace on behalf of Children's Television Workshop (CTW).

SRCD appointments include Pamela Reid as a member of the Program Committee; Linda Burton as a member of the Publications Committee; Algea Harrison and Deborah Johnson as members of the International Affairs Committee; William Cross as a member of the History Committee; John Ogbu as a member of the Interdisciplinary Affairs Committee; Vonnie McLoyd and Senobia Crawford as members of the Social Policy Committee.

Suzanne Randolph provides artwork for the SRCD 1995 Conference Program material.

Diana Slaughter-Defoe is appointed Associate Editor of *Child Development* by incoming editor, Marc Bornstein. Caucus members who are appointed to the standing editorial review panel by Slaughter-Defoe are Deborah Johnson, Mary Lou de Leon Siantz, Diane Scott-Jones, Margaret Beale Spencer, and Melvin N. Wilson.

Diane Scott-Jones becomes a member of SRCD Ethics Committee.

Maxine L. Clark, faculty member at Virginia Commonwealth University, dies. Her research interests included children's peer relations.

1995–1997, Ura Jean Oyemade-Bailey, Chair

1996   Margaret Spencer is a candidate for at-large member of SRCD Governing Council.

Harriette McAdoo is a candidate for President-Elect of SRCD.

1997   Vonnie McLoyd is the recipient of the MacArthur Foundation "Genius" award. The Caucus, led by her former graduate student Suzanne Randolph, celebrates this award on the Tuesday evening before the fifth Pre-Conference in Washington, DC. Fifth pre-conference of the SRCD Black Caucus: "The Pursuit of Talent Development: An Approach To Optimizing Child Development," in Washington, DC (Ura Jean Oyemade Bailey, Program Chair; Co-Sponsor: Center for Drug Abuse, National Institute on Drug Abuse, Howard University and The Center for Research on the Education of Students Placed at Risk (CRESPAR), Howard University).

CONCLUDING REMARKS

The above timeline sketches only a few of events that had great significance to the majority of SRCD Black Caucus members between 1973 and 1997. More details about many of the events described here are presented in volume chapters. Note that at this writing, in 2002, the Black Caucus of SRCD continues its membership growth and its biennial pre-conferences. Members of the Caucus are involved in the Society's governance, with membership on the Governing Council and the various committees. Caucus members are featured in the Society's biennial meeting program.

APPENDIX B
SUSTAINING BLACK CAUCUS MEMBERS, 1973–1997

SUSTAINING MEMBERS OF THE BLACK CAUCUS PAID CAUCUS DUES ON AT
LEAST THREE OR MORE BIENNIAL OCCASIONS BETWEEN 1973 AND 1997

Bonita Allen
Larue Allen
Michelle Allen
Walter Allen
Kevin Allison
Lester Alston
Oscar Barbarin
William Curtis Banks
Denise Banks-White
Patricia Barnes-McConnell
Micheline Bean
Loren Blanchard
Geraldine Kearse Brookins
Enora Brown
Ernestine Brown
Jean Carew
Grace (Massey) Carroll
John Chambers
Michelle Chargois
B. Mawiyah Clayborne
Deborah Coates
Gabrielle M. Cobbs
Beverly Colwell-Adams
Mary M. Cross
William Cross
Michael Cunningham
Jessica H. Daniel
Anita DeFrantz
Rodney Dennis

John Dill
Phyllis Dukes
Patricia Edwards
Mary L. Ennis
Cheryl A. Evans
Lillian Filmore
Harold Freeman
Vivian Gadsden
Juarlyn L. Gaiter
Pamela Garner
Aline M. Garrett
Robert L. Gatson
Victoria Goodard-Truitt
Wanda Grant
Sherryl Browne Graves
Sadie A. Grimmett
Gladys Hall
Priscilla Hambrick-Dixon
Mary Harper
Violet J. Harris
Yvette Harris
Algea O. Harrison-Hale
Hope Hill
Asa Hilliard
Ivy Hinton
Bertha Holliday
Carrell Horton
Cynthia Hudley
Andrea Hunter

Eben Ingram
Aeolian Jackson
Jacquelyne Faye Jackson
Robert Jackson
Roberta Jackson
Robert Jagers
Carol Johnson
Deborah J. Johnson
Elaine Jones
Mario Kelly
Jackie Kimbrough
Kimberly Kinsler
Velma LaPoint
Gwendolyn Laroche
Valerie W. Lawrence
Marjorie W. Lee
Rachel Lindsey
Valeria Lovelace
Arthur Mathis
Harriette McAdoo
John McAdoo
Vonnie C. McLoyd
Fayneese Miller
Dalton Miller-Jones
Evelyn Moore
Elsie C. J. Moore
Angela Neal (Barnett)
Sharon Nelson-LeGall
John Ogbu
Corann Okorodudu
Ura Jean Oyemade Bailey
Glendora Patterson
Marie Peters
Carol Phillips
Layli Dumbleton Phillips
Ellen Pinderhughes

Karabelle Pizzigati
Suzanne Randolph
Aisha Ray
Pamela T. Reid
Fariyal Ross-Sheriff
Martin D. Ruck
Barbara Scott
Doris E. Scott
Diane Scott-Jones
Belinda Sims
Diana T. Slaughter-Defoe
Henrietta Smith
Robin E. Soler
Margaret Beale Spencer
Joseph Stevens
Dena Swanson
Ron Taylor
Mona W. Thornton
Rosa Trapp-Dukes
Sherry Turner
Patricia Wallace
Alan J. Ward
Lucretia Ward
Ernest D. Washington
Valora Washington
Janice Wells
Marsha Williams
Constance Williams
Madge Willis
Clancie F. Wilson
Melvin N. Wilson
Linda F. Winfield
Allen Wood
Karen F. Wyche
James Young

ACKNOWLEDGMENTS

Members of the Black Caucus of the Society for Research in Child Development (SRCD) began writing this *Monograph* with no knowledge of where or how it would be published. Special thanks are due to all authors, who took the time to write and to assume the initial costs of chapters with no real assurances that they would ever appear in print.

Early inspiration for the document came from Harriette McAdoo and Valora Washington. Gratitude is extended for their continued support during critical moments in the production process.

Of the many persons who contributed to the support of the Black Caucus within the SRCD parent organization, perhaps none have been as instrumental as its two Executive Officers, Dorothy Eichorn and John Hagen. Much appreciation is extended for their understanding the importance of including diverse voices within SRCD, and for their willingness to reinforce the understanding with specific opportunities for Caucus members to serve SRCD and the cause of benefiting America's children. Moreover, the heroic efforts of John Hagen led to the fiscal resources that enabled production of this volume.

Because of their courage, their spirit of optimism, their efforts at inclusion, and their scientific integrity, the *Monograph* is dedicated to Jean Carew, Mary Ainsworth, Bettye Caldwell, Esther Thelen, Althea Huston, and Sandra Graham. It is also dedicated to the many SRCD members of color. In particular, an earlier, thoughtful account by Marla McDaniel of the significance of Margaret Beale Spencer's published research to her own early initiation to the field was a source of inspiration for discussions of the important role of cross-age mentoring.

Special gratitude is expressed for the essential editorial consultation and proactive support of Jeff Cooper and Diane Eyer. Both consultants helped to bring a complex and unwieldy text reflecting diverse voices to a readable, integrated, and productive document that should advance our scientific field. We are also grateful for the valuable comments of John P. Jackson concerning the thematic content of the volume.

The production of this *Monograph* was made considerably easier by the dedicated support of several individuals, notably Tondra Loder, Janean Williams, Birgit Swanson, Patricia Settimi, Stephanie Church, Jennifer Bateman, and Crystal Aderson.

Finally, Suzanne Randolph's permission to reproduce the text of her poem in the *Monograph* is genuinely appreciated. The poem captures the sentiments of the contributors, and of Caucus members generally, as they sought to benefit a neglected group of America's children.

—*Diana T. Slaughter-Defoe and Aline M. Garrett*

This *Monograph* is an expression of gratitude and obligation to the first African American member of SRCD, Henrietta Smith, as well as all past, present, and future African American members. Special recognition is given to the efforts of Jeff Cooper, a remarkable scholar and gentleman. Importantly, acknowledgment is granted to John Hagen for his integrity, diplomatic skills, and hard work that made this publication possible. The late Esther Thelen, who devoted time to this manuscript during her presidency, and others too numerous to mention who worked with us over the years to increase the diversity of SRCD. Finally, this edition is dedicated to future members of SRCD and social scientists devoted to the welfare of children, who will enjoy a more diverse membership in SRCD while confronting the challenges and accepting the rewards of their careers.

—*Algea O. Harrison-Hale*

CONGRATULATIONS

Harriette Pipes McAdoo

It is great news that this history of the African American involvement in the Society for Research in Child Development (SRCD) is now available. This has been a dream of mine and others for a long time. I was the first African American who was on the Governing Council of SRCD. I was also the first on the Publication Committee. As a group, the Black Caucus existed for a while and people had membership for a long time. I have had almost 40 years of active membership within this organization. I was on the Governing Council because certain persons who were on influential committees had decided that it was time for Black involvement. There was the expectation that it would not be possible for one of us to get elected directly by the membership.

Therefore, my presence was because of the forward thinking of a few individuals who were very supportive of Black involvement, who appointed me to the Governing Council, specifically for my racial group identification. These people, among several others, were Mary Ainsworth, Betty Cardwell, Dorothy Eichorn, and Francis Horowitz. We should not forget the great work and dedication that these people showed. As the first Black on the Council and Publication Board, my job on both organizations was to quietly observe the dynamics, to learn the traditions, to learn the processes, and to become aware of the many politics that were at play. I was then able to pass on to the others who followed me. After my years on the Council, we decided to place a spot on the ballot that would ensure that a Black would get elected. Therefore, two were placed on a ballet slot, who were also Black. That would guarantee that at least for another 6 years there would be a Black presence. This therefore was the process that we used to become involved in the workings of SRCD.

This volume represents mostly the writings of the senior Black members of SRCD. We started our memberships as students in doctoral programs, especially at The University of Michigan, Harvard University, and the University of Chicago. These persons over time went on to become professors at universities all over the country. Many of these elders went on to sit on endowed chairs and to become distinguished university professors at major universities. They were joined by the second and third generation of professors from a variety of colleges and universities. At one point, the Black members could sit in one hotel room at the conference. We now have grown to have Pre-Conferences and to have several symposia at a conference. Many of our elders are nearing retirement and a few have died. We all feel proud of the work and research that we have done. The one thing that is special about oral histories is that the contents are influenced by their writers. The chapters in this volume reflect the many schools where we attended. These differences are the result of our training, our career paths, and experiences that we have had as Blacks in Black universities and in predominately White universities. Therefore, there is not complete agreement between these chapters. We want you to read these as a collection of experiences that reflect the many voices that form the African Americans who are intimately involved within the SRCD.

FUTURE VISIONS OF THE BLACK CAUCUS OF SRCD

Melvin N. Wilson

In thinking about the future of the Black Caucus of the Society for Research in Child Development (SRCD), it is appropriate to consider the scientific criticism provided by Thomas Kuhn (1970). Kuhn outlined the process of knowledge accumulation in science and the role that revolution plays in scientific discovery. Accordingly, science is represented by a community of scholars who are committed to pursue solutions to prescribed problems within a set of established rules that govern the development, collection, analysis, and communication of evident results. Central to a Kuhnian perspective is the paradigm that provides a system of developing and implementing theory, law, method, and applications of a problem-solving model while directing the activity of the paradigm and unifying a scientific discipline around agreed upon fundamentals. Kuhn has suggested that a *paradigm* can be divided into *exemplars* or models of problem solving and their *disciplinary matrixes* or the prescribed processes for solving problems, including operational criteria and methodological steps of problem solving, the qualifications and training of researchers, and the appropriate means for communicating paradigmatic solutions and activities. The successful implementation of paradigmatic activities means that qualified scholars are addressing important problems, deriving solutions that are communicated to a community of scholars.

A crisis occurs when any part of the system of doing science results in anomalous findings or activities. Once anomalies occur, science then enters a revolutionary phase that results in a new promising paradigm replacing the old. It was the anomalies surrounding the absence of cultural context in child and family research and limited opportunities for minority researchers that led to the emergence of the Black Caucus of SRCD. Specifically, two critical anomalies spurred the development of the Black Caucus: the strict application of developmental stages and processes that were based largely on White middle-class American families to low-income African American families and children; and the limited opportunities for African American scholars to present alternative culturally sensitive research to a community of scholars.

The Black Caucus addressed the anomalies in four specific ways. It provided an organization and structure of common interest, afforded opportunity for professional development, assisted in identifying appropriate communication vehicles for many young scholars, and, equally important, encouraged the exploration of culture in the lives of African-American children and their families. As a community of scholars, the Black Caucus of SRCD performed a vitally important advocatory role regarding research and social issues affecting African Americans and other ethnic Americans. Black Caucus members not only raised questions regarding the appropriate analysis of Black children, but also developed innovative research models and plausible alternative accounts of the normative development of children and families of color.

The future of meaningful scholarship involving African American children and their families requires an ongoing adjustment, a dynamic that befits the rapidly changing lives of African American children, perhaps even in the context of other groups of color and their dynamics. The demographics among African Americans in relation to other groups of color, particularly the fast-growing population of Latinos, means the Black Caucus may advance multigroup research to address new anomalies.

An important wisdom of Kuhnian analysis is the understanding that paradigmatic activity produces successes by accounting for failures or anomalies. Kuhn discussed the activities of the professional organization as an important aspect of the paradigmatic conduct of science. Activities like meetings, publications, and advocacy are examples of what the organization does to promote its paradigm. In the midst of doing science on questions relevant to Black child development and family life, African American scholars were faced with limited arenas in which to present their work. The Black Caucus initiated its Pre-Conference meeting to coincide with the SRCD biennial meeting. It was a smashing success, and the Caucus institutionalized its Pre-Conference as a vital part of SRCD's biennial conference.

The Black Caucus has developed a tradition of undertaking applied and policy-related scholarship and advocacy within itself. These activities should be relevant to the parent organization as well, because new scholars are often isolated from applied and policy-related activities during their academic training. The development of research on African-American children and families necessitates a link between scholarship per se and its application. The Black Caucus has laid a solid foundation that focuses on promoting socially responsible and culturally sensitive research and intervention, fostering a highly extensive and integrated informal

215

professional support network, and advocating a greater visibility and representation of African American members within the parent organization.

As long as American society uses race as a division, there will be urgency for the Black Caucus to take a firm stand with respect to the African American population's participation in basic and applied research. The reemergence of genetic and biological determinism, and of racial and ethnic group comparison studies, has spurred a pressing need for organized countermeasures. Those research developments should not in and of themselves serve as "the alarm calling us to action." The issue raised by the deterministic and race-comparative studies centers on the accompanying adverse psychological, political, and social interpretations that naturally ensue from such research perspectives. Although the Black Caucus is proceeding to develop viable alternative theories and research models, its members must remain vigilant and responsive during this resurgent trend of deficit-oriented research and intervention practices.

Achieving the visions of Black Caucus will undoubtedly depend upon the group's ability to recognize anomalies and address them. The new multicultural sensitivity that is developing throughout the social sciences will probably yield new unexplainable outcomes that will take courage to confront. The future of the Black Caucus *must* include the following paradigmatic activities: (a) continue to provide an ongoing review of and reflection on theoretical, methodological, and statistical assumptions in a manner that contributes toward preserving the scientific integrity of the field; (b) continue to support the professional development of young scholars; and (c) continue its role as a critical participant in the structural aspects of SRCD.

The Black Caucus must also maintain two important products that are recognized by both Black Caucus members and other SRCD members as critical communication vehicles for African American professionals: the Caucus Pre-Conference and the Caucus newsletter. It should not escape attention that when the flyer announcing our biennial Pre-Conference is distributed, members and nonmembers of the Caucus respond. Since its initiation, the Black Caucus Pre-Conference has become a respected, valued tradition. The newsletter also represents a vital function in keeping valued lines of communication open. Nonetheless, we must do more. The Black Caucus not only is charged with advancing the knowledge base of child development and fostering the professional development of young scholars, but also is responsible for protecting the integrity and soul of African American communities.

In the final analysis, the Black Caucus of SRCD has become a community of scholars who are committed to the pursuit of knowledge for the advancement of humankind. Our community has prescribed a set of rules that govern the scientific activities and scholarly behaviors affecting children and families of color. The Black Caucus has constructed an organization that is vital in its contribution to the understanding of all people. Victory is the good work that the Black Caucus members continue to do.

REFERENCE

Kuhn, T. (1970). *The structure of scientific revolution* (2nd ed.). Chicago: University of Chicago Press.

THE HISTORICAL CONTEXT OF THE AFRICAN AMERICAN SOCIAL SCIENTIST

John P. Jackson, Jr.

This volume consists of very personal histories of the Black Caucus of the Society for Research in Child Development (SRCD). The professional experiences of these pioneering social scientists underscored what current ethnic studies scholars often call the invisibility of whiteness. Developmental psychologists had focused on the experiences of White children as if such experiences could translate unproblematically to children of color. Whiteness, for mainstream social science, was invisible and no thought was given to the notion that science derived solely from White experiences could fully explain Black experiences.

The founders of the Black Caucus knew better. Coming from a variety of backgrounds, the founders all shared, in the words of Margaret Beale Spencer, "a spirit of commitment and steady engagement to the task of insuring that the experiences of children of color would not be ignored in the written and spoken representations of developmental science." They gathered and formed the Black Caucus and created a network of like-minded scholars who shared a common interest in advancing developmental science through attention to the lived experiences of African-American children. The success of the Black Caucus can often be seen in these pages through off-hand comments. For example, in her chapter recounting her early collaborations with Jean V. Carew, Diana T. Slaughter-Defoe notes casually that such collaborations were made possible because "Fortunately, we knew each other" because of their early involvement in the Black Caucus.

Not that the road traveled by the Caucus has been an easy one. One of the central difficulties the Black Caucus has faced, and undoubtedly will continue to face was the reluctance of White scholars to recognize the very personal nature of knowledge production in social science. Many social scientists who believed that psychology could be made more "scientific" by divorcing social science from social values, did not take kindly to Black scholars pointing out that White perspectives on Black experiences could be limited by a *racial* perspective. In her contribution to this volume, Algea O. Harrison-Hale noted that a driving concern of the Black Caucus has been "a major concern about articles on Black children and families published in SRCD journals and in the literature of developmental psychology. Black scholars thought these writings distorted the Black experience and lacked validity. Relying on both their professional observations and their personal experience of life in their communities, Black researchers perceived a gap between their own perspective of events in the Black community and that expounded by White researchers."

The notion that Black scholars could bring a unique and valuable perspective to the scientific study of racial problems has a long history in the United States. W.E.B. Du Bois was one of the finest intellects the United States ever produced. In a life that spanned nearly a century, it was impossible for an intellectual to seriously discuss race relations in the United States without taking note of the breadth and depth of Du Bois's scholarship on the subject (Lewis, 1993, 2000). Perhaps he is best remembered for his declaration at the dawn of the previous century that "the problem of the Twentieth century is the problem of the color line (1903/1994, p. v)." Some years before his famous declaration, however, Du Bois had pinpointed one specific problem that would confront African American scholars who looked to science as a source of liberation. At the end of the 19th century, Du Bois had been commissioned to undertake a sociological study of the "Philadelphia Negro." Du Bois's project stood at a crossroads in social science. As Du Bois's biographer noted, "The armchair celebrations of sociology's great nineteenth-century system builders—Auguste Comte, Karl Marx, and Herbert Spencer—would continue to inform, challenge, and inspire, but the watchword of the discipline was becoming *investigation*, followed by induction—facts before theory (Lewis, 1993, p. 202). Du Bois embraced the new investigative methodology with gusto, visiting hundreds of homes in Philadelphia and compiling a massive book of statistical and economic analysis dedicated to understanding the social position of Philadelphia's African Americans. In framing his results for the reader, Du Bois's (1899/1967) cautioned that in undertaking a scientific investigation, the social scientist "must ever tremble lest some personal bias, some moral conviction or some unconscious trend of thought because of previous training, has to a degree distorted the picture in his view" (p. 3).

Du Bois was reflecting a common idea regarding the nature of scientific objectivity which is that reliable knowledge can only be achieved when the investigator denies that she or he has any standpoint on the issues being investigated—what Daston (1992) has called "aperspectival" objectivity. Philosopher Thomas Nagel (1986) called this idea that the world can only be understood if investigators removed their own perspective "the view from nowhere." Somewhat more slyly, Donna Haraway (1991) dubbed the same idea the "god trick" (p. 193). At least since the influential work of Thomas Kuhn (1970) if not before, scholars have raised serious questions if a scientist can ever completely remove their own perspective from their investigation, even in the exemplar sciences of physics or chemistry.

The aperspectival view of objectivity, however, poses particular problems for African-American scholars. Throughout the 20th century African-American social scientists were, more or less, forced into the study of racial problems, the one area where their objectivity would be most suspect precisely because White Americans generally believed that African Americans would be unable to put aside their own social position when investigating racial problems (Holloway, 2002). The obverse proposition, however, that White Americans would be influenced by their own position in society, was seldom raised. The unstated assumption was that White meant neutral, simply because Whiteness was not seen as itself a racial identity—to be White was assumed to be neutral with no racial identity.

The result was that African-American social scientists were often ignored, regardless of the quality of their scientific output. For example, African-American scholars were some of the earliest and most vocal critics of the racial interpretation of IQ tests, but White scholars often viewed their claims as too self-interested to take seriously. In retrospect, of course, their claims have been proven to be amazingly prescient (Jackson, 2004). However, in the early days of the 20th century, when Du Bois was an active social scientist, it was assumed by many members of the scientific community that members of racially suspect groups: African Americans, American Jew, or "provisionally white" groups of recent immigrants could not possibly be objective scientists. The point was made starkly by Madison Grant on the founding of the Galton Society in 1918. Grant, an armchair anthropologist, was concerned by the increasing dominance in anthropology of Franz Boas and his students. For Grant the rise of the Boasians, many of whom were, like Boas Jewish, served to "confirm me in the belief that you must have at the head of any anthropological work a member of the North European race, who has no bias in favor of helots or mongrels" (quoted in Spiro, 2002, p. 39). Grant, who prided himself on being of pure Nordic blood, never questioned his own racial identity or its relationship to his anthropological science.

The idea that African Americans could not put aside their own perspective on American race relations rose again in the 1930s when the Carnegie Foundation funded a major sociological investigation into American race relations. Carnegie's directors passed over Du Bois because they believed he could not set aside his political wishes which were then much better known than when Du Bois penned *The Philadelphia Negro*. To their credit, Carnegie also passed over many White investigators for the same reason they passed over Du Bois: they believed that White Americans would be as unable as Black Americans to put aside their own views when conducting scientific investigations on race. Carnegie, however, did not abandon the notion that the best social scientific investigation should be conducted by someone disengaged from the society under study, which led them to seek out a foreign scholar from a country with no colonial tradition who would, presumably, have no perspective to bring to an investigation of American race relations. The person they eventually chose was Gunnar Myrdal, who may not have had a view from nowhere, but did have a view from Sweden, which in terms of American race relations may have been very close (Jackson, 1990).

The resulting study, Myrdal's (1944) *An American Dilemma*, set the stage for social scientific research on race for two decades. Myrdal's outlook assumed that Blacks could assimilate into White society if only the barriers of discrimination and prejudice could be eliminated. A central point of Myrdal's agenda was that the social ills that beset Black culture were the result of White discrimination and the result was a pathological culture. Myrdal (1944) argued that:

> The instability of the Negro family, the inadequacy of educational facilities for Negroes, the emotionalism in the Negro church, the insufficiency and unwholesomeness of Negro recreational activity, the plethora of Negro sociable organizations, the narrowness of interests of the average Negro, the provincialism of his political speculation, the high Negro crime rate, the cultivation of the arts to the neglect of other fields, superstition, personality difficulties, and other characteristic traits are mainly forms of social pathology which, for the most part, are created by caste pressures (pp. 928–929).

Myrdal called for African Americans to fully assimilate into White society and was severely critical of White racism that prevented such assimilation. Myrdal's assimilationist and universalist outlook dominated social scientific research for two decades following World War II (Jackson, 1990, 2001; King, 2004).

In the mid-1960s, the Myrdalian consensus about both assimilation of Blacks into White culture and the pathology of Black culture collapsed. The 1960s saw a large scale shift from universalist and assimilationist models of liberation toward particularist and pluralist models (King, 2004). In the 1950s, scholars often embraced universalism because they were fighting against segregation and discrimination based on drawing differences between perceived races. In the 1960s, and the collapse of "respectable" racism (Jackson, 2005), scholars interested in racial liberation began viewing assimilation as a dangerous snare that perpetually held out a promise that could never be fulfilled. The assimilationists' views of the pathology of Black culture was increasingly seen as are all "too obvious extensions of the process of degradation by other means, and have always functioned as an indispensable element in the vicious cycle that perpetuates white supremacy through the systematic exploitation of black people" (Murray, 1973, p. 98).

Taking inspiration from the anti-colonial movements of the so-called "Third World" African Americans began to call for self-determination in the face of White racism. Where Myrdal had seen social structures blocking Black advancement owing to White's racially prejudiced attitudes, scholars inspired by the rise of the Black Power movement spoke increasingly of *institutional racism* that did not depend on White attitudes but on the mere continuation of White power structures (Jackson & Weidman, 2004). An example of how the new political atmosphere changed notions of scientific objectivity is that provided by pioneering African American psychologist, Kenneth B. Clark, often viewed as the ultimate integrationist. The key social scientist in the 1950s worked with the NAACP to fight school segregation (Jackson, 2001), in the 1960s, Clark began writing of the need for Black self-determination and the need for the social scientist to fully embrace her or his own position in society. Writing in his landmark book, *The Dark Ghetto*, Clark (1965) argued that the "*facts* of the ghetto are not necessarily synonymous with the *truth* of the ghetto" (p. xxiii). For Clark, socially active social scientists must fully acknowledge their own position in relation to the subjects of study in order to discover the truth. A concomitant belief is that the search for neutrality by pretending one is not part of the society under study is a futile search indeed (Phillips, 2000).

It is from this milieu that the Black Caucus of the SRCD emerged. In these pages, the reader can see the emergence of an organization that recognized that the search for a socially responsible science of child development must account for the truth of the lived experience of African Americans. The founders and first generation scholars of the Black Caucus clearly reject the notion that an objectivity based on political and epistemological neutrality is the only way to study child development. Rather, they realize that the social position of the researcher will influence how the researcher investigates and understands children. The careful reader will find here a clear rejection of racial essentialism: no one argued during the formation of the Black Caucus that White investigators were incapable of understanding Black Children. Rather early researchers questioned whether Black investigators were not better equipped to understand the special problems and needs of Black children because of the shared experiences between researcher and subject.

Regardless of disciplinary affiliation, history, psychology, sociology; those portraying African Americans walk a tightrope. Fall one direction and you focus too much on the ugly truth of racial oppression: and African-American life and culture becomes merely a "pathological" version of the dominant culture. Fall the other, and focus on the agency of African

Americans and you write a celebratory account that fails to recognize the realities of the racist society of the United States. One must constantly recognize that African Americans create their own culture and social space within a racially oppressive system. Here the Black Caucus tells its story of walking that tightrope. Would that we all could walk is as successfully as they have.

References

Clark, K. B. (1965). *Dark Ghetto: Dilemmas of social power*. New York: Harper and Row.

Daston, L. (1992). Objectivity and the escape from perspective. *Social Studies of Science*, **22**, 597–618.

Du Bois, W. E. B. (1967). *The Philadelphia Negro*. New York: Schocken (original work published in 1899).

Du Bois, W. E. B. (1994). *The souls of Black folk*. New York: Dover (original work published 1903).

Haraway, D. (1991). *Simians, cyborgs, and women*. New York: Routledge.

Holloway, J. S. (2002). *Confronting the veil: Abram Harris, Jr., E. Franklin Frazier, and Ralph Bunche, 1919–1941*. Chapel Hill: University of North Carolina Press.

Jackson, W. A. (1990). *Gunnar Myrdal and America's conscience: Social engineering and racial liberalism, 1938–1987*. Chapel Hill: University of North Carolina Press.

Jackson, J. P. Jr. (2001). *Social scientists for social justice: Making the case against segregation*. New York: New York University Press.

Jackson, J. P. Jr. (2004). Racially stuffed shirts and other enemies of mankind: Horace Mann Bond's parody of segregationist psychology in the 1950s. In A. S. Winston (Ed.), *Measure of difference: Historical perspectives on psychology, race, and racism* (pp. 261–283). Washington, DC: American Psychological Association.

Jackson, J. P. Jr. (2005). *Science for segregation: Race, law, and the case against Brown v. Board of Education*. New York: New York University Press.

Jackson, J. P. Jr., & Weidman, N. M. (2004). *Race, racism, and science: Social impact and interaction*. Santa Barbara: ABC-Clio Press.

King, R. H. (2004). *Race, culture, and the intellectuals, 1940–1970*. Baltimore: Johns Hopkins University Press.

Kuhn, T. S. (1970). *Structure of scientific revolutions*. Chicago: University of Chicago Press.

Lewis, D. L. (1993). *W.E.B. Du Bois: Biography of a race, 1868–1919*. New York: Henry Holt.

Lewis, D. L. (2000). *W.E.B. Du Bois: The fight for equality and the American century, 1919–1963*. New York: Henry Holt.

Murray, A. (1973). White norms, black deviance. In J. Ladner (Ed.), *The death of White sociology* (pp. 96–113). New York: Vintage.

Myrdal, G. (1944). *An American dilemma: The Negro problem and modern democracy*. New York, NY: Harper & Brothers Publishers.

Nagel, T. (1986). *The view from nowhere*. New York: Oxford University Press.

Phillips, L. (2000). Recontextualizing Kenneth B. Clark: An Afrocentric perspective on the paradoxical legacy of a model psychologist-activist. *History of Psychology*, **3**, 142–167.

Spiro, J. P. (2002). Nordic vs. Anti-Nordic: The Galton society and the American Anthropological Association. *Patterns of Prejudice*, **36**, 35–48.

FOR BLACK CAUCUS

John W. Hagen

The Society for Research in Child Development (SRCD) was founded in 1933, following several developments in the 1920s. During the 1920s the movement for establishing a systematic study of child development in order to improve health, rearing, education, and the legal treatment of children in the United States gained momentum (Siegel & White, 1982). The U.S. Children's Bureau was established and many prominent scientists devoted their efforts to better understand children's development. Further, there was an urgency that resulted from the recognition that many of America's youth were not "fit" when thousands of young men failed the entry tests for the draft for World War I (Hagen & Townsend, 2004).

The status of the field was recognized by the formation of the Committee on child development in 1922–1923 by the National Research Council of the National Academy of Sciences. Its activities included conferences, establishing a directory of researchers, and beginning publications. The journal *Child Development* was established in 1930. Private funding was obtained for supporting activities, and a multidisciplinary approach was required from the beginning: members of the committee came from anthropology, mental hygiene, physical growth, and psychology. With the formation of the SRCD , its first conference was held in 1934, and its program reflected both the multidisciplinary approach and the inclusion of both basic and applied issues. During the 1930s the society flourished, membership increased and many universities as well as free-standing institutes were founded to promote the movement of research in children's development. However, because of World War II, the field as well as SRCD lost many earlier gains during the 1940s. Following the conclusion of the war, university enrollments burgeoned and new efforts to launch programs and departments on child development and families were highly successful.

The field of child development, as we know it, really has its roots in the time of growth beginning in the mid-1950s and expanding rapidly in the

1960s. Psychology became the dominant discipline. The twin goals of SRCD, to be multidisciplinary and to be concerned with both basic and applied research, were seriously challenged. It should be noted that up to this time, a review of the literature and archives show virtually no mention of issues pertaining to race or ethnicity of the children studied. Journal editors were under no instruction to publish research dealing with differences among children because of these factors, and there was not a concern with paying attention to children from other nationalities or countries. However, by the 1970s, the Governing Council of SRCD began to recognize the importance of issues that had not been a focus previously. In 1977, three new committees were established to be the integral parts of the Society: ethnic and racial issues, history and archives, and policy and communications (this committee also worked directly with the newly established Washington, DC Office). In 1981, the Ethical Conduct Committee began and in 1988, the International Affairs Committee was established. These committees remain intact and viable today.

The Black Caucus of SRCD was founded by members of SRCD who recognized the need for a formal voice for researchers concerned with issues of Black children as well as children of the Black community. Independent of the formal organizational structure of the society, the Caucus provided a forum that served several roles for its members. The *Monograph* of the Black Caucus tells the story of the motivation for its founding as well as the critical role that its members played in the early years in interacting with the governance of SRCD.

The conservative stance of the governance of SRCD began to be challenged in several ways in the 1970s. Harold Stevenson served as president for the 1971 biennial meetings, and instead of a presidential address, he held a symposium titled Child Development and the National Scene. Speakers included (then) Senator Walter Mondale of Minnesota and Congressman Orval Hansen of Idaho as well as Edward Zigler, director of the newly established Office of Child Development in Washington, DC and several prominent scholars in the field. The message was a call for a major shift, not only within SRCD but in the work of researchers in the field. Research should be used to influence policy, and children of all backgrounds were to be served. Charles Super (1982) showed that most studies published in Child Development were either of White, middle-class children or race and ethnicity could not be identified at all. What studies there were of minority children were often comparative and supported a "deficit" model. Applied work was not well informed by findings of top-notch research. Thus, the Black Caucus began its activities in a time of concern, criticism, and counter-criticism.

Chapter III, Letters from Mary, draws from exchanges between Mary Ainsworth, who served as president of the Society from 1977 to 1979.

Harrison-Hale says, "little is known about her (Ainsworth's) role as a social force for change within SRCD." Ainsworth's views, strategies for accomplishing change, as well as her frustrations are illustrated in the letters between her and the Black Caucus during these years. Many of the very positive changes that exist today, in the governance, publications and the biennial meetings, can be traced directly to the her leadership and the skills and determination of members of the Caucus.

I believe that SRCD today is one of the most vital forces in child development, in terms of its stances, activities, and successes in increasing membership, journals, and size and quality of its biennial meetings. We are viewed as a leader in promoting diversity, and over the past decade or so our journals and meetings show great increases in studies published or presented of children of diverse race and ethnicity, social class, nationality, and range of "normalcy." The Black Caucus of SRCD has played critical roles in advocating for and achieving these gains, and the Society owes a debt of gratitude to the many members who have been involved in these efforts over the past 30 years.

CONTRIBUTORS

Ura Jean Oyemade Bailey, Graduate Professor of Human Development and Director of the Center for Drug Abuse Research, Howard University.

Geraldine Kearse Brookins, President of Changing Dynamics, Jackson, Mississippi, and past Director of the Merrill-Palmer Institute, Wayne State University.

Grace Carroll, Education Consultant based in Oakland, California.

Aline M. Garrett, Retired Professor and Head, Psychology Department, University of Louisiana at Lafayette.

Sandra Graham, Professor, Department of Education, UCLA.

John W. Hagen, Executive Officer, Society for Research in Child Development.

Algea O. Harrison-Hale, Professor of Psychology, Oakland University.

John P. Jackson, Jr., Assistant Professor, Department of Communication, University of Colorado, Boulder.

Deborah J. Johnson, Professor of Family and Child Ecology, Michigan State University.

Velma LaPoint, Professor of Human Development and Psychoeducational Studies, School of Education, Howard University.

Harriette Pipes McAdoo, University Distinguished Professor, Department of Family and Child Ecology, Michigan State University.

Vonnie C. McLoyd, Professor of Psychology and Senior Research Scientist at the Center for Developmental Science, University of North Carolina, Chapel Hill.

Suzanne M. Randolph, Associate Professor, Department of Family Studies, University of Maryland, College Park.

Diana T. Slaughter-Defoe, Constance E. Clayton Professor in Urban Education, Graduate School of Education, University of Pennsylvania.

Margaret Beale Spencer, Board of Overseers Professor of Applied Psychology and Human Development, University of Pennsylvania.

Veronica G. Thomas, Professor, Department of Human Development and Psychoeducational Studies, School of Education, Howard University.

Valora Washington, Professor and Director of Center for Children, Families and Public Policy, Lesley University.

Trellis Waxler, Retired Education Specialist for the Head Start Bureau, Administration for Children and Families, U.S. Department of Health and Human Services.

Melvin Wilson, Professor of Psychology, University of Virginia, Charlottesville.

Monographs of the Society for Research in Child Development (ISSN 0037-976X), one of two publications of Society of Research in Child Development, is published three times a year by Blackwell Publishing with offices at 350 Main St., Malden, MA 02148 and PO Box 1354, Garsington Rd, Oxford, OX4 2DQ, UK and PO Box 378 Carlton South, 3053 Victoria, Australia. A subscription to *Monographs of the SRCD* comes with a subscription to *Child Development* (published bimonthly).

INFORMATION FOR SUBSCRIBERS For new orders, renewals, sample copy requests, claims, changes of address and all other subscription correspondences please contact the Journals Department at your nearest Blackwell office (address details listed above). UK office phone: +44 (0) 1865-778315, Fax: +44 (0) 1865-471775, Email: customerservices@ blackwellpublishing.com; US office phone: 800-835-6770 or 781-388-8599, Fax: 781-388-8232, Email: customerservices@blackwellpublishing.com; Asia office phone: +65 6511 8000, Fax: +61 3 8359 1120, Email: customerservices@blackwellpublishing.com

INSTITUTIONAL PREMIUM RATES* FOR MONOGRAPHS OF THE SRCD/CHILD DEVELOPMENT 2005 The Americas $471, Rest of World £335. Customers in Canada should add 7% GST to The Americas price or provide evidence of entitlement to exemption. Customers in the UK and EU should add VAT at 5% or provide a VAT registration number or evidence of entitlement to exemption.

*A Premium Institutional Subscription includes online access to full text articles from 1997 to present, where available. Print and online-only rates are also available.

BACK ISSUES Back issues are available from the publisher at the current single issue rate.

MICROFORM The journal is available on microfilm. For microfilm service, address inquiries to ProQuest Information and Learning, 300 North Zeeb Road, Ann Arbor, MI 48106-1346, USA. Bell and Howell Serials Customer Service Department: (800) 521-0600 × 2873.

MAILING Periodical postage paid at Boston, MA and additional offices. Mailing to rest of world by DHL Smart & Global Mail. Canadian mail is sent by Canadian publications mail agreement number 40573520. Postmaster: Send all address changes to *Monographs of the Society for Research in Child Development*, Blackwell Publishing Inc., Journals Subscription Department, 350 Main St., Malden, MA 02148-5020.

 Sign up to receive Blackwell *Synergy* free e-mail alerts with complete *Monographs of the SRCD* tables of contents and quick links to article abstracts from the most current issue. Simply go to www.blackwell synergy.com, select the journal from the list of journals, and click on "Sign-up" for FREE email table of contents alerts.

COPYRIGHT AND PHOTOCOPYING © 2006 Society for Research in Child Development, Inc. All rights reserved. No part of this publication may be reproduced, stored or transmitted in any form or by any means without the prior permission in writing from the copyright holder. Authorization to photocopy items for internal and personal use is granted by the copyright holder for libraries and other users registered with their local Reproduction Rights Organization (RRO), e.g. Copyright Clearance Center (CCC), 222 Rosewood Drive, Danvers, MA 01923(www.copyright.com), provided the appropriate fee is paid directly to the RRO. This consent does not extend to other kinds of copying such as copying for general distribution, for advertising or promotional purposes, for creating new collective works or for resale. Special requests should be addressed to Blackwell Publishing at: journals-rights@oxon.blackwellpublishing.com.

© 2006 Society for Research in Child Development

CURRENT